CHASING
THE DRAM

CHASING
THE DREAM

FINDING THE LIFE

RACHEL McADAM

CHASING THE DRAM

FINDING THE SPIRIT OF WHISKY

RACHEL McCORMACK

**SIMON &
SCHUSTER**

London · New York · Sydney · Toronto · New Delhi

A CBS COMPANY

First published in Great Britain by Simon & Schuster UK Ltd, 2017
A CBS COMPANY

1 3 5 7 9 10 8 6 4 2

Simon & Schuster UK Ltd
1st Floor
222 Gray's Inn Road
London WC1X 8HB

www.simonandschuster.co.uk
www.simonandschuster.com.au
www.simonandschuster.co.in

Simon & Schuster Australia, Sydney
Simon & Schuster India, New Delhi

The author and publishers have made all reasonable efforts to contact
copyright-holders for permission, and apologise for any omissions or errors in
the form of credits given. Corrections may be made to future printings.

While every care has been taken in compiling the recipes for this book,
the author and publishers cannot accept responsibility for any errors or omissions,
inadvertent or not, that may be found in the recipes or text, nor for any problems
that may arise as a result of preparing one of these recipes. If you are pregnant or
breastfeeding or have any special dietary requirements or medical conditions,
it is advisable to consult a medical professional before following any of
the recipes contained in this book.

A CIP catalogue record for this book
is available from the British Library

Hardback ISBN: 978-1-4711-5722-6
eBook ISBN: 978-1-4711-5724-0

Typeset in the UK by M Rules
Printed and bound by CPI Group (UK) Ltd, Croydon, CR0 4YY

Simon & Schuster UK Ltd are committed to sourcing paper
that is made from wood grown in sustainable forests and support the Forest
Stewardship Council, the leading international forest certification organisation.
Our books displaying the FSC logo are printed on FSC certified paper.

To André Dang, without whom this book
would never have been conceived

(blank page)

Contents

INTRODUCTION

'So, I got another rejection for my book on Spain, Dad. It seems that there's no market for a Spanish cookbook in the UK. No one buys them.'

'That's not good.'

'No, but I gave my agent another idea and publishers seem to like this one.'

'Uh-huh. And what's that one on?'

'Cooking and whisky.'

'Cooking and whisky? Like malt whisky? Like the stuff you've been drinking since you were 15 and I would give you in hot toddies for your colds?'

'Yes, Dad, that stuff.'

'And they want you to write a book on that?'

'It seems so.'

'And they'll pay you for it?'

'So it would appear.'

'Aye, well that's no' bad, is it?'

Despite a Catholic upbringing, my father, like almost all Scots, is a cultural Presbyterian. This Presbyterianism makes us a people who could never be accused of exaggerated enthusiasm about ourselves or others.

A friend from Manchester once said to me that I wasn't a person who gave out a lot of compliments. I was highly insulted as I had told him only three months previously that having one of his poems inscribed onto a wall in a Yorkshire university building complete with a big ceremonial unveiling was really quite good. I mean, what more did he want?

I think it may be something that is either put in the water or what happens when you get rained on as often as we do. A Hindu from Edinburgh was once telling me about a contract she was about to complete. I asked her if she was excited about it. 'Well yes,' she said. 'But the Edinburgh Presbyterian in me won't believe it until it's signed and the money is in the bank.'

You can be Catholic, Hindu, Muslim, Jewish or atheist Scot, but part of you will always be Presbyterian. With this information in mind you have to return to my father's phrase, 'Aye, that's no' bad, is it?'

This, for a postwar West of Scotland man, is the highest compliment that could be paid to anyone about anything. No' bad is way beyond Californian awesome. It's awesome with chest bumps, high-fiving, running around like an aeroplane, screaming woohoo and generally making a rather loud spectacle of yourself. No' bad, in short, is quite good.

The above, I feel, constitutes fair warning as to the contents of this book. It will not be full of praise and glory and, unless a burning bush talks to me on a hill on the Isle of Arran, the word awesome will not be applied to anything. But whisky is good, and some bottles are better than others. Food is good. Mostly. I mean even when food's rubbish it's reasonably good as it keeps you from starvation. Combined they could be no' bad at all.

The first time I left Scotland, aged 19, I went to Spain with every intention of becoming Spanish and never, ever going back. In the years I lived there, mostly in Barcelona, I learned all about the food, the culture and two of the languages. It became my calling card when I moved to London; it got me my first job there and then, when I went into the world of food and drink, Spanish, and particularly Catalan, food was what I became known for. If you ever hear a Scottish woman on the radio who seems to know a lot about Spanish and Catalan food, it'll be me.

It was eight years ago that I left Scotland for a second time and moved south. London is a funny city. It is the most international and cosmopolitan yet utterly small and parochial place I have ever lived in. It is, often quite rightly, the focus of blame by the rest of the UK for its absorbing centralism, its stranglehold of UK cultural and political power and being virtually the only place with decent jobs.

The thing is, there is a sense of possibility in London that other places don't have. You can do things here. If you live on a Highland croft your life revolves around doing any and all jobs to be able to stay where you want to live. London offers rubbish and hideously expensive places to live in, but also a chance to do things you can't do anywhere else. You have to decide what payoff you want, and for how long.

In the years since I left for London, both the political and gastronomic landscapes of Scotland have changed irrevocably. And while I can watch the former easily online – and it often looks far more fractious than it is in reality on the ground – one cannot eat or drink via a computer screen. There's a whisky explosion going on, with new boutique distillers opening and big distilleries are creating new lines all the time.

I want to go and see what is happening with whisky and I want to put it in food. Whisky in Scotland is like heat in Australia – it's everywhere. Whisky production is the third biggest industry after oil and technology and there are 118 working distilleries, with another 30 being built across the country at the moment. Its exports earn £125 every second and it directly employs over 10,000 people.

The GMB union estimates that 120,000 jobs UK-wide are connected with whisky production and export and at least 7,000 of these are in rural areas where other work is hard to find. Everyone in Scotland has some connection with whisky, even if they think they don't: their school was opposite a whisky company's office; they live near a whisky warehouse; they pass a distillery on their way to work. It's unavoidable.

While most of the whisky we make is exported, Scots still account for about 20 per cent of the UK's whisky consumption. For every dram an English or Welsh person has, someone in Scotland has two. Whisky in Scotland is more than a drink. People identify with it as part of them, far more than the English do gin and more than the Spanish do wine.

Whenever Scots go abroad whisky is the first thing that foreigners mention. When I went to live in Spain all anyone did on meeting me was ask which whisky they should buy. I knew from my father that they had to buy a malt and I knew that his favourite malt was Macallan, so that is what I told them.

The first year I lived there I had a flatmate who was a great connoisseur of wines and spirits, but he told me he didn't like whisky. I refused to believe this. No one could like the range of rums that he did and not like whisky; he just hadn't tried the right one. I told him to wait until my father came over with some Macallan. When my father arrived on a visit, Ramón dutifully sat there and took some whisky, trying not to screw up his face in disgust. He then got a proper whiff and looked really shocked. He tried it, held up the glass to his eyes to get a better look, raised his eyebrows, looked at my father and me and said: 'Well.'

He took another sip: 'That . . . well that . . . is . . . really good.'

During the remainder of my time in Spain, I became a whisky and wine mule between Ramón and my father, taking wine back to Scotland and different types of malt whisky to Spain for Ramón. I took him Talisker, Auchentoshan, Bowmore, and when I moved home to Scotland I would bring him still more whisky on my trips back to Barcelona. His favourite thing ever was a Glenmorangie tasting glass with a glass lid, which I still see in its box in his house whenever I visit.

Scotch whisky ranges in price in the UK from £10 for a 70cl bottle of supermarket label blended whisky, to £150,000 for a 54-year-old bottle of black Bowmore. There is something for everyone who drinks alcohol within that price range, although if you only like bottles at around the £100k price mark I suggest you find a less expensive hobby, like collecting vintage cars or transatlantic yacht racing.

Whisky has garnered a small army of passionate advocates among the great and the good. In a 1978 episode of the Radio 4 programme *Desert Island Discs*, the late Labour peer Manny Shinwell chose a case of Scotch whisky as his luxury to keep him going while marooned on a tropical island.

A few years later, on 14 December 1983 during a debate in the House of Lords, Lord Shinwell claimed that when he was an MP and part of the Labour government in 1948, he tried to get whisky made available on prescription during the creation of the NHS. According to the Hansard record he then suggested that it be made freely available to members of the House of Lords 'since many of them cannot do without it because it is in the nature of a medicine'. Sadly for the lords, Shinwell was as successful at making it free for peers of the realm as he had been at making it available on the NHS, but both remain good ideas to contemplate.

If you aren't convinced by any of this, if you are shuddering at the idea of whisky on a desert island, if you have never met a whisky you liked, let me tell you that you just haven't met a whisky you like *yet*. You are like Ramón before he met me. Don't be like Ramón. Improve the quality of your life with a decent dram.

One of the problems people have is assuming that the whisky your pal likes is one that you will like too. Whisky is a bit like finding a spouse – one type doesn't fit all. You could be the happiest husband in the entire world, your wife's mere presence could be enough to make you happy and fill your life with meaning. That doesn't mean she would suit me. For a start, I like men. I wouldn't want to marry a woman. I have no objection to anyone marrying a woman. I do not think it is a stain on their character. I just don't want to marry one myself. Thus it is with whisky. You have to find the one that suits you.

The other thing about whisky is that polygamy is encouraged. People now ask me what my favourite whisky is and I give them at least ten answers. Then someone names another one and I say: 'Oh yeah, I really like that too.' You can have as many whisky favourites as you like and there is always a new one to discover. Keep your eyes open for whisky tastings, shows and events near you and go and have a try. You may have to kiss a lot of whisky frogs, but you will eventually find your dram prince or princess, and soon enough you'll have an entire royal collection.

There is no tradition of drinking whisky with food and no tradition of cooking with whisky in Scotland. We have a very strong Presbyterian idea that whisky should be drunk on its own or with a wee bit of water. It's like our traditional attitude to sex – lights off, one position and never admit that you are actually enjoying it. No Kama Sutra for us; and no variety with our whisky.

It is about time that changed. Whisky can add a depth and flavour to dishes that nothing else can, and as there is such a variety of whiskies, different ones can give you vastly different results. They are a great addition to all kinds of food, both sweet and savoury.

Drinking whisky with food is also a good thing to do. A whisky and soda is generally much better with really spicy food than wine, and whisky goes well with a wide range of dishes. The recipes and the ideas for whisky matching are completely personal to me or people I've met in the course of researching this book. The idea is for you to have a go at making your own. The Chinese have whisky with green tea, Brazilians with fresh coconut water, Indians with spicy lamb chops. Why should they get to have all the fun?

This is the story of my trips round Scotland's five whisky regions, learning about whisky, putting it in food, drinking it in new ways, meeting all kinds of people and catching up with old friends. It's the story of me working out what whisky means to Scotland, and what Scotland means to whisky.

1

WHISKY CITIES

*'While I can't walk on water, I can
certainly wobble on whisky.'*

ASHWIN SANGHI

Go anywhere in a wine-producing area and you expect locally produced wine to be available, be it good, bad or indifferent. But whisky, despite all the nonsense expounded by the overly romantic, doesn't have a terroir. The process of fermentation and distillation and the cask that stores the whisky afterwards are far more important than the softness of the water or the provenance of the barley.

However there are some basics about whisky that you should know from the outset. There are five recognised whisky-producing regions in Scotland: the Highlands, the Lowlands, Islay, Campbeltown and Speyside. Speyside is part of the Highlands but due to the number of distilleries there, over 50, it is considered a region of its own. Generally speaking the lightest whiskies are Lowland and the heaviest, smokiest, peatiest whiskies are Islay and the further west you go in the Highlands, the more the whisky tends to get smokier and peatier. But with distilleries producing new and different whisky types – for example Islay distillery Bruichladdich produces an unpeated whisky – these are guidelines rather than hard and fast rules.

Single malt Scotch whisky comes from Scotland and the grain used in the pot still is barley that's been malted. Some whiskies are produced by blending single malts and they are known as vatted or blended malts.

Grain whisky is also made in Scotland, more of it than malt, and it hardly involves barley. Grain whiskies, produced in skyscraper stills, form the base for blended whiskies, with malts then being added to enhance taste.

Long-standing legal definitions were drawn up in 1909 after much controversy and scandal by a Royal Commission on Whiskey (*sic*). It found that the term whisky could apply to products made of barley, wheat or maize. However, by 1916 a spirit could only be called whisky if it had aged in a wooden cask for a minimum of three years. This has a significant effect on the final product. Whisky does not age once it is put in a bottle. The ageing all happens in the cask.

Right now you might be shouting at me inside your head: 'But Rachel, that can't be true. I've read dozens of articles about whisky having terroir; I've been told how important the water is at a distillery. It must be of major importance.' And I want you to know that I hear you.

Whisky is a bit like tartan, bagpipes and deep-fried Mars bars. We all just know that these things are completely Scottish, we know that they are traditional; we don't know or care about the truth of them. If you want to belong to a clan and have your own tartan, it will take a tartan seller on the Royal Mile in Edinburgh five minutes to find that your surname vaguely translated into English or Gaelic with a Mc or Mac slapped in front of it gives you a claim to the Scottish surname that also happens to have the tartan that you like the best. Much to your delight, this happy coincidence means that you can justify buying the scarves, the hats, the tartan whisky flasks as well as clan tartan outfits for every single child in your extended family.

And so it is with whisky. Mrs Molino from Spain will spend her entire life happy that she is also a MacMiller and entitled to wear their tartan, and you will spend your life happy thinking that part of the distinctive taste in your Islay whisky is due to the peatiness of the water. If this thought adds a little more weight to the measure of your happiness, then far be it for me to deprive you of one of the small pleasures that life is offering you. But it really doesn't make a difference to the taste.

Lastly, no one knows why whisky tastes exactly as it does. People may tell you that they do, but it's not true. One expert dubbed it the result of 'nature and nurture'. The mystery is part of the fun.

There are lots of myths and misconceptions around the whisky business. I know because I had a few myself when it came to writing this book.

In my mind's eye I saw myself visiting distilleries set in

beautiful countryside while you, dear reader, suffered a crowded commuter train on your way to the office.

For me, there would be lines of crystal glasses containing outstanding examples of whiskies you'll never drink. As a reader you would have been forced to read odes and rhapsodies to simply the finest dram known to humankind in full awareness that you will never, ever get your nose within a whiff of it.

You would be disconsolately turning pages before walking to the office, contemplating the standard 10-year-old single malt waiting for you at home, with a slightly more sluggish step in the full knowledge that when the winners in the lottery of life were picked, you were not among them.

Sadly for me, it didn't exactly pan out like that. But I've some experience of dram envy due to reading Derek Cooper.

The late-lamented Derek was a god of food broadcasting and writing throughout Britain. Founder of Radio 4's *The Food Programme*, he also wrote extensively on all aspects of food production during a period of over 30 years. If you are interested in erudite, witty, fun and hard-hitting food writing, the anthology, *Snail Eggs and Samphire*, is a book you must read.

Lesser known to the food-obsessed public is Derek's Scottish writing. His mother's family were from the Western Isles and he wrote extensively about the Hebrides, the Highlands and the national drink. The books are great. Once you've finished this one, get on your phone and order one of his from a second-hand bookshop. I started with *Hebridean Connection* and was captivated by page three.

But before you get too enamoured with Mr Cooper and his

wit and writing, here is an extract from his 1989 book *A Taste of Scotch*. It's etched on my brain, as he did that thing whisky writers do. While you read the following excerpt, try not to spit with envy and, remember, I've had to write this out and read it loads of times while proofreading this book. You can read it just the once, go a bit green and move on.

A remarkable whisky was offered to me on a winter's morning in 1988 in the Glasgow blending rooms of Lang Brothers. The bottle had been recovered from the Indian Ocean in 1961, part of a consignment of Macallan which had gone down with a ship in 1857, the year of the siege of Lucknow and the Cawnpore massacre. This pre-Mutiny dram, at least 131 years old, was amber in hue, full-bodied and memorably mellow.

Despite this, he did, of course, remain someone I admire. And I encountered other heroes during my research. But even then it didn't turn out quite like I planned.

On one of my first trips to Edinburgh I had met broadcaster and writer Billy Kay. Billy has spent his life studying Scotland and the Scots, our drinking habits, our language, our diaspora. He knows his stuff. I remembered him presenting programmes on Scottish television in the eighties, in the days when STV still did cultural programmes, and before meeting up with him I rewatched a number of them on YouTube. He was at the National Library to give a talk on the history of claret drinking in Scotland and had suggested we meet beforehand.

They say never meet your heroes, but when it comes to the heroes of your inner teenager, there should be a compulsory health warning. It doesn't go very well.

I was sitting at a table near the entrance of the library when Billy walked in dressed in a grey tweed jacket and with a full head of white hair. It was the same hair that I had seen on YouTube a few weeks previously. The same hair that I had watched interview cultural figures from across Scotland on my telly when I was about 13.

He was here, with his hair, to speak to me and give me information that I could put in my book.

Out comes my inner 13-year-old. My mouth is dry, I am sweating, and all that I can hear is a hysterical voice repeatedly screaming, 'The man off the telly! He is HERE to talk to ME!'

This voice is very loud and distracting, but I pull myself together, stand up, smile and go to say hello.

Now Billy Kay is not just a hairdo, that would do him an extreme disservice. Billy is also a voice. It's a deep, low, warm, authoritative voice, like an old sherried single cask malt. It's a voice that, when broadcast over the airwaves on Radio Scotland, the fish in the deepest waters near Ullapool recognise as Billy Kay. If God ever chose to reveal himself to mortals at the top of a Scottish mountain his best chance of convincing atheists of his existence would be to use Billy Kay's voice.

Billy starts to tell me of stories about whisky and I sit, rapt, trying unsuccessfully to shut up the frenzied teenager inside me. Like most of the people around his age he remembers the importance of the bottle at New Year, and he told me about his first taste of what is now one of his favourite whiskies. The first in his family to go to university, Billy was at the Traverse theatre bar while studying languages at Edinburgh.

'I asked the barman for a whisky, he poured me a Glenlivet and said, "Try this." I phoned home the next day and told my father that I had found us a new whisky.'

The Glenlivet is one of the oldest legal whiskies around and has been in production since 1824, and I can imagine Billy's moment of wonder on first trying one. It's a soft Speyside whisky and different expressions have different tastes, but if Billy had only tasted old-fashioned smoky blended whisky before, he would have been taken aback by the vanilla and soft nutty taste of Glenlivet, so completely different to his previous experience and expectation of whisky.

The voice of Scottish God – let me assure you, he really would sound like this – regaled me with lots of other things that day, but I was so engrossed that, while he was talking to me, I didn't take down any notes. He told me about writers and stories and things to investigate; he told me how painters at the Johnnie Walker bottling plant in the fifties used to dip clean paintbrushes into barrels and then wipe them into buckets in order to steal whisky; he told me to get everyone on my travels to tell me how people used to steal whisky in the old days.

He told me about a family in Jerez called the Fergusons, Diego and his daughter Macarena Ferguson, people whose ancestors from Banffshire went to southern Spain in the 19th century to send sherry casks to Scotland. Yet my memory of my conversation with Billy consists of just three names, one book and the fact that Banffshire, where a lot of the Speyside distilleries are located, was predominantly Catholic. All of these things were prompted by Billy saying, 'Make sure you write this bit down.' He must have thought me a very strange writer who took no notes and sat there looking like a rabbit in the headlights, staring at him and trying to get some words of her own out.

One of the writers he recommended turned out to be a joy. David Daiches was the son of an Edinburgh-based rabbi and grew up in the interwar period. His memoir, *Two Worlds*, tells of the small group of practising Jews in Edinburgh along with anecdotes of him growing up in 1920s and 30s Presbyterian Edinburgh. Daiches went on to become a highly respected literary critic and scholar, specialising in Scottish culture and literature, and, as well as various biographies of Scottish literary figures such as Sir Walter Scott and Robert Louis Stevenson, he wrote a book on whisky.

In the 1950s and 60s there was a fashion for the erudite British male scholar to write a whisky book, and sadly most of them should have stuck to drinking the stuff, but Daiches' book is an exception. When I bought it in a second-hand bookshop in Glasgow, Caledonia Books, the shop owner commented, 'Aye, that book always sells quickly whenever it comes in. Naeb'dy really bothers with similar ones.'

If you want a guide to whisky in the sixties and the earlier history of what was in your glass, Daiches is yer man. If you want a biography of any of the great men of Scottish literary history, he's yer man for that too. If you want a biography of any of the great women of Scottish literary history, his daughter, Jenni Calder, has continued and expanded on his work.

Daiches describes cultural whisky better than anyone else: 'The proper drinking of Scotch whisky is more than indulgence: it is a toast to civilization, a tribute to the continuity of culture, a manifesto of man's determination to use the resources of nature to refresh mind and body and enjoy to the full the senses with which he has been endowed.'

If you are ever in the company of Scots drinking good whisky, read out Daiches' words – all of them will raise a glass and more than one will well up, I guarantee you. Daiches, who died in 2005, would have been saddened at the way the Jewish communities of both Glasgow and Edinburgh are shrinking. Never more than six thousand, Glasgow's Jews now number about one thousand, partly due to the migratory nature of Scots (out of the six cousins in my Scottish family, none of us lives here). Then there are the difficulties of keeping religious traditions alive and the problematic nature of living in such a small community.

I was telling a Jewish Glaswegian friend who lives in London how small I was finding Scotland as I was travelling around the country. Everyone but me knew everyone else, and when anyone told me a story they'd start it off with, 'Do you know . . . ?' When I began a story they'd interrupt with, 'Oh so-and-so? Aye, I know them.'

She looked at me with disdain. 'Try being Scottish and Jewish then you'll know what small is. You know what, go and have Friday dinner at my parents' house; my dad will talk to you about whisky.'

So I went off on a Friday evening to a house on the south side of Glasgow. My friend's mother asked me not to say whose house it was in case every Jewish household in Glasgow reads this book and then tells her she served me all the wrong things. If you are a Glasgow Jew, I had very nice Jewish food that you normally have on a Friday. I am sure, had I been at your house, the food would have been better, there would have been more of it and the hospitality would have been of a superior quality, but I had what I had and it was very good.

Her father told me about his life growing up in Glasgow and how, now that malt whisky is such a big thing, a wedding in Scotland for the black-hat brigade is a must-visit.

'You mean Orthodox Jews? Glasgow has Orthodox Jews?'

'Aye, most of them have moved to Manchester or London as there arenae enough of them up here, but there are a few. And when they have a wedding they come from all over. Tel Aviv, New York, Jerusalem, they're all here. I mean, they come for the wedding, but mostly they come for the whisky. You have to have a big table full of malt whisky for a black-hat wedding at the synagogue.'

He went on to tell me how the synagogue hosted malt whisky tastings for the congregation, and how they were very well attended, usually with more than a few extra family members who just happened to be up visiting from elsewhere.

The next day my friend texted me to find out how I had got on, and more importantly what her dad had given me to drink.

'Aberlour 18? That's what he gave you? What are you,

Rachel – royalty? Even I don't get the Aberlour 18 when I visit!' Like Glenlivet, Aberlour is a Speyside malt, the two distilleries are just 13 miles apart. And Aberlour 18 is one of the glories of Speyside. A relatively expensive bottle, available only in the French market until 2008, it is not for everyday drinking; you may even choose to keep it for visiting royalty. It's got the creamy smoothness you want from a Speyside and a smell of prunes and Armagnac, the expensive kind, a hint of sherry and a proper caramel taste at the end.

If you are a whisky fan and not bound by your religion to follow certain food rules, then you can freely avail yourself of all the whisky Scotland's capital city has to offer without worrying what you are going to eat.

Edinburgh is full of shops selling whisky to tourists and locals alike. The pubs in the Royal Mile, the main tourist street, are full of malt and blended whiskies and cold-looking tourists in waterproof jackets eagerly trying them all, but it wasn't always thus. Until well into the 19th century Scotland's capital drank claret.

Whisky was seen as an uncouth abomination from the wild north and no self-respecting Edinburgh inhabitant would drink it. The old pubs and taverns in Edinburgh traded in wine via the port of Leith, mostly from Bordeaux, until various wars between the British and the French managed to bring it to an end.

Scottish people, especially those in Edinburgh, like to claim a lot of kinship with the French. We call it the Auld Alliance, something we think on fondly as a time of unbound affection between the two countries. We love the French, we drank their claret and even named our food after theirs – our lamb comes in gigots, our serving dishes are ashets, from *assiette*, and even our stovies are supposed to be named after the French *étuve*.

One wonders how we managed to eat without them.

The reality of all this French–Scottish love was often somewhat different. The medieval French historian and author Jean Froissart wrote this about a campaign in 1385 when some French soldiers arrived to help the Scots repel the English.

News soon spread throughout Scotland that a large body of men-at-arms from France were arrived in the country. Some began to murmur and say, 'What the devil has brought them here?' or, 'Who has sent for them? Cannot we carry on our wars with England without their assistance?'

The French themselves were less than enamoured of being in the country.

In Scotland you will never find a man of any worth: they are like savages, who wish not to be acquainted with anyone, and are too envious of the good fortune of others, and suspicious of losing anything themselves, for their country is very poor.

Froissart continues in this delighted manner, sharing the opinions of the soldiers.

They said they had never suffered so much in any expedition and wished the King of France make a truce with the English for two or three years, then march to Scotland and utterly destroy it: for never had they seen such wicked people, nor such ignorant hypocrites and traitors.

You know things are not going well when a Frenchman calls you a hypocrite and a traitor.

But Edinburgh has in the 21st century put aside the love of claret and claimed ownership of that other favourite drink of the French, malt whisky. The French drink more per head than anyone else, probably more than us, so Edinburgh, possibly unknown to most of its inhabitants, is strengthening the bonds of the Auld Alliance with its newfound love of whisky.

Another thing that Edinburgh is great for is cocktails, and obviously Scotland's capital prides itself on its whisky ones.

Old men in pubs across Scotland will scowl and draw their breath in heavily at the idea of using good whisky in a cocktail, but every expert agrees that quality ingredients are vital. A good cocktail is something that takes real skill to make. I have spent my time researching and trying out various cocktail experiments and inventions and nothing has worked better than following to the letter the advice of a well-known cocktail maker. A teaspoonful of something unexpected, or using a completely different whisky, can totally change the flavour of a cocktail. I make a very small range of them and take the measurements very seriously.

One of my favourite cocktails to make at home, generally only on special occasions, is a whisky version of a French

75. The Bon Vivant bar in Edinburgh makes them using Talisker whisky – produced on the Isle of Skye – and honey. Meanwhile, the Central hotel bar near Glasgow's main station used to have them on their menu using Johnnie Walker. Just after the 2014 independence referendum they called it a Salmond 45 – and then it disappeared from their menu.

You need a smoky whisky for this, so a blend like Johnnie Walker, or almost any malt west Glenmorangie (lovely as it is, it's a bit too sweet for this) would be good.

I've called it an Auld Alliance, obviously.

The Auld Alliance

Serves 1

25ml whisky
10ml freshly squeezed lemon juice
2 teaspoons superfine sugar (I like mine quite tart; add
    more sugar if you like it sweeter)
crushed ice
50ml champagne (enough to top up a champagne flute)

Put the whisky, lemon juice and sugar in a cocktail shaker (I once used a radio producer's baby's plastic beaker for this; you can also stir frantically in a jug) with some ice.

Strain the liquid into a flute glass and top up with champagne.

In Glasgow the whisky aficionado will beat a path to the Pot Still, the Bon Accord or the Ben Nevis, all pubs with a fabulous array of whiskies for sale. While the capital was a late adopter of whisky, Glasgow, with its Highland immigrants sent down to work in its factories and the smuggling of illegal whisky from places like Arran, has been drinking it for a lot longer.

What is really noticeable is that none of these places are great for food. The Pot Still sells pies that they keep warm on a bar top oven, the Bon Accord serves old-fashioned pub food at very cheap prices. Neither place is actively bad for food, but they're afterthoughts, dishes that you eat because it's a mealtime and you don't want to leave, rather than interesting menus in themselves.

In the Pot Still one afternoon I met a Californian man who was on a business trip to Poland and had specifically flown over to Glasgow for the afternoon to drink Port Ellen whisky – it would never have occurred to him to have an amazing meal with it.

Part of the issue, I think, is the drinking culture in Scotland.

Drinking whisky is very much seen as a man's tradition, and this is partly to do with the temperance movement. Drunkenness among the established classes of Edinburgh in the 18th century was seen as a societal right and a bit of fun, but once it spread to the lower orders of Glasgow it became a societal menace. Temperance movements, much like drug enforcement agencies today, focused on the drinking of the working classes as a cause of their misery and not a symptom.

Historian Tom Devine pointed out that the only long-term success of temperance was to stop women drinking in pubs, which then simply turned into drinking men's dens.

Women didn't go to pubs at all until the 1960s, and even then they were expected to drink sweet sherry not beer or hard liquor. Things changed reasonably quickly and, in the late 1970s when I was growing up, whisky and soda was a normal drink for a middle-class woman to ask for from a living-room drinks trolley.

My parents drank gin and tonic, but among their friends were two couples and the wives both drank whisky and soda. The two women happened to be tall and both of them called Helen. It never occurred to me that whisky was a man's drink but, as my parents are both small, I did think it was for a tall woman. Gin was the choice for wee people.

While researching for this book, I have sat in pubs in Glasgow looking at whisky drinkers and realised they are still mostly men. The owner of the whisky shop in Oban told me that, due to the craft gin movement, gin sales to men and women are now 50:50, while his whisky sales are still 85 per cent for men. Distillery tour guides have all told me that when it comes to tasting whisky at the end of a tour women often say, 'Oh, I don't like whisky, my husband does.' But when they taste it they really enjoy it. Who knows how many women there are out there who just don't realise they like whisky?

Spending time in Glasgow, I have taken a number of women to the Pot Still, which has over 700 whiskies, to see if my Whisky Whisperer powers work, and I've not failed yet.

The trick is to ask them what they don't like about whisky and what other tastes they do like. There will be something for them. There always is.

I wonder if one of the reasons for women thinking they don't like whisky is that they do other things for a thrill in middle age which clubbing used to offer. Also, there is no kudos in society for women to know about whisky the way there is for men. You never hear women, unless they are professionally involved in food and drink, say, 'I really should get into whisky.'

British and American television dramas tend to emphasise this. Whisky-drinking female characters are women who have 'made it' in a man's world; they are the chief of police, the high-powered lawyers with their power outfits and elegant glasses of Scotch. They have won in a man's world and are therefore entitled to its privileges, one of which is whisky. The whisky-drinking women are never young, bubbly women in pink.

Paradoxically, the industry is full of women: some of the best-known and most highly qualified blenders in the business are women; there are women distillers, whisky writers, bloggers and experts. When you get involved with proper buffs, the people who see Glasgow as merely a series of whisky pubs to visit on their way to a whisky festival, women make up about 40 per cent of them. Yet spend an afternoon and evening in a whisky pub in Glasgow and it's mostly men. For now.

But the profile of a typical Scotch drinker is getting ever further from scowling men in tweed caps.

In India, a country where hard liquor is far more popular

than beer or wine, Johnnie Walker is the unofficial national drink. Having it on the table, especially at a wedding or other big event, implies great prestige, the 'striding forward' slogan of the product's cartoon namesake being seen as something aspirational. Johnnie Walker appears regularly in Bollywood films and not simply as product placement. It's a brand that has a lot of meaning in Indian popular culture, similar to the hard men of fifties American films drinking their Scotch on the rocks.

A whisky fiend Indian friend of mine told me that anytime her father visits her in London he is delighted to try her wide collection of malts, as well as other whisky in bars across town. He has a great time, tells her how fascinating it is and then buys nothing but Johnnie Walker at the airport. Every single time.

When I was in Sri Lanka's main airport, the duty-free shop was full of whisky. It had all kinds of malts and blends, but over half of the space selling whisky was given over to Johnnie Walker. I asked the shop assistant why and she told me that they sold far more of it than all the rest of the brands put together.

If Johnnie Walker is the national drink of India, then what better accompaniment than a biryani, and one using venison, one of the iconic meats of Scotland.

Indian cookery writer Mallika Basu very kindly gave me her biryani recipe to share with you. This is not a simple weekday recipe and will require some thought and forward planning. It is, however, a relatively straightforward version of what is known to be a very complicated dish. Mallika has made it her mission in life to simplify Indian cooking while ensuring that it still tastes great.

If you want to be properly Indian, serve this with Johnnie Walker and ice and soda.

Venison Biryani

This is a home-style version of the regal dish dating from the Mughal Empire in India. A biryani is vastly different from a pulao, namely in the number of spices it uses, its fragrant aroma and the layering of rice and meat. Using turmeric is unusual, and normally limited to biryani hailing from Kolkata in West Bengal. But worse crimes have been committed in the name of Indian cooking, and I do think it works very well to mask the gamey smell of venison and help it do better justice to the spices.

You will need a heavy-based casserole dish.

Serves 4, generously

For the meat
500g venison haunch, cubed
¼ teaspoon turmeric
½ teaspoon chilli powder
1 tablespoon chopped coriander
½ tablespoon chopped mint
4 tablespoons natural yoghurt

½ teaspoon salt

1 teaspoon garam masala

For the rice

400g long-grain basmati rice

4 black cardamoms

5cm cinnamon stick

8 cloves

8 whole black peppercorns

1 teaspoon ghee or salted butter

2 teaspoons salt

To finish

6 tablespoons neutral oil, such as sunflower or rapeseed

3 medium onions, finely sliced

2 pinches of salt

3 tablespoons whole milk

2 pinches of saffron

2 teaspoons ghee or salted butter

¼ whole nutmeg

sprinkling of rose water (optional)

In a glass or ceramic mixing bowl, stir the meat ingredients together and leave to sit.

Now, wash the rice in a sieve until the water that seeps through runs clear. Leave the drained rice to sit in the sieve.

Heat the oil in a large frying pan or sauté pan and add the onions. Cook on a medium heat with a couple of pinches of salt until caramelised. This will take a good 15 minutes and you need to stir from time to time. Turn the heat off and move the pan onto a cold hob. Warm the milk quickly in a microwave, stir in the saffron and set aside.

Preheat the oven to 190°C/fan 170°C/gas 5 and start the rice in a saucepan. Bring a litre of cold water to the boil with the cardamoms, cinnamon, cloves and black peppercorns. When it starts bubbling, stir in the washed rice and ghee and bring back to the boil. Boil for 2 minutes, then drain, reserving the water, and keep the rice in the sieve.

Time to assemble your biryani. Smear the base of a casserole dish evenly with a teaspoon of the ghee or butter. Add the venison cubes with all of the marinade, pressing down and arranging the pieces until the base is covered.

Sprinkle the salt onto the rice and then spoon half of it onto the meat. Then top with half the caramelised onions, a grating of the nutmeg, a dotting of half the saffron-infused milk and the remaining teaspoon of ghee or butter. Sprinkle a tablespoon of the reserved rice water on top.

Then repeat with the remaining rice (apart from the ghee or butter), ensuring all the saffron strands have been evenly distributed. If using the rose water, sprinkle it over the top, then seal tightly with foil, then the casserole lid, and oven bake for 45–50 minutes.

When the time is up, leave the biryani to settle for 5 minutes before you lift the lid off the dish and savour its contents.

Glasgow is awash with whisky dinners. Together with whisky tastings and distillery tours, these are big business in Scotland where back in the day gaunt salesmen haunting public events would have given small samples away to potential customers.

Now, brand ambassadors showcase their whiskies and pair them with food, so more people are seeing the possibilities of drinking whisky with food here as well as in India. Wine appreciation in Scotland is very much a middle- and upper-class thing, while everyone likes a good whisky. Spending money on a whisky in Scotland means you have more of it than any kind of class signifier, and as more women go to the dinners, more women get into whisky.

But if you are not fortunate enough to live near Glasgow or Edinburgh, where do you go for a good whisky?

For my very first outing for this book I said to a German friend who I had worked with when I last lived up here that we needed to go out in Glasgow to some whisky pubs. When he immediately asked me how many whiskies a bar needed to have to be so called I was somewhat taken aback.

It was a very exact question. Maybe when Bertolt Brecht wrote 'show me the way to the next whisky bar' in the 'Alabama Song' in 1925, later immortalised by The Doors and David Bowie, he really meant 'and a whisky bar, mind, not pub with beer and vodka, a proper whisky one'.

It is a question I have mulled over and I have decided that a whisky bar or pub needs to have more varieties of whisky in it that you would like to drink than you can in one night. This does not necessarily make it a good whisky bar, but it qualifies. If it means that the best whisky bar locally to you is your house, so be it. You can have people round and have a fun night tasting. In the end, the spirit of whisky is to be found with people having a good time.

The Scots Martini

The Blythswood hotel in Glasgow makes this and it is one of the best riffs on a martini I have ever had.

I belong to the Noël Coward school of martinis where you pour gin into a glass and then shake some dry white vermouth in the general direction of Italy, but at the Blythswood they make their martinis with five parts gin to one part dry white vermouth.

Serves 1

5 parts gin
1 part dry white vermouth

crushed or cubed ice
curl of lemon peel
Ardbeg whisky in a spray bottle

Measure the gin and the vermouth and pour into a
cocktail shaker filled with ice.

Shake vigorously then pour into a glass with the lemon
peel and then spray the whisky on top.

2

STILL SO MUCH TO LEARN

*'Always carry a large flagon of whisky in case of snakebite
and furthermore always carry a small snake.'*
W.C. FIELDS

Now you know a bit more about why people drink Scotch.
But why don't the Scots themselves have a more thriving
tradition of cooking with whisky? One of the main reasons
for that is the cost. The Union of the Crowns of Scotland and
England in 1707 meant an immediate increase in the tax on
malt and thus heralded the beginning of the end of whisky
as a cottage industry. Taxes on malt and later on whisky continued to rise and whisky became less and less affordable, so
it was no longer on hand in the kitchen.

During the 19th century, when places like Spain and
France were developing cottage industries and co-ops for
winemaking and also brandy distilling, Scotland's whisky

business was already far larger and more industrial in scale. This meant that bottles had to be purchased rather than made and were also pricey. Unlike the Normans, who often add Calvados to dishes, and the Spanish, who in old recipes often don't discriminate between using wine or brandy in recipes, the chances of the Scots developing a tradition of adding whisky to food were slim to none.

Home distilling was also made illegal – more of this later – so any illicit whisky proved likewise too treasured to be used in cooking.

If the poor didn't have the opportunity to cook with whisky, what about the rich? The really rich in Scotland, the landed gentry, were either absent landlords – so not creating any kind of culinary culture – or heavily influenced by the London season, with all sophistication leading to France and its cuisine. The not-quite-as-wealthy arrivistes wanted to be like the aristocrats so they emulated them in all matters, including the culinary.

When you look at old Scottish cookbooks you will see dishes with claret, brandy or sweet sherry in them. You rarely, if at all, find whisky, unless it is a base to make medicinal bitters. Thankfully, times are changing, and if you are still reading, you must also agree that a new tradition of whisky in food would be a good thing. One of my first opportunities to find more people willing to try whisky in food came about via a whisky tasting.

For the passionate about whisky, the whisky calendar presents various opportunities to drink and be merry with like-minded people. There are whisky shows all over the world where, for a fee, you can go and spend a day trying all kinds of whiskies from all kinds of brands. Everyone is there, from the big players who have stands with classic cars and fully stocked bars making cocktails, to wee tiny whisky companies who have a table, a couple of bottles and someone in a pair of jeans and a polo shirt pouring drams.

If you are interested in learning about whisky, a whisky show is a great place to go and discover something new. A few pointers will help you at a show:

1. Start with lighter Speysides, Lowland whiskies and blends before moving on to heavier Highland or Islay whisky. It is hard to move from a deep and peaty Laphroaig straight back to a lighter sherry-cask Glen Grant.

2. Don't try stuff you know you like until last. The aim is to discover new whiskies. You know what you like; you may even have it at home or you order it regularly in the pub. Try things you have never heard of, different cask finishes, ages, 'solera' methods or small-brand blends.

3. Take less than half of what is poured into your glass. Whisky is not beer. The point is to be able to taste what you are drinking at the end of the day and to be able to walk out of the show rather than stagger. You want to taste as many as possible and have an opinion on them. You can get drunk on a cheap bottle at home.

For the really serious whisky aficionado, a mere day show is not enough. They want at least a weekend festival. Early on in my research I realised I was going to have to go to one of these festivals to see what they were like. I know, I suffer for you, dear reader.

The biggest one in Scotland is the week-long Fèis Ìle, the Islay whisky and music festival. It's been going since 2000 when the distilleries on the island joined in with the already existing festival and is ridiculously popular. Camper-vanloads of Scandinavians and Dutch, all in black polo necks, all searching for the peatiest malt in existence, spend the week going from distillery to distillery for their open days, drinking whisky, listening to music, and generally being thrilled to be there. The Fèis Ìle is so successful that Campbeltown holds its whisky festival a few days before, so that some extra-keen festival goers can stop off there on their way to Kennacraig to catch the Islay ferry.

Speyside now has a similar festival. It starts just before the tourist season really kicks in and is full of whisky writers and obsessives giving talks, doing demos, with distilleries all showcasing anything new and innovative or old and unusual that they might have.

All these area-specific festivals are great, but not much good to you if you can't get to Islay or Speyside or anywhere else in Scotland for a whisky festival because you live in Australia. While the spirit of whisky will definitely be found at all of those festivals, is it only there that you will find it? Do you have to go all the way to Islay or Aberdeenshire to discover the spirit of whisky? Are those the only festivals that count?

I then found out about another one in the Netherlands called Maltstock. Some 350 Dutch whisky fans go camping every year and drink whisky and talk about it. I hate camping, and 350 tall people all talking about the same subject intensely all day, who I then have to sleep beside in my own tent, is my idea of hell. So that was not happening.

Salvation came in the form of Jason Standing.

I met him on a plane to Islay when I had gone on the trip there. We sat beside each other and he told me how much he loved whisky. When I told him I was writing this book, he got quite excited and then reeled off a big list of whisky people based in Scotland, none of whom I had heard of.

He looked a bit confused.

'The thing is,' I tried to explain, 'I'm Scottish. We know about whisky the way you Australians know about heat. Even if you're not an expert on it, it's just there around you, omnipresent.'

That seemed to satisfy him and he told me all about the worst of whisky geeks who appear when he and his friend Billy run tastings. Almost exclusively men, they treat a blind tasting as a pissing contest and, instead of enjoying the dram that they are given, are simply determined to guess what whisky it is.

While Jason is asking them about flavour profile, they are shrieking, 'Highland Park 12, I *know* it's a Highland Park 12! Am I right? I am right, amn't I?!'

We bonded by guffawing at such behaviour, me safe in the knowledge that I would never want to do such a thing, that as someone with a lot of experience in food tasting and flavour I would only ever be interested in the flavour of a whisky and would never be so stupid as to turn tasting into a guessing game or a pissing contest.

Then he told me about Dramboree.

Jason and another whisky pal realised that a lot of people had bottles of whisky that they wanted to drink with people that might really appreciate them and talk about them, so they organised a weekend where this could happen. You go to Dramboree, take a bottle and talk about it. It doesn't have to be an expensive bottle; it can be something outlandishly odd, a real classic or even supermarket whisky. The point is that it's something you want to share.

He said it had become really popular, now attended by about 60 people, sometimes from as far away as Dubai. It normally took place in a hostel of some kind, so no camping, and various whisky companies had got involved with tastings.

This was the kind of thing I could go to. It is the sort of thing that could be set up anywhere in the world. Get together some pals who you know are whisky fans, head to a venue that will feed you and house you for the weekend, and drink whisky together. This could even work with virtual pals, ones you only know from online and want to meet over whisky, rather than real ones who are suspicious of any alcohol that isn't vodka.

Like Bible camp but about booze and with no tents.

You just know you want to.

I offered to do a cooking with whisky demo at the upcoming Dramboree as it would be a great chance to see what whiskies went with which foods with a bunch of people rather than just me tasting and working it out at home. The venue was the youth hostel at the top of Loch Lomond, several whisky companies were coming, we were going on a distillery visit, I'd come back with some more food and whisky ideas. It was all fantastic.

I've been up past Loch Lomond countless times; it's where you have to drive past from Glasgow to get to almost anywhere in the West Highlands and is also a popular destination for anyone who lives in and around north Glasgow. On a sunny Sunday in July, Loch Lomond can be as busy as any shopping centre at Christmas, as everyone goes there for the day.

The Sunday run is a post-World War 2 institution and came about due to a combination of increased car ownership and strange Scottish licensing laws. No one in Scotland could buy a drink in a public place on a Sunday unless they were a bona fide traveller – which meant having travelled a distance of over 20 miles. All of a sudden, people could travel on a Sunday distances that their thirsty parents could only have dreamed of and the Sunday run began. You can still see large inns in unexpected places in Scotland and, if you look at them on a map, many are just outwith the 20-mile boundary of a big city. They were all places families would drive to in order to have an alcoholic drink. Even though drink-driving laws have entirely changed and the quaint habit of driving 20 miles, going to a pub and, as no one under 18 was allowed in them, leaving the children in the car with crisps and lemonade has long disappeared, the Sunday run is still a Scottish institution.

When I meet someone from Glasgow and ask them where they grew up, if their parents had a car I can almost always guess correctly where they went on their Sunday run. If they lived to the west of the city then they almost certainly went to Loch Lomond.

When I got to the bus station I met some of the whisky people. They all seemed to know each other from whisky festivals and other events, and as we left Glasgow and went up the familiar road towards Loch Lomond, I was beginning to regret my decision to spend a whole weekend doing this. I was having flashbacks to school trips and the horror of being an entire weekend in an isolated location with people I didn't know, with nowhere to escape to. It had sounded like a fun idea when Jason mentioned it, but what if I got on with no one, what if they treated my lack of whisky knowledge with disdain? I was about to settle into a nostalgic teenage wallow of self-pity and woe when I got a whiff of peat and realised that someone had opened a really good-quality whisky to drink on the bus, and it shook me out of myself. Coffee or cheap beer are normal on a bus, but there is an entertaining cognitive dissonance to be on a stagecoach and get a whiff of expensive whisky. I was a fully grown woman on a research trip for my work, which involved spending an entire weekend drinking whisky in the middle of the summer in Scotland right beside one of its most beautiful lochs. I really needed to pull myself together. It might be an idea for Scottish tourist buses to pump the smell of good whisky through their air-con.

We crossed the loch by boat as the coach cannot get along the tiny one-track road to Rowardennan, and we walked up to the youth hostel. There were no shops aside from the hostel and the nearest village was eight miles away. Clearly we were all going to have to get on.

I took a good look at the people who were spending the weekend in a youth hostel drinking whisky. There were a surprising number of women, around 40 per cent. Clearly they hadn't been reading the articles that I had, saying that there was something almost amounting to a social stigma with a woman drinking whisky that had to be overcome.

A lot of the attendees worked in IT, and the academics were all in science. If you have ever been to visit a whisky distillery and wondered who buys the whisky-branded jackets, polo shirts and jumpers, these are the people. Almost everyone was wearing something with a logo. There were Ardbeg jackets, Laphroaig baseball caps and Glenfiddich t-shirts everywhere you looked. I was feeling slightly out of place in a dress.

The whisky bottles were put on the table. Everyone had brought at least one bottle and a lot of people two or three. There was a mind-blowing array, ranging from a 1970s Whyte & Mackay and almost every age-statement malt from everywhere, to an Australian whisky and even an Icelandic one. I had no idea where to begin.

The start, though, had been organised for us, with a tasting of six whiskies by three private bottlers. Private bottlers vary in size from a small group of people who buy casks and bottle them for themselves to big companies.

One of the biggest and most influential of the private bottlers is the relative newcomer, The Scotch Malt Whisky Society. Both a private bottlers and a club, the society has in the past 30 years had a huge influence on the whisky world and in Edinburgh an entire generation of whisky experts started their training there.

If you ever wander round a whisky shop or, in certain

parts of Scotland, a big supermarket, you might see a bottle of whisky from a distillery you know but with completely different branding. You might wonder how on earth that happened and why there is an Auchentoshan 18-year-old that says Douglas Laing on the label. This is the work of private bottlers.

Whisky was originally blended, bottled and sold by grocers who bought their whisky directly from the distillers. In many ways, private bottlers are the inheritors of this trade. They buy casks either via whisky brokers or directly from distilleries, keep them, then bottle and sell the whisky. This substantially increases the range of whiskies on the market.

Nowadays, the best way to think of a private bottler is as the diametric opposite of a blend. If you buy a bottle of Famous Grouse, Chivas or Ballantine's, you expect the taste to be exactly the same whether you bought the bottle in Inverness or in Singapore. You also expect the bottle you just bought to taste the same as the one you bought last year. You are putting your trust in a team of blenders to create a consistent taste for you. You'd be disappointed if they didn't do their job.

With a private bottler it's almost the opposite. A bottle from them is made using a much smaller number of casks, often just a single one, so what you are getting is a snapshot of a distillery at one specific point in time. What they are selling is uniqueness and small scale.

The society was founded in Leith in 1983 and now has another premises in the New Town in Edinburgh as well as branches and associates all over the world, all of which are great places for whisky-lover spotting.

Unlike any other private bottler, their labels have two identification numbers. The first is the distillery the whisky came from, the second the cask number. For example, the label 110:234 is the 110th distillery the society purchased from and the 234th cask from that distillery. You can easily find out the name of the distillery online – 110 is Oban, for example – but what the society does is focus on taste rather than regions and distilleries. Two casks filled at the same time from the same distillery can taste quite different one from the other and the tasting notes on the bottle reflect that.

The three private bottlers for this tasting were Berry Bros, founded in London in 1698 by a woman known only as 'the Widow Bourne' and the oldest bottler in the UK; Cadenhead's – the oldest independent bottler in Scotland – based in Campbeltown; and Gordon & MacPhail, viewed as whisky royalty.

I had been to a number of tastings, but never with so many people who knew so much about whisky and were so serious about it. In the first hour I was there, I met at least three people who I knew from social media as proper whisky geeks, people whose Twitter handles were whisky something, who tweet about whisky purchases at 8.30 in the morning and seem to spend every evening either at tastings or running them.

The first thing I can say is that whisky geeks on a tasting during a fun weekend Do Not Spit. There were six glasses put out in front of us, each with a generous measure of whisky, and a spittoon on each table that no one used.

I am not used to this. At wine tastings people spit. I have

been to tastings where I've sampled more than 40 wines. After 20, all I can taste is wine and have no idea of any of the flavours in the glass, but I spit them out. I can walk away from a wine tasting completely sober.

Clearly that is not happening here.

The three men running the tasting know most of these people. There's a distiller, half a dozen whisky writers, several members of various international whisky prize-judging panels, three people who own whisky shops in the Netherlands, a scientist who is giving up academic life to become a private bottler and distiller, and a couple of brand ambassadors from other whisky companies.

Not an easy crowd, especially when they have no intention of spitting out a drop of the whisky they have. All three of them know what they are doing, though; they use the right buzzwords that keep the crowd happy. There is no chill filtration in any of the whiskies. By the nods and the murmurs I understand this is a good thing.

Chill filtration is a process whereby the whisky is chilled to $-1°C$ and then filtered to remove certain compounds, esters and proteins that can produce sediment in a bottle stored at a low temperature and can make a whisky go cloudy if you add ice. The American market didn't like its Scotch on the rocks going cloudy, and so many whisky companies started chill filtering to make sure their whisky was clear at lower temperatures.

When it is time for Rob from Berry Bros to present his whisky, he goes as far as to describe chill filtering as childish, and everyone agrees.

Childish it may be, but it actually makes very little or no difference to the taste and has made a big difference to the general popularity of whisky. There is no need to be put off by whisky turning cloudy when you add ice to it, or by discovering some sediment in a bottle you have left outside in Siberia or Alaska in January, but if you do find it disconcerting, chill-filtered whisky is for you.

What I was learning at this tasting was that my whisky palate had a long, long way to go before I could even consider myself to be one of them properly. Stephen from Gordon & MacPhail brought a Clynelish 2000 Brora matured by MacPhail in an ex-oloroso sherry cask. The ABV – or alcohol by volume, the number of millilitres of pure ethanol present in 100 millilitres of solution at 20°C – was 46 per cent and someone complained that it had been watered down as it is of a type that drinks really well straight from the cask. Someone else said that adding water to it made it taste like rhubarb.

Cask-strength whisky is becoming increasingly popular; people like to add their own water or even drink it neat. Most whiskies are sold at 40 per cent and have some water added to them between coming from the cask and going into the bottle, but cask-strength means it goes in the bottle the way it comes out of the cask, and the younger the whisky, the stronger it is. People often find themselves putting more water than they would normally when drinking a cask-strength whisky, which is a completely sensible thing to do even if others are saying it makes the whisky taste like rhubarb – like that was a bad thing. That day I was just thinking that adding a couple of drops of water to it was making it slightly less fiery and more aromatic.

Then we got the last whisky, the one which would separate the eloquent from the inarticulate, the wheat from the chaff; the one that left me convinced that I was pure chaff. It was Rob from Berry Bros again.

He built it up well, telling us it was grain whisky from 1982 from a closed distillery and that a sure-fire way to make your whisky very popular was to close your distillery, as the price per bottle just rocketed. Everyone was trying to work out which one it was. It turned out to be Lochside, a distillery that closed in 1992, and one that I have not heard of before or since. No one was able to guess it.

People were smelling the whisky and raving about it, uttering words like nutmeg, walnuts, nutty fudge, amontil-lado sherry. I overheard someone saying it was deliciously fruity and wine-like. All I could taste was stale body odour and smelly feet. This makes it sound more awful than it was. It wasn't a bad taste; it was similar to the flavour in red wine that people describe as chicken shit. But it was nothing like walnuts or nutmeg.

I know that palates are individual and I am very aware that one woman's smelly feet is another woman's walnut, but here I genuinely think my inexperienced palate played a big part. While people have individual tastes, there are those who have developed better palates than others. They have tried more things, be it food or wine or whisky, educated themselves, and they do simply know better. They can appreciate nuances that other people can't; they are also aware of what is their personal taste and what is objective quality. I agree with whisky experts who say that if we all liked the same whisky there would be one bottle on the table, but I also think that experience and education show.

That tasting was the first time I realised why people who don't have the money to show off do spend £300 and £400 on bottles of whisky and why they like private bottlers. Private bottlers are not the cheap end of the whisky market, the entry-level price for most of their bottles is £50, although some companies, like Wemyss Malts, are selling blended malts for around £40.

Where they come into their own is the upper end of the range. Gordon & MacPhail have a 70-year-old Macallan, the oldest Macallan in the world, and they sell it for £5,000, whereas the top end of the Macallan range from Macallan sells for £17,000 a bottle. Even around the £100 price point, a private bottler is usually better value for money than direct from the whisky company, but for me £100 a bottle is far more than I have.

We finished the tasting and moved on to dinner, where people were chatting about their favourite and discussing alcohol percentage points. I felt like someone had just handed me a radiograph of a hand and asked me to see if it was healthy, while all I could do was admire that it was a hand.

Which would all be fine, I was there to learn, I was unaware of the existence of private bottlers until a few months previously, but the next afternoon I was doing a demo. I was supposed to be telling all these people about whisky and food and taste. I went to my bed more than slightly nervous.

Chocolate and Whisky Macarons

I asked Scotland's best pastry chef, Helen Vass, for her whisky macaron recipe. Making macarons is not for the faint-hearted. You have to really know your stuff to do this; you also need a temperature probe and a proper mixing bowl. The measurements in this recipe are really exact, they need to be. Fifty-five grams is approximately two egg whites, but an egg white can weigh from 30–45g so it is essential that you weigh everything exactly as Helen has stated.

When you can make macarons as good as Helen's, you know you have reached the baking equivalent of true whisky aficionado status.

Invert sugar is sucrose that has been broken down into free fructose and free glucose; you can buy invert sugar from specialist pastry shops. The crystals are smaller than in table sugar and means the ganache has a smoother texture. For the ganache to reach optimum consistency for piping, it needs to be left overnight to crystallise.

Makes approx. 25 macarons

For the Italian meringue
150g caster sugar
37ml water
55g egg whites

For the macaron base
150g ground almonds
150g icing sugar
55g egg whites

For the chocolate and whisky ganache
75g whipping cream
37g invert sugar
250g dark chocolate (at least 55% cocoa solids)
40ml good whisky (one you really like the taste of)

To make the meringue, gently dissolve the sugar in
the water in a saucepan on a low heat. Once dissolved,
turn up the heat and bring the sugar syrup up to 118°C.
When the sugar syrup reaches 115°C, start whisking the
egg whites in a free-standing electric mixer, ensuring
that the bowl is completely clean and grease-free.

When the sugar syrup has reached 118°C, add it gradually
to the mixer, whisking the egg whites at the same time.
Keep whisking until the meringue has cooled.

Preheat the oven to 150°C/fan 130°C/gas 2 and line a
baking tray with baking parchment.

In a large bowl, sift the ground almonds and icing sugar
and mix together. Add the egg whites and mix well to
make a marzipan. Fold in the Italian meringue and mix
until the batter reaches the ribbon stage.

Pipe circles of the macaron batter onto the prepared baking tray, ensuring they are similar in size. Once all the mixture is piped, give the tray a good tap on the work surface. Leave the macarons to rest for at least 30 minutes until a skin has formed on the outside then bake in the preheated oven for around 10 minutes. Once baked, remove from the oven and leave to cool.

To make the ganache, heat the cream and invert sugar in a saucepan until the mixture comes to the boil. Put the chocolate in a heatproof bowl and pour the hot cream over it. Leave for a few moments so the heat of the cream can melt the chocolate. Using a spatula, mix together. When it is all mixed, add the whisky and stir. Pour the ganache into a tub and cover with cling film, making sure the film is in contact with the ganache. Leave to crystallise overnight in the fridge before piping onto the macarons and sandwiching them together.

3

THE RELUCTANT WHISKY COOK

*'A good gulp of hot whiskey at bedtime – it's
not very scientific, but it helps.'*
ALEXANDER FLEMING

A name like Loch Lomond whisky conjures up an image of a tiny distillery with freshly painted white walls, Victorian pagoda chimneys and a view onto the largest bit of fresh water in Scotland. Against the backdrop of Ben Lomond, you imagine this picturesque distillery reflected in the water, nestling between hills ablaze with heather with a startled deer's head poking through. It's not like that.

Although it's only a 30-minute walk to the edge of the loch, the Loch Lomond distillery is at the back of an industrial estate in Alexandria, beside a shop which last had a stock change when Madonna was a virgin and a devolved Scottish parliament was the dream of madmen. Although the distillery has a history dating back to the 18th century, this particular building was built in 1964 and I am not sure even the most hardcore brutalist architecture fan would be able to love it.

My mother's first job as a head teacher was at the primary school in Alexandria, and I remember it chiefly as a place with a really good fishmonger, especially for squat lobsters. They are small brown creatures, like a cross between a large prawn and a tiny lobster. The by-catch of langoustines, no one in the early nineties wanted to eat them, so they were dirt cheap. My mother and I loved them so much that she bought them every week, and there was a hotline between the fishmonger and the primary school office as he would phone her whenever he had them in.

My mother is famous among her friends and family for her love of langoustines and squat lobsters. I once brought her langoustine cutters back from Spain and she kept them in her handbag for nearly a decade in case of a langoustine emergency. Even today, restaurants all over the UK give you lobster cutters for langoustines, and they are too big for a langoustine claw. At a time when they were still reasonably affordable, my mother would order them in every restaurant where they were available, and would take her own pliers out of her handbag to use.

If you are a fan of langoustines they are well worth purchasing; especially now, as they come at such a price you want to get every tiny piece of meat out of them. Nowadays, she only eats them at home and only on very rare occasions.

If you want a whisky to drink while you eat them, then something like Old Pulteney or Tobermory would be good. If you want to be like my mother, have rosé wine, as that is what she has with everything, except when she has Glenkinchie or Auchentoshan three wood.

The Alexandria distillery exists as the apex of an almost unknown whisky triangle to the north of Glasgow and south-west of Loch Lomond. The bottling plant for Ballantine's, the second most popular blend of Scotch whisky in the world, is at one corner; and, if you ever take the road to the town of Helensburgh, you drive past miles of warehouses containing almost the entire output of the 13 distilleries that Pernod Ricard own, all of it in barrels, all of it waiting for the years to pass until it's bottled and enjoyed in far-off parts of the world.

Once you start noticing whisky warehouses in Scotland you realise there are more of them than practically everything else in the Scottish landscape except for grouse bred for rich people to come and shoot. The barrels probably outnumber grain-fed grouse released into the wilds of a carefully managed estate by at least three to one.

Loch Lomond has most of its storage warehouses in North Ayrshire, but there's still a large racked warehouse on site and it's the first place we walk into. Everyone is really impressed to be there on this Dramboree trip. Loch Lomond has a grain still, two types of pot stills, its own cooperage, and a small tasting room, none of which is normally open to the public, and we are going to see them all. Like a murder mystery trip on a corporate day out we are divided into four groups, and my group is left in the warehouse so we can have a look at all the barrels stacked up to the ceiling, before moving on to the cooperage.

Thanks to last century's lawmakers, Scotch whisky can't be called whisky until it has been in an oak barrel for more than three years. From the time it comes out of the still until it is three years old, it is called new-make spirit, and while after those three years it is legally whisky, it may take many more years before you get something that you want to drink. No matter what you are told, whisky doesn't mature in a bottle; it only matures in a cask, and the only cask in which you are allowed to mature your whisky in Scotland is one made of oak.

Scotch whisky has some of the strictest rules and regulations of any drink, and they all need to be followed in order to be able to call your whisky Scotch. Some of the newer companies complain about these restrictions, but a lot also feel that they keep standards at a certain level and mean that customers can be sure of what they are getting from something bearing the name Scotch.

I was on the side of the innovators and disrupters, wondering if the rules really had to be that tight, but then I got skin-on sliced potatoes instead of proper chips (more of that later) and realised that the Scotch Whisky Association has a very good point with is zealotry.

Oak barrels are used to mature and store all kinds of drinks and almost all of the barrels used to mature whisky have been used for storing some other alcohol beforehand. For many years, the most popular maturing cask for whisky was a sherry cask, and its addition to the flavour of a whisky was thought to be so important that up until the 1960s both new and used casks were coated with Paxarette, a blended sweet dark sherry developed specifically for the purpose of conditioning casks.

Blender William Sanderson, who went on to create the once-ubiquitous Vat 69, was a fan of the sherry effect. As he experimented in 1864, he wrote:

> It is well known that whisky stored in sherry casks soon acquires a mellow softness which it does not get when put into new casks; in fact the latter if not well seasoned will impart a woodiness much condemned by the practised palate. In sherry casks the spirit like-wise acquires a pleasing tinge of colour which is much sought for.

Nowadays, most barrels used are former bourbon casks, although sherry barrels are still popular. But bourbon casks are more prolific.

In 1935, under pressure from both the coopers' union and the lumber industry, the Federal Alcohol Administration Act in the United States decreed that all bourbon had to be matured in new oak casks, and a great trade in importing used bourbon casks to Scotland began. They arrive here pulled apart and flat-packed, like the furniture you buy in IKEA. Unlike the furniture you get in IKEA, putting them back together so that they are liquid-tight and suitable for maturing whisky is the job of a cooper and requires a four-year apprenticeship.

Once the staves and the lids have been put together by the cooper, the cask is charred on the inside, and then steam pressure is applied to make sure it is watertight. A cooper also has to check empty barrels that have been previously filled with whisky and replace and repair staves and make sure the cask is suitable to be reused. In the Scotch whisky industry, barrels can be used various times and it's up to the cooper to declare them fit for purpose or not. One of the oldest barrels we saw that day was from the Stitzel-Weller distillery and had first been filled with bourbon 50 years previously, on 8 November 1966.

We were free to wander round the cooperage, take photos and ask questions. We didn't want to disturb the men and it took me a good 10 minutes to realise that they weren't really working; they were there for our benefit. It was a Saturday, the cooperage wasn't normally open at the weekend; they were working for us.

Watching them work I suddenly understood one of the reasons for the popularity of programmes like *Bake Off* and *The Great British Sewing Bee*. Most of us don't make things either as a job or even as a hobby. We spend our days in front of computers and buy things we need. Part of the joy of *Bake Off* and the *Sewing Bee* is that people are making and using their hands. The drama is in whether they will work or not – will the clothes fit, will the sponge rise? The biggest crime is a soggy bottom rather than a shattered dream. It's about what people make; real skills with your hands. No soft skill in the world can help your chocolate fondant melt in the mouth – you need to be good with your hands.

Watching the men at the cooperage, and now that *Bake Off* has moved channels, my money is on the next big programme on TV being *The Great British Cask Off*. A middle-ranking manager from Suffolk, an accountant from Bath and a GP from Manchester could compete alongside a call centre manager from Greenock to learn a four-year apprenticeship in six weeks, all culminating in making the perfect whisky barrel. On the side, they could learn to produce some of the tourist tat made out of individual staves that ends up on sale in whisky shops across Scotland, and we can discover more about the liquid contained in the barrels.

In the way that food from professional kitchens has been fetishised and chefs are now celebrities and kitchens mythologised, it's about time we did the same with the whisky industry. It is only a matter of time before a writer goes off to learn how to be a cooper or a coppersmith or a distiller with the aim of writing a book the way so many have about kitchens. The BBC could get in early with a reality TV competition.

Coopers used to be paid per finished cask and would often end up getting work-related injuries very quickly, due to the speed at which they worked to maximise their earnings and the little care they took for their own safety. Now coopers are mostly in salaried positions and great care is taken to ensure that they do not end up with career-ending injuries such as repetitive strain.

There is a romanticism about the old ways of working in distilleries when nothing was automated, all the tasks were done by hand and men got a dram at the end of the day. The problem was, the drams could get more frequent as the work got harder or the boss's back was turned and more than one distillery worker became dependent on the whisky that he was making. It kept the workers docile and from asking for better pay and conditions while their families suffered the havoc that alcoholism wreaks. Working in a distillery is now a job, like other ones, with decent pay and good conditions, and while workers may get discounts on the whisky they make, payment is not made in the stuff. It seems to me that both the business and its employees are a lot better for it.

Someone who did not fetishise distillery work was writer Agnes Owens. She was based in Alexandria until her death in 2014, and is one of the great unsung heroes of Scottish literature. Owens wrote about the small people on the edges of life, the ones most people only see out of the side of their eye. Her characters are the middle-aged women who clean the pubs when they're closed, the men who spend their days sitting on park benches drinking cheap fortified wine wishing it was whisky, and young men with skills but no jobs.

In *Gentlemen of the West*, first published in 1984, a 22-year-old bricklayer called Mac spends his life looking for employment, or dodging it. While he had dreamed at school of becoming a veterinary surgeon and his pal McCluskie a fireman, he becomes an apprentice brickie, and McCluskie goes to work in the distillery. The only advantage McCluskie has over the narrator is that distillery work is mostly inside and he can also smuggle out some new make off the stills every so often. The reader is introduced to McCluskie as he has just got out of jail after being inside for manslaughter that everyone says was actually murder.

Darkly comic, I wondered what Owens would have made of the Dramboree visit to the distillery in her town with us all standing and staring in wonder at coopers, all thrilled to be there.

Our group left to see the stills and then we went to see my favourite person in the whisky industry. (If you are reading this and you are in the whisky industry and I met you while researching this book, don't worry, you are my second favourite person in the whisky industry; it's just she is first.)

With its grain still, Loch Lomond produces vodka and gin as well as whisky. All of the new-make from all the stills has to be analysed and recorded to make sure it stays consistent, to ensure its chemical components are the same, and that it will have the flavour you want when you drink it in 10 or 20 years.

The person in charge of all this is a wee bird-like woman with curly hair and glasses called Lorna Buchanan.

I love scientists. People in fancy designer suits and power shift dresses from Hugo Boss never impress me; even a gangster can buy fancy tailoring, but you have to earn a white coat and a place at the head of a laboratory.

I have spent my working life dealing with people or systems that other people have created, from teaching or learning languages to organising payments via a financial apparatus that is as synthetic, and as vulnerable, as the old Politburo system in the Soviet Union. Scientists deal in how the world works as opposed to people. If something doesn't turn out the way they expect then, once human error has been discounted, once they have got rid of the people, scientists are faced with the entire universe to deal with and try to figure out.

I am rubbish at the scientific universe. Emboldened by a radio producer, I once attempted to explain the difference between baking soda and baking powder in public at a radio recording. I got a painstakingly clear explanation from a scientist friend of what their differences were and what they each did as raising agents. I copied out the explanation and learned it by heart.

I then messed up on the first line, saying it was an acid when it was an alkali. Or the other way round. Anyway, surprisingly enough, it didn't make the edit.

Science is not, and has never been, my forte. My abiding memory of science at school was having the head of the science department as a teacher and us doing illegal experiments. In the mid-1980s, what was then the Scottish Office had banned a whole load of chemicals for use in the classroom. My science teacher did what every other sensible science teacher in Scotland did. He took them home, put them in his garage and brought them back on the days when he wanted to show us an experiment. Some days, science lessons would start like this:

'So, eh, you don't have to do this experiment for yer O grade.'

He would look from side to side.

'In fact, yer no' really supposed tae dae this experiment.'

He'd raise his shoulders up to his ears.

'In fact, don't tell anyone we're dain' this.'

We all convinced ourselves that the regular visits from lab technicians were really just to check that he hadn't blown us all up. He hadn't. He never did. And none of us ever told anyone what banned experiments we did in the name of science. In fact, I am not even telling you now.

The sad thing is that even this did not instil in me an abiding love for the subject. I am far better at getting people to do things with substances that are banned in many countries than I am at understanding the basic science behind baking powder.

Scientists don't think like the rest of us; even our questions can make no sense to them. If you ask a historian a question about what happened in a certain village in northern England in 1828, the answer will depend on their particular area of interest. It might be about working lives, politics, gender behaviour or food, but it will be something that the layperson can grasp. Talk to a scientist and you can often get a completely baffling answer until you ask what is for you the same question in a slightly different way, but for the scientist a totally separate one.

As none of us likes to be confused, there aren't nearly enough scientists in public life helping us to see how they think, and they certainly don't get paid remotely what they're worth, but they will be the only ones left standing when climate change has drowned all the financiers and property magnates.

Lorna is the epitome of the best in science. Modest about her work and her achievements and proud of her small team, she takes the time with us all to explain what components are in each of the new-makes she tests and analyses. She hands round six different glasses with new-make spirit so that we can all smell the differences, and she explains what flavours will develop in barrels and which ones will dissipate.

How the taste of whisky changes as it develops in a barrel

has to be one of the most fascinating things about this drink. Straight from a still, the liquid tastes like a yeasty not-very-good grappa or orujo. Even the most pleasant new-make I have tasted was still nowhere near as good as a decent orujo or grappa.

Thus we learned that there is something about a barrel that completely changes the taste (although we still don't know exactly why), and turns whisky into the world's favourite spirit. That people like Lorna exist and know what something coming off the still will taste like from a barrel leaves me in awe.

It's more than no' bad, it's positively quite good.

The distillery visit over, we went back to the hostel and I stood in the communal kitchen and panicked.

I have being doing cooking classes and demos for over six years, during which time I have taught people how to light fires with sugar and a tiny gas blowtorch; I have barbecued lamb chops in the dark using a phone torch as a light; I have made Catalan sauces in front of Catalans and had them tell me it was better than their grandmothers'. I talk about food and food culture regularly on BBC Radio, and no audience that we have ever recorded in front of has ever freaked me out like this one.

These people taste walnuts and dried fruit when I taste feet. They can tell the alcohol percentage point of a whisky by smell, and this is the audience that I am supposed to be teaching something to.

I was lucky that the brand ambassador whose whisky I was using was also there, and I wanted him to tell everyone about the distillery that R&B were building on Raasay. New distilleries in unexpected places are always of interest to any whisky fan and an island that has never had a legal distillery on it especially so. The other story about the distillery is that the area they wanted to build over turned out to be home to a colony of a protected species of bat, and so they immediately had to change plans and work out how to build around them.

Then he stopped speaking and it was my turn.

They all looked at me expectantly, so I thought I'd better ask them about cooking with whisky. Very few of them ever did any. Someone said they added cheap stuff to a chilli, someone else always added a decent whisky, blend or malt, to a chocolate mousse. Most of them hadn't even thought about it.

I had the two while-we-wait whiskies from R&B to use, both the peated and the unpeated. Although 70 per cent of the flavour of whisky comes from a barrel, the most noticeable immediate difference in taste between whiskies is peat. Peat gives such a distinctive flavour that it cannot be ignored and is something that non-whisky drinkers often think is in all whiskies.

Having a peated and an unpeated whisky gave them the chance to decide what worked better in a dish and what was personal preference. First up was gravadlax. Everyone thought that peated whisky was better with gravadlax than unpeated. Peated whiskies do tend to work really well with oily fish and heavy seafood in general, and if you are making gravadlax and are not sure which whisky to use, just imagine

70 whisky geeks standing behind you whispering the word peat into your ears.

It was the same with the steamed salmon – almost full agreement, peated whisky is better.

Then we came to the Caledonia cream.

If you only ever make one thing from this book in your entire life, make this. It is gobsmackingly easy and will delight your friends and family when you offer them a real adult dessert. Cream is something that the UK food media has fallen out of love with. If you look at magazines and newspaper columns, the writers are all in love with almonds, polenta and yoghurt for making desserts, but supermarkets all have shelves full of cream, so everyone is still using it, and for more than just putting on top of strawberries. This dessert also has the joy of matching any and every whisky in your collection. The Dramboree crowd were split down the middle and decided that the whisky that goes in this dish is completely personal. Also, if you don't like marmalade, replace it with jam, or fruit in syrup.

Caledonia Cream

Serves 4

300ml double or whipping cream
150g cream cheese or crowdie
2 tablespoons bitter orange marmalade
3 tablespoons whisky
juice of ½ lemon
25g caster sugar (optional)

To serve
mandarin segments
shortbread biscuits

In a big bowl whip the cream until it's in stiff peaks,
then whip in the cream cheese or crowdie. Whip in the
marmalade and whisky, and then add in 2 teaspoons of
the lemon juice, while whipping.

Taste and see if you want to add in the sugar (it depends
on the sweetness of the marmalade and your preference),
or a tiny bit more lemon juice or whisky, and if you do
whip that in too.

Put in the fridge until you want to eat, then spoon into
glasses, pop a segment of mandarin on top and serve
with a shortbread biscuit.

They were now in the swing of things, telling me what they
thought would make the gravadlax better, how the steamed
salmon would be great with a citrus flavour and informing
each other about what whisky they'd use in a Caledonia
cream.

I breathed a very heavy sigh of relief and got out the cheese.

Blue cheese and peated whisky taste like they are made for
each other and every whisky fan should insist on it instead of
port, Marsala or some other drink rich British people thought
would annoy Napoleon and which they foisted upon the
aspiring lower orders.

Lagavulin, Machrie Moor, Ledaig should be what you drink with Stilton, or any other blue cheese. No one should make you drink oversweet red wine with cheese. If we all start insisting on it in friends' houses and restaurants we could create a new culinary tradition far more in keeping with modern times and tastes. We would free ourselves of badly thought-out combinations originally designed as propaganda tools and have a new tradition based on conviviality and pleasure rather than one based on pissing off the French. Given how much the British pissed off the French, and the rest of the EU, in June 2016 now would be a good time to get rid of outmoded traditions rooted in old enmities. We can do it one drink at a time.

Lastly, we did a whisky and chocolate tasting. Almost every distillery that is open to visitors has the option of a whisky and chocolate tasting. They go together really well. I had several different types of chocolate: chilli, lime, plain and, ironically, the one I bought just for a laugh was the one that went with both whiskies the best. It was dark chocolate and coconut, like an upmarket red label Bounty bar, and everyone said it was the best match.

I later mentioned this to someone who works with flavour profiling as a professor in a university and so must know what he is talking about, and he waxed lyrical about coconut flavours in whisky because of the charring in the casks. I say this means that you should try whisky with anything and everything and see what you think of it. Whisky and pumpkin as a match hasn't convinced me so far, but one day someone will make an amazing pumpkin pie with whisky, or a pumpkin curry to eat while drinking whisky and soda, and prove me wrong. If that is you, please invite me round, or at least send me a recipe and some photos so that I can drool.

My demo was done, no one had complained, and while I was clearing up people were coming up to me with ideas and suggestions and thanks. I went back to the common room and the whisky table and got a dram.

The people at Dramboree, the IT specialists and the scientists, were very exact, more intense and above all a lot less self-obsessed than most of the folk I normally deal with. It even turned out there was someone there who I had known from my early years in London. Billy Abbot had worked near to my offices and we used to have occasional lunch meet-ups with other people from social media and while we were all obsessed with food, Billy was obsessed with beer and whisky. He got his dream job writing for an online whisky shop and disappeared from my world and there he reappeared at Dramboree, revered as one of the main experts during the weekend, and is back in my life as my whisky guru and my main back-up when I need to ask for whisky advice and help.

Everyone there, not just Billy, was friendly and happy to explain to me all the whisky on the table, trying to get me to see the difference between really old whisky that had been bottled in the 1970s (lots of smoke – the stills were all heated by coal and oil back then, so whisky tasted different) and stuff that was newer and had been matured in sherry casks.

I was still getting a bit lost. There were too many bottles

and we all drank too much, but I managed to pick up some things.

Whisky geeks love whisky that was bottled 30 years ago. Becoming obsessed with Scotch seems to mean that you also develop that Scottish habit of nostalgia, so no whisky brand or blend is really the same as it was. After Dramboree, some of the people I became friends with on Facebook went to a special White Horse lunch where they tasted a range of the blended whisky from the late sixties onwards. For four days I saw photos of this lunch on Facebook, with various bottles of White Horse and long discussion threads about which ones were the best. There were explanations about the difference between each year and the disappointment for many that the oldest ones weren't just the best by merit of age.

They may be right – the Dramboree crowd generally are when it comes to whisky.

Charles MacLean, one of the world's great whisky experts, says that whenever he does blind tastings with older and newer versions of the same whisky, the older one always wins. The problem, as with most things, is the cost. A 12-year-old Glenlivet that you can buy in a shop will cost you a fraction of a 12-year-old Glenlivet from the early seventies that you can only get at auction. You have to decide if the increase in cost is worth the increase in pleasure. Personally, I owe my mother far too much money to be able to even think of buying whisky bottled in the 1970s, and so I am determined to squeeze as much pleasure as possible out of the entry-level whiskies and the supermarket special offers as I can.

Scots Gravadlax

The complete lack of any Scottish tradition of cooking with whisky is even more incomprehensible when you realise that our closest neighbours to the north, the Scandinavians, regularly use their aquavit to marinate salmon and make gravadlax.

We have a long tradition of smoking salmon, albeit with a much stronger smoke than is currently common in Scotland, and we once had a massive herring industry with a workforce of women salting the herring on the shore, so it does seem extremely strange that we never developed a dish using whisky to cure salmon.

The best we can do is appropriate a Scandinavian recipe and use whisky instead of aquavit. You really want to use a whisky with some peat in it but not one that is really heavily peated, so I'd recommend either Springbank or, if you want to be more like a proper Viking, Highland Park from Orkney.

Norwegian gravadlax is quite sweet and the ratio of sugar to salt they use is the opposite to this recipe. If we are going to make gravadlax Scottish, it would better suit our character to have it salty rather than sweet.

Serves 8–10

approx. 1kg side of salmon, properly boned
150g demerara sugar
200g coarse sea salt

5g roughly ground black pepper
6 tablespoons Springbank or Highland Park
15g dill, roughly chopped

Get some tweezers and carefully search the salmon and remove any bones, especially the almost invisible pin ones.

Lay the salmon skin side down, in two pieces if it is too long, in a glass dish or stainless steel or enamel tin.

Put the sugar, salt, peppercorns, dill and whisky in a mixing bowl.

Stir all the ingredients together.

Spread the mixture over the fish and rub it in well with your hand. Cover the dish with clingfilm and place a small chopping board and a few cans on top to weigh the fish down.

Put in the fridge and leave to cure for between 48 hours and 4 days.

Remove from the fridge and pour away the liquid released from the salmon and scrape away the marinade. Cut the fish into thin strips and serve with the whisky you used in the cure.

4

A MALT DRINK

'And malt does more than Milton can
To justify God's ways to man.'
A.E. HOUSMAN

Islay – as we will see, the Hebridean crofter's source of choice
for whisky – lies off the coast of Argyll and is one of the islands
in the Inner Hebrides. If you are Scottish it's just another island,
one of many that are a pain to get to with a car as you have to
drive halfway down the Argyll peninsula to get the ferry, or
go to Oban on one of three days in a week and get one there.

It has the same activities available as other islands: beaches,
birdwatching, hill walking. It has the same problems as other
islands: bad land distribution, lack of affordable housing,
lack of jobs. It occupies about the same geographical space as
Toronto, but Toronto has over 2.5 million people. Islay has
just over three thousand.

What Islay has in abundance is whisky. At the moment it has eight distilleries with at least another two under construction, and it produces about a quarter of Scotland's malt whisky exports. If there was any justice in the world, and increasingly there isn't, the British government would give every islander a Mercedes and a mansion on their 18th birthday out of sheer gratitude for the amount of tax that Islay's whisky production contributes to the public coffers.

Islay's distilleries have a long legal history and in 2016 both Laphroaig and Lagavulin celebrated their 200-year anniversary, while Bowmore got its legal licence in 1779. The long-standing legal distilleries are partly due to the availability of barley that wasn't needed for food after Daniel Campbell bought Islay in 1726 and modernised agricultural practices.

Campbell was a Glasgow merchant, one of the many who made their money from tobacco, cotton and other produce that relied on slave labour in the Americas. As a younger son, he had no chance of a proper inheritance and went off to New England, initially trading illegally with the English colonies. He later came back to Glasgow and was quickly one of the richest men in Scotland. He eventually became a member of the Scottish parliament, was one of the negotiators of the terms of the Act of Union in 1707 and richly rewarded for it.

Like most merchants, he built an ostentatious house. His was called the Shawfield Mansion, and it was badly damaged in a riot in 1725 which was triggered by the imposition of a malt tax that would greatly increase the cost of ale and whisky. The government decided that the Glasgow city officials were responsible for 'favouring the mob' and ordered that they recompense Campbell to the tune of £7,000, despite the reported damage to the mansion costing far less than half that to repair. That £7,000 formed the bulk of the £12,000 he used to buy the entire fertile island of Islay, which nowadays has whisky that can sell for £150,000 a bottle.

Personally, I like to think of Campbell's time on Islay as repentance for a life lived enslaving, benefiting from the produce of slaves and always making sure he was on the side of the powerful and corrupt. He initiated many agricultural reforms which hugely increased the level of production of barley and enabled farmers to use spare barley to make whisky, which kick-started whisky production on the island.

Campbell's descendants added to his reforms, building planned villages like Bowmore and Port Ellen, and so successful were they at developing the island and creating work that by 1831 Islay had 15,000 inhabitants, five times today's population.

Like so much of the Highlands and Islands, prosperity ended after the Napoleonic Wars when crop and cattle prices dropped dramatically. In 1846 the potato blight that caused terrible hardship in Ireland appeared in western Scotland, affecting some 200,000 people. It led to destitution rather than starvation, with the Kirk and others promptly intervening with aid. But a decade of poor harvests thereafter accelerated population decline.

Now Islay is heavily dependent on whisky and whisky tourism. Without it the population would probably be around a third less than it is now, and if you ever meet anyone from Islay either they or one of their family members are or were involved in the whisky industry.

However, there is a difference, almost a disconnect, between Whisky Scotland and Actual Scotland.

I was in a pub in Glasgow recently and bought a Bowmore and a Kilchoman whisky, two Islay whiskies. The young woman behind the bar beamed at me and said: 'I'm from Islay. I love it when anyone buys Islay whisky; it makes me think they're connected to home.'

I smiled and wondered if she fully appreciated Islay involvement in the whisky business. I imagined taking her to all the bars in all the world that stocked Ardbeg, Lagavulin, Bunnahabhain, Laphroaig and all the other Islay whiskies. I wanted to make her realise that producing a quarter of the malt of the third biggest industry in Scotland was a really big deal and that people came from all over the world to her wee island on pilgrimage. I wanted to tell her stories about gruff American male journalists drinking Port Ellen whisky outside the old distillery in the sun and crying with the joy of it; about a Spaniard saying that one of the best moments of his life was drinking Ardbeg by the fire in the rain in the cottage beside the distillery. But the whisky industry goes on selling itself to the world as part and parcel of Scottish culture, and Scots still think it's a tiny thing that's ours, having no real concept of just how big it is and what it means to other people.

The disconnect isn't restricted to Islay. When people think of Scotland and whisky tours, they do not think of towns in decline with no industry, or big cities with traffic jams and pollution. They think of wild landscapes and hills, lochs, deep blue sea and sheep. No one drinks a Ballantine's imagining a bottling plant on a massive industrial estate.

People want to believe, and the marketing people want to convince them, that their whisky tastes a bit salty because it has been made in a distillery beside the sea and then stored for a decade in barrels in a warehouse near the beach. The reality is that new-make, the liquid that comes directly from the still, often gets put straight into a tanker and then driven somewhere quite far inland to be put into barrels and stored. The more you keep your eyes open as you go round Scotland, the more you become aware just how much land is taken up with whisky storage space.

Although they only tend to be part of the story, a lot of distilleries are in beautiful rural settings where often they are about the only source of employment.

All the whisky made on Islay is malt whisky, and so someone needs to make the malt. A few distilleries still malt their own barley, notably Springbank and Highland Park, but most buy it in from professional maltsters and one of the biggest in Europe is the Port Ellen maltings on Islay.

Malted barley is not used exclusively in malt whisky. It's also used in beer, bread, the hot drink that my grandmother used to inflict on me and another drink less known in Britain called Vitamalt, one in my view that smells and tastes of baby sick but is very popular in other corners of the globe. Its success in the English-speaking Caribbean and West Africa seems to be down to it being sold as a health drink. Honestly, if you want to drink malt, drink whisky; if you don't want to drink alcohol, drink water. Do not let unfermented whisky wort touch your lips.

It was on Islay that I got the whole malting process explained to me by a big tall beaming man called Gordon.

His wife was eight and a half months pregnant with their first child and, whenever he changed from the subject of malting, it was to say how well he had done for himself with his wife, and what a great place to bring up kids Islay would be. He had been running the Port Ellen maltings for eight weeks and had found the perfect job in the perfect place. He was from Aberdeenshire, his wife was from a tiny island of 70 people off the coast further north; he said she needed to live on an island in the west and he needed her.

His knowledge of malting was exquisitely detailed. He explained how, when barley is taken off a field, it's about 20 per cent moisture. That figure has to be reduced to about 12 per cent for storage, so that it isn't plagued by bugs or any other undesirables.

At that point the barley is in dormancy, it's sleeping. So then it has to be kicked back into life to start the growth.

'We get 1,700 tonnes of barley delivered to us every two weeks for the maltings,' Gordon explained. 'Distillers will distil 420 litres of alcohol per tonne of malt, and we'll steep a mixture of English and Scottish barley.'

Traditionally, most of the barley grown in Scotland was given over to whisky production and south of the border it went to beer. As the whisky industry has developed and grown, that border has moved further and further south. But times have changed, not least to fulfil the high demands of quality control for Scotch-making. Now it is recognised that you are better off with good-quality malt from further away than using a bad harvest from the field next door, and any barley of lesser quality than required for whisky production is used for the manufacture of other products, mostly beer and bread.

With malting the idea is to allow the crop to grow – and then halt the process at the right moment. Permitting the plant to germinate for five days naturally breaks down the starch that's held in the middle of the grain, because that grain needs the sugar for energy. It begins with a rigorous steeping schedule.

'We soak the barley in water at about 14 degrees. In winter we have to use a boiler for about six hours to get moisture to penetrate the husk,' said Gordon. 'Then we drain it, and give it an air rest so that it can start to breathe. We leave the grain breathing for 12 or 13 hours and then we repeat the process twice more.'

By the end of the third and final process, the moisture content in that grain has gone up to 46 per cent and a wee root is visible on the grain, called the chit or culm. For germination to continue, the aim is to replicate springtime. To do this the barley used to be spread on the malting floor and left for five days. The key to making good malt is a nice slow cool germination.

During growth spurts it's giving off heat, so all the windows are usually opened as excess heat can cause the grain to sweat. This can speed the growing process, causing a chain reaction, and all the little rootlets will start tying together to form one big mat. Left untouched, there would be a foul-smelling carpet of golden malt.

To prevent this, the grain is regularly turned. Traditionally, this was the most intensive part of the malting process – and some producers still insist on this method. Workers walk the floor all day, turning the grain with pitchforks, ending up with one pronounced forearm and shoulder from the pressure of lifting and turning. That is where the term monkey shoulder comes from – there's even a whisky named after their arms.

Most whisky makers don't do any of this anymore and malting floors lie empty or have been remodelled to be visitor centres and cafes. They get their barley malted to their specifications by people like Gordon, and Port Ellen maltings is one of the biggest in Europe.

Gordon explains: 'At the maltings in Port Ellen we do vat sizes of 56 tonnes and we do 13 batches a week. We don't have enough floor space to spread all this barley out, so in the sixties and seventies they started building drum maltings, and nowadays rather than spread the barley out we cast it into a big drum.

'The germinating barley sits in that drum with fans blowing cool air to enable a nice slow germination and every 12 hours we turn the drums really slowly using a cog and wheel function.'

The drums are checked daily, the same way as maltsters using a traditional malting floor would. If the germination is racing on – very common in the heat of summer – it's cooled, or the steeping schedule is changed. It's a very reactive process and can vary day to day.

After five days on a malting floor, or in a rotating drum, the grain should feel soft and silky smooth. As so-called green malt, it is ready to go into the kiln.

The idea of the kilning is to heat the malt to a point where it's going to be sufficiently dry for milling. The way the kiln is heated has a direct result on the flavour of the whisky. On Islay, peat has been a traditional fuel, giving off a distinctive 'peat reek'. Although peat is not the source of the heat, it remains the root of the flavour. In the case of almost all Islay whiskies, you get the peat smoke stuck to the husk as well and this further weighs on the taste buds. Selecting the peat is a science in itself.

'Now, although peat to most people is the same everywhere we need to be careful because different peats have different phenols,' Gordon said. 'Coastal peat is very iodine, salty and briny, while mainland peat is a bit drier and burns completely differently, giving a slightly different flavour profile. The skill of the malting guy is to understand that; he needs to know where the peats come from and know what kind of fire he'll get to bring consistency to products.

'We don't get any heat from the peat; we just want smoke to flavour the barley. Different distilleries on the island request different phenol rates: Ardbeg ask for the highest phenol count, about 55 parts per million, while Lagavulin currently are about 38 ppm.

'The strength of the barley that goes into the distillery is far higher than that which ends up in the bottle. The ppm in the bottle ends up at about a third of what started off in the grain. Even then there are only so many ppms that can actually be absorbed into the main spirit, so we say it's 38 ppm in the barley; in reality the whisky is probably nearer to 18.'

Drying malt in the kiln occurs in two stages. The first 12 to 14 hours is free-drying the malt to about 50°C to get rid of the moisture, and that's the time when lots of peat goes up in smoke.

Gordon explained 'We want lots of smoke going up in underneath the malt so that the smoke can stick to the grain.'

After about 14 hours in the kiln the temperature is ramped up to 60°C for a further 14 hours. At this stage there is no point in using any peat as it is rendered ineffective.

'Our kilning process takes about 28 hours, after which we'll analyse the phenol spec and then send the malt off to the distillers to start the distilling process,' said Gordon.

In recent years ppm has become a kind of Holy Grail for a certain type of whisky obsessive. Liking whisky with a high ppm turned into a whisky-based masculinity contest. Someone in the industry called it the Friday night curry factor, where after 15 pints out with the boys the only suitable thing to do is see who can eat the hottest curry possible. And so it has been with peaty whiskies. The problem with drinking a really ultra-peaty whisky is that there is no taste other than peat and, once you've twisted your face and said, 'Oh, that is really peaty', there is nothing left to say, and nothing left to enjoy.

If you are tasting a wide range of whiskies at any one time, any professional tasting will start off with lighter Speyside whiskies and end with the heavier peated ones. The less imaginative whisky fan has possibly assumed that meant they were ending a tasting with the best, rather than simply the strongest-tasting.

If you think that you do not like whisky because it is too smoky for you, Islay whisky is not a good place to start trying to prove yourself wrong. Once you get a taste for whisky, it might be worth trying a peated again to see, but if it is not for you, there is no shame in it. Islay has plenty of fans, and there are plenty of other whiskies to enjoy.

I was on Islay with some journalists who, like me, were based in London, some of whom I already knew. If I was describing Scotland in terms of distilleries, this was the ultimate whisky Scotland trip. It was the only reason we were all on Islay and what we were all bonding over. Journalists, though, are inquisitive types, but they were so focused on whisky that they didn't seem to be interested in much else.

Kenny, the minibus driver who chauffered us round, was an ardent supporter of Scottish independence who had given up watching BBC News and thought that Russia Today provided him with better coverage, but no one argued the point with him as no one found out. Emma, who ran the guesthouse we all stayed in, had recently brought her family back to Islay after many years in Glasgow. Her father had been the manager at one of the distilleries and she and her family were making a lot of their living from corporate visits and press trips paid directly by whisky companies. We were all finding the complete lack of mobile phone reception very disconcerting. Emma explained to me that everyone on the island communicated by Facebook and if they weren't at home would run into cafes or pubs or anywhere else with Wi-Fi to send someone a message. Sometimes I felt I was the group's official interpreter for non-whisky knowledge.

I've since wondered if we had been sharing accommodation with some nature journalists, who are about the only non-whisky journalists who would visit the land, how we might have judged each other. They would have talked about gannets, oystercatchers and the migration patterns of barnacle geese, while we waxed lyrical about malting grain, the effect the size of a still has on taste and how good the distillers' selection Lagavulin was. They would have smiled politely and thought, 'These people are quite mad, it's all whisky.' We would have thought, 'What a bunch of weirdos with such an obsession with birds.' We would all have been right.

Presbyterian Porridge with a Twist

While at the Glenegedale guesthouse, Emma told us all at breakfast to put a teaspoon of whisky in our porridge. Her husband spent two hours every morning making porridge using just oats and salt and water. I tried this at home and it is better than my usual oats, water, salt and three minutes in the microwave, but I do not have two hours every morning to dedicate to making porridge.

If you want a special porridge at the weekend the best thing is to make proper Presbyterian porridge with salt, water and oats. Once it is cooked, put it in a bowl and have a small dish of freshly whipped cream on the side then add a teaspoon of Islay whisky to the porridge. Don't put more than a teaspoon or you will ruin it. Stir the whisky through the porridge and then take half a spoonful of porridge and half a spoonful of cream at the same time.

Neo-Presbyterian Risotto

The change a teaspoon of peaty whisky can make to porridge was really intriguing (yes, this is the kind of thing that food obsessives think about at great length) and so I have spent a while experimenting with risotto. There is a version of risotto where white wine, instead of being added to stock, is put in each individual dish and the risotto is served on top. It's eaten by digging the fork to the bottom of the dish each time and gives you an almost bubbly taste.

After several attempts, some of which were dreadfully bland and others too strong, I have got it right.

You need a really simple risotto, just onions, garlic, rice and chicken stock will do. Don't use peas, mushrooms or asparagus. It really is best with a good chicken or vegetable stock and onions. Be brave and leave the rest of the stuff out.

In each serving bowl add 2 teaspoons of an Islay whisky and 2 teaspoons of soda water, and serve the risotto on top. Eat it as above, by digging the fork to the bottom of the dish each time to mix the whisky and the soda in with the rice.

Personally, I would never start someone's whisky journey with an Islay, but then someone told me that they fell in love with whisky after tasting peat, and someone else tweeted me that they really didn't like whisky but were enjoying Laphroaig (one of the strongest-tasting and peatiest whiskies in the mainstream) and did I think that was OK? In the end we know very little about ourselves and even less about other people.

Islay's Lagavulin whisky was a fundamental constituent of White Horse, once one of Britain's favourite whiskies. The origin of the name lies in the White Horse Inn in Canongate, Edinburgh. However, the whisky, first produced in 1861, was made in Glasgow by Mackie & Co. The company took over the Lagavulin distillery in 1888 and benefited for the next 30 years or more from a fondness developed for the blend by British soldiers.

Almost the only place in the UK that you can find White Horse now is a hotel bar on Islay. The once popular UK blend is now only sold abroad, mostly in Russia, but as Lagavulin is such an important component of it and there is a long tradition of White Horse drinking on Islay, they still sell it to one hotel on the island.

The Islay whisky I have had the most difficult relationship with has been Laphroaig. People find it very divisive. It has a really deep, strong flavour that is almost like Germoline, along with lots of peat and seaweed. Some people gag at the smell, others cannot get enough of it. My issue with it is different.

Now, my father will tell you I am talking nonsense, that

he never said such a thing in his life and that this is akin to false memory syndrome, but I swear to you he did this. One evening, when I was about 16, he was in the kitchen getting an after-dinner Macallan and shaking his head and tutting.

'Laphroaig,' he said. 'Laphroaig. Naebdy but public school eejits who don't know anything but how to take control and invade places drink Laphroaig.'

As someone who never went to public school, has no idea how to take control, has never invaded anywhere, but prides herself on knowing a thing or two, I knew Laphroaig wasn't for me. So much so that I never even tried it until I was in my late thirties.

It took me years to realise why my father said what he did. My first inkling of it was seeing the crest of the Prince of Wales on the bottle I tried. I didn't have much idea what it meant beyond it had some kind of royal connection, but I knew that would not have impressed my father. He is, was and always will be a convinced republican so any kind of royal association would not have thrilled him in any way, shape or form.

It turned out that the royal warrant was the least of it, and that Prince Charles was famous on Islay for crashing his plane at the airport in 1994 when he tried to land at too high a speed in a tailwind when he was going to the Laphroaig distillery on a visit. Laphroaig is apparently Prince Charles's favourite whisky. My father must have read it somewhere the day he was in the kitchen muttering, and that was how a great aversion to it was born.

5

THE BARLEY WATER STORY

*'Too much of anything is bad, but too much
of good whiskey is barely enough.'*
MARK TWAIN

In 1982 the American writer Paul Theroux travelled round
the coast of Great Britain. It was the time of the Falklands War
and the year Prince William was born. That summer, while
I was sitting in a fold-out paddling pool in a back garden in
suburban Glasgow, Theroux was admiring Edinburgh and
pondering the perils of Tartan Special.

Scotland seems to confuse him. He finds it too empty; the
west coast landscape has too many inlets and sea lochs and they
disrupt his journey walking round the coast by adding unexpected length. He speaks almost exclusively to old men, for they
are the ones who take public transport in such an empty area
as the West Highlands, and he finds them strange.

'The Scots had a nervous way with a joke. Their wit was aggressive and unsmiling. I kept wondering: Was that meant to be funny?'

Theroux has long been regarded as one of the most grumpy, curmudgeonly, gripe-ridden travel writers in the English language, something that, in these days of PR-controlled travel blogs and Instagram feeds, I greatly admire him for. So I find myself slightly perplexed by his lack of understanding of us. For surely we Scots are his spiritual brethren? I have travelled the world through Theroux's books and his miserablist, irascible views remind me of so many Scotsmen of his generation that I was rather shocked on a recent rereading of *The Kingdom by the Sea* that he hadn't wanted to move there immediately. Perhaps people don't like mirrors.

Reading his description of Oban in 2016 is also slightly troubling:

Oban was made of stone. It was Scottish and solid ... a town of cold bright rooms, with rosy-cheeked people in sweaters sitting inside and rubbing their hands; it had fresh air and freezing water ...

In Oban it struck me that most Scottish buildings looked as durable as banks. Here the dull clean town was on a coast of wild water and islands. Some of these Scottish coastal towns looked as if they had been thrown out of the ground.

As soon as I arrived in Oban I looked nervously around the town for signs of physical collapse needing urgent government intervention. But Theroux was talking in terms of different banks, in a simpler time. The town looked as solid and durable as ever.

I went to Oban over Easter with Sheri, one of my oldest friends. We are now so old that we have known each other for nearly 20 years and she and I shared the last flat in Barcelona that I lived in.

The big mission for Sheri when we shared a flat was to get us invites and VIP tickets to every and any club that we wanted to go to on a Saturday night. By the Wednesday we'd decide where we wanted to go and then Sheri would take on the challenge. Occasionally, I would get a phone call on a Thursday afternoon.

'You know, I don't think I can do this, I might not be able to get us in.'

'Oh come on, Sheri, if anyone in this city can get us free passes, you can!'

'You know, you're right, I shouldn't give in like this! Let me see who else I might know.'

It never, ever failed.

Saturday was the single most important event of the week. Not going out on a Saturday night was a sign of serious illness. Saturday made the week with its dull job paying not enough money worthwhile, and was something I started anticipating on early Wednesday afternoon. The music we played while getting ready to go out had to match the venue we were going to. Cuban music clashed with dance which clashed with hip-hop. The getting ready and the music meant that our Saturday nights would start at about 9pm in the flat and finish with an early-morning metro at about eight o'clock the next day. By that time our make-up had gone grey, body glitter had turned to grit, sunglasses were superglued to our faces, and small children on their way to the beach with their grandparents were suitably scared.

Now when I go to Barcelona and see Sheri we sometimes spend three days convincing each other that we will go to the best new club and show everyone there how it should be done. We get dressed up for it and put on even more make-up and glitter than we did when this was a weekly occurrence, then we go and sit in her friend's bar and talk about going clubbing. The bar closes at three and we always go back home, because we choose to. We could go clubbing if we really wanted.

Last year we went to a daytime party at some DJ friends of hers and the music was almost exactly the same as the music I remembered from Barcelona 1999. The only thing missing was the Matinée Group remix of Whitney Houston's 'It's Not Right but It's Okay' to complete the 16-year-old vibe. I asked Sheri what was going on.

'Our stuff is back in as retro for new kids going clubbing.'

I stared at her. 'Our stuff is the new *retro*?'

'Yeah, but it was better when we did it.'

Sheri now runs a Bollywood dance school in Barcelona and DJs at Indian club nights all across Spain. Yet despite being a major representative of South Asian culture Sheri doesn't like whisky. She drinks gin or wine. She just wanted to come along and see some of Scotland and have a holiday. I warned her it would be cold, but 20 years in Barcelona have left her with quite different ideas about that definition from mine.

To test her on whisky, when she arrived in Scotland I got her to try a Laphroaig, just to see what she made of it. She screwed up her face and nearly spat it out.

'Oh, that is gross, I mean absolutely hideous.'

'Well, it was once described as tasting like cheap perfume strained through a peat bog.'

'I can see why.'

Our trip to Oban was delayed by a day as I had to go and talk about Spanish Easter food on the radio, so rather than taking the train up north we went to the BBC Scotland studios on the banks of the Clyde, a building that looks like a beehive. After telling Scottish radio listeners about marzipan sweets shaped to look like saints' finger bones complete with red fruit marrow, we headed into the centre of Glasgow for an event. But we got to the venue too early, so decided to go to the Indian restaurant across the road for a drink and a snack.

This presents a problem. If you are a person of Pakistani or Indian origin, apparently the Eighth Wonder of the World is a Scottish Asian. Sheri is from Manchester. Her parents are from the Pakistani Punjab. She once came back to Barcelona from a family visit, having watched a television programme featuring Scottish Asians. 'They looked like me and spoke like you! It was so strange and funny, and actually quite sexy.'

This fascination is not limited to the diaspora.

I have a friend in Karachi who watches Scottish political programmes if MSP Humza Yousaf is on them even though she has no interest at all in Scottish politics. She puts videos on Facebook of Scottish programmes if they feature an Asian, and loads of Pakistanis leave messages about how much they love the accent.

It is evidently 'a thing'. The whisky industry would do well to sponsor a big Bollywood wedding film and have a story about a Scottish Asian working in the whisky industry and a lovestruck Bollywood star. It would make a mint and sell even more whisky.

We went into the restaurant, with Sheri under strict instructions not to laugh, and were greeted by a huge Punjabi Scot singing 'Lady in Red' at me for wearing a red coat and seating us at a great table by the window as we'd only be there for half an hour.

The all-male front of house staff were enamoured by Sheri and the way she constantly smiled at them and took photos. They asked about Barcelona, and chatted about Glasgow and how lovely Oban and Mull were. They told Sheri where all the objects in the restaurant had come from and where the photos on the walls were taken. She told them about her trips to India; they all agreed that I should go and visit.

The whole time I was terrified that she was not going to be able to contain herself, talking to Glaswegian Asians. On leaving, as soon as the restaurant door closed behind us, she turned to me and said, 'You see – I didn't laugh once. You should trust me more!'

We didn't have pakora there; they didn't even have any on the menu. In Glasgow, pakora can have a bad name as too often in restaurants it is reheated and dried out, so new hip places might not necessarily even serve it. Sheri, however, makes the best pakora I have ever had in my life. Even if you come back from a night out to find some left on a plate, from a batch she made about eight hours previously, cold and exposed to the elements, it will still be far better than most of the pakora you will have eaten in restaurants.

Getting the recipe for it is a problem, though. It's not that Sheri is too secretive to give it to me; the problem is she's too Spanish. Spanish people do recipes the old way. Most of them didn't learn how to cook from books. You will rarely hear a Spaniard say at a dinner table that the lamb you are eating is from a recipe by a TV chef or food writer. Someone in their family, or a friend, will have told them what to do, or they might have had a conversation about it in a restaurant, or talked to someone in the food market – and the most exact measurement given is 'enough'.

It becomes such a normal way of cooking that discovering that other people cook recipes from books can come as quite a shock. I still find it strange that food writers I know cook complete recipes from someone else's book. I do sometimes and I always feel like I'm serving someone else's food, having had no input or understanding of how the dish came about; I'm just following instructions in blind faith.

The food writer Claudia Roden talks on an old *Desert Island Discs* programme about starting to collect recipes from friends and family, exiled from Egypt after the Suez crisis, who were passing through London on their way to more permanent new homes. There were never any exact weights – with a certain type of dough the most accurate measurement she could get was to make it so that it felt like an earlobe when you pressed it. She had to work things out and then carefully record weights and measures to compose the recipes so that others could replicate the food of faraway friends and family.

If you have ever eaten houmous, tahini or pitta bread in the UK it is thanks to Claudia. She was the first person to introduce the food of the Middle East to an audience outside of tiny pockets of diaspora in London. Her food writing isn't about a twist on something or a hasty put-together of ingredients from a trip to the supermarket. All her books are about the people who make the food, where they are from, how the food got there, why they cook as they do. Claudia is as likely to tell you about the hidden fourth wives who did all the cooking in traditional Moroccan households as she is the ideal cut of lamb for a tagine. If you want to understand a people and their food and Claudia has written a book about them, her book is for you. She will also save you a lot of trouble turning information like Sheri's into a proper recipe as she will have done the work for you.

A Pakora Recipe Written by Me Pretending to Be Claudia Roden

Makes around 12

100g chickpea (gram) flour, plus more if needed
200g (2 medium-sized) onions, finely chopped
220g peeled and chopped potatoes
100g chopped spinach

½ teaspoon each of ground coriander, chilli powder,
  ground fenugreek and cumin seeds
1 teaspoon salt
handful of finely chopped coriander
1 litre sunflower oil, for deep-frying

To serve
natural yoghurt
chopped fresh mint

Sift the chickpea flour into a bowl and add all the
vegetables and spices, the salt and coriander. Add enough
water to make a stiff batter. If you think the vegetables
aren't coated in enough flour, add some more.

Heat the oil in a deep, heavy-based frying pan. If you
don't have a temperature probe then after a few minutes
drop in a tiny piece of onion and, once it fizzes and rises
to the surface, the oil is ready.

Fry the pakora in batches until they are brown and
crispy, about a dessertspoonful for each one, then drain
on some kitchen paper.

Serve with yoghurt and fresh mint mixed together and a
good whisky.

Although the above recipe is what I have taken from
Sheri's advice, she also said:

'Remember, there is no right or wrong way to make pakora. Some families like the crunch of dried pomegranate seeds in the pakoras, while others love to add a few cauliflower florets. If you like more spice, just add more.

The whisky event that we finally attended started with Sheri announcing to the Glengoyne brand ambassador that she really liked theirs as it tasted just like Jack Daniel's rather than whisky, and ended with us organising, over a lot of gin, a trip to Barcelona with two women we'd never met before, so it was quite a success.

The next morning was not so good, so we got the later train to Oban, arriving there in the late afternoon. The place was full of Easter tourists, Europeans wrapped up in outdoor clothes and Glaswegian women with fake tans, high heels and leopard print drowning themselves in Pinot Grigio.

Oban itself was established round the distillery, which was founded in 1794. It's been in the same place since it was built, although the distillery was rebuilt in 1883. It's another example of how important whisky has been to Scotland for over 200 years, since the town wouldn't exist without the distillery.

Shipping came and went, various wars left their mark when its port had strategic importance, but now it's the biggest terminal for ferries to the Western Isles. Modern Oban lives off tourism, which has been important for the town since the railway arrived in the late 19th century. The buildings do look thrown out of the ground, as Theroux wrote, and by the time we had climbed to the top of the town to our guesthouse, which overlooked the bay and the distillery, we weren't fit for much more.

The next morning we went on the ferry to Mull.

If you are familiar at all with the children's television programme *Balamory*, you'll have seen Mull and its capital Tobermory. Although Archie the Inventor is now hosting *The News Quiz* on Radio 4 and Suzie Sweet is dead, Tobermory still has life-size photos of the *Balamory* characters you can pose beside. It must also have the highest percentage of craft shops per head of population in the entire world.

The brightly painted houses facing the bay are all given over to shops selling island-made wind catchers, jewellery and paintings of the town. You cannot buy toilet roll or a bottle of washing-up liquid anywhere on the front, but there is a shop that sells only horn craft and walking sticks. You can buy all kinds of hand-crafted heads for your walking sticks and kit to put them together and make them for yourself; the same shop also sells candelabras made out of antlers. The island has a population of less than three thousand, so everyone living there must have a hand-crafted walking stick and an antler candelabra in their house, as well as a load of dirty dishes because they've run out of detergent.

Mull has just one distillery. It's on the seafront at Tobermory, beside the pier and the bus stop. It was originally built in 1798 by merchant John Sinclair, marking the lifting of the restriction on grain use in Britain imposed during its conflict with France.

Like most distilleries in Scotland it has changed ownership

many times over the decades and was closed entirely for 41 years in the 20th century, reflecting the economic times. Even when it reopened, its future was far from secure. Another short-term closure in 1975 led to 14 people being suddenly made redundant. That number of lost jobs on an island of less than three thousand inhabitants has a massive impact on the local economy and is one of the problems of international ownership. Distilleries can be bought and sold or even closed down for reasons of international competition or company-wide efficiency that have nothing to do with a local area but have a huge effect on it. When Bruichladdich distillery on Islay reopened in 2000, having been closed in 1994 as 'surplus to requirements', one of their new employees had been made redundant from the same distillery at least four times.

By the time the Tobermory distillery opened again in 1989 the warehouse behind it had been converted into flats, so all of its output is matured off site. It is now owned by a South African-based company which also owns Bunnahabhain on Islay and Deanston distillery near Stirling.

When you sit in New York or Hong Kong enjoying Tobermory whisky, it is quite strange to think that someone in Stellenbosch, South Africa, has decided to invest enough money in marketing and production to enable you to drink the product of the island of Mull's only distillery. Your taste for Black Bottle, the blend that uses a lot of Tobermory malt, keeps various families on the island, and is vital in saving the population of Mull from becoming just a group of pensioners living a Scottish Highland fantasy.

When you buy a bottle of Ledaig (meaning 'safe haven' in Gaelic) you are helping the distillery guide – a young woman from the isle of Lewis who is a biologist but there were no jobs left at the aquarium – make a life for herself on Mull. It's good to know that you are drinking something that is so important to the livelihoods of people in distant places, but it also makes them very vulnerable to both your tastes and a far-off company's commercial strategy.

Apart from Sheri and me, the other visitors were mostly walkers who had never been to a whisky distillery but were looking for something to do on a non-hill climbing day. They looked rather bemused throughout, yet many were convinced enough to buy some Tobermory whisky at the end of the visit, so something must have sunk in.

The Tobermory distillery produces about 800,000 litres a year, while the average malt distillery in Scotland does 4–5 million litres. They make Tobermory in the first half of the year, and their peated brand, Ledaig, in the second.

They get the peated barley for the Ledaig from Gordon at the Port Ellen maltings on Islay. It is delivered by boat then ground down into a grist in the distillery. Tobermory, like almost all the older Scottish distilleries I've been to, uses a Porteus mill to grind the malt. These mills were so effective and so well made that the company went bust because no one needed new ones or replacement parts. More than one technology company has learned from such a mistake and now deliberately builds in obsolescence.

Once the barley has been milled, it goes into a mash tun to convert the starch to sugar so that it can ferment. Water is added three separate times to the barley to maximise the sugar extraction. Distillers get measured by their bosses, on their efficiency of alcohol output compared to weight of barley, and at Tobermory the first two lots of water are sent to the fermentation tanks while the third is sent back to be used with the next lot of barley.

The barley water is then cooled and filtered through to the fermentation tanks. The barley that is left over from the filtering is sold on to farmers for cattle feed and, if you ever eat Isle of Mull Cheddar, the cows being milked for it have been reared on the by-product of the whisky-making process.

The fermentation tanks hold 27,000 litres, and 100kg of distillers' yeast is added to each one. The tanks, or washbacks, can be made of wood or stainless steel. Many distilleries are loath to replace old wooden washbacks with stainless steel as they are concerned that this may affect the flavour of their whisky. Fermentation can last anything from 48 to over 90 hours and the length of the fermentation also affects taste and character.

If you ever look up the technical details of a distillery, some of the things you will discover are which type of washbacks are used and how long the fermentation time is. Whisky geeks have very serious discussions about how exactly taste is affected by the different variables.

The first thing that hits you when you open a fermentation tank is CO_2, and if you stick your head into the tank too quickly you can end up sprawled on the floor gasping for breath. There is a law of the universe that states that no matter how often a distillery guide tells people to be careful and not to stick their head into a fermentation tank too soon, someone always does and is overcome by the smell of yeast and fermenting barley as well as the CO_2. When you do visit a whisky distillery, just try to make sure that it's not you.

Once the barley has been fermented, it then needs to be distilled.

In most of Scotland the distillation is a double process. The fermented liquid, called wash, is distilled and then the resulting spirit is distilled. A few distilleries, notably Auchentoshan, triple distil, but that is more of an Irish technique than a Scottish one.

The shape of these stills is of utmost importance as the wash is heated and the vapours are captured and condensed back into liquid. Shorter stills get a heavier vapour, while taller stills generally create a lighter liquid. The stills at Glenmorangie, for example, are as tall as giraffes and the whisky they produce is famously light.

The wash is heated in the still, the vapours collected and condensed, and then the distilled wash, called low wine, is put in a tank to go back into the smaller (except at Dailuaine) spirit still.

From a second distillation you get three products. About the first 5 per cent is called the foreshot. It's too heavy and has too much methanol in it, so it goes back into the low wines to be distilled again. The centre cut, about 70 per cent of the liquid, is the new-make spirit and goes to be casked and become whisky. The last part of the distillation process produces feints, which are too watery and too low in alcohol to make decent whisky, so they get put back into the low wines mix to be redistilled as well.

Every malt distillery you visit employs the same basic method as the one at Tobermory. They all make a liquid with mashed-up malted barley, ferment that liquid to make a type of beer then distil it. I never get bored of going to a distillery to watch the process and see how it's done. I like learning about the tiny idiosyncrasies of each distillery, what it is they do that makes them unique. The visits to loads of different distilleries have been one of the joys of researching this book, but while they are where whisky is made, they are not the best places to find the spirit of whisky. They are places of work and of tourism; for a real whisky lover they are also places of pilgrimage; they are great places to learn about whisky, but you don't find out what whisky really means in any of them.

We left the distillery and headed to the ferry terminal on the island double-decker bus to catch the boat back to Oban. It was a Saturday night and we were planning to go out on the town.

Among our choices of venues for the evening were two places catering for foreign tourists in search of an authentic Scottish experience by threatening to have ceilidhs, and a pub that did food that promised to have a DJ from 10. Broadcaster Tom Morton had suggested via Twitter that we go to the Lorne bar, telling me that it was famous for being one of the hangouts of the late singer, Jackie Leven. Described as a cross between Van Morrison and a psychopath, his friend Ian Rankin used one of his lyrics as the title of a Rebus book, *Saints of the Shadow Bible*.

Not only was the Lorne one of Leven's places, Tom was warned when he went there 'never to tell anyone about this place'. Psychopaths, book titles of works by famous authors and warnings to keep quiet were far too much mythical Scotland for one bar to carry off, so we avoided the Lorne.

We went to the pub where you could eat and which promised a DJ in time for last food orders, and sat at the only available table, cramped between the kitchen door and the men's toilets. The place was half people in late middle age in full make-up and good jumpers who lived in Oban, and half tourists in jeans and big anoraks. Men with bursting bladders were continuously walking past and having a good stare either at us or our food. Eventually one stopped.

'Youse awww right, ladies?'

Sheri turned around and smiled.

'Youse enjoying yer dinner?'

A small stocky bald man with a green t-shirt and faded jeans stood in front of us swaying slightly, with his hands in his pockets and an attempt at a debonair smile on his face.

'Whit's yer names?'

We told him and asked him what his was. He punched a clenched fist out in the middle of the table between us and barked, 'Hovis'. On closer inspection each letter was tattooed on a knuckle, so the air-punching was proof of identity rather than an empty gesture.

Hovis had not limited his tattoos to a mere nametag; he had more inks on his arms than anyone I have ever seen. I hang around with a lot of chefs, I know tattoos, but this was special. Every single bit of his arms was covered in them. He had gone as far as having a life-size can of Irn-Bru tattooed on the inside of his left arm. That is commitment to both tattoos and Scotland's national soft drink.

'We're bikers ye see,' he slurred, while motioning with his right hand to another corner of the pub.

'We're here for ma pal's 50th birthday. It was too wet tae bike up fae Glasgow but we came up anyways.'

At the best of times a strong Glaswegian accent can be hard to comprehend. We sound like someone has stolen all our consonants; they were possibly nicked by the Portuguese who use only them to speak. Hovis was no exception. Added to that, he had had more than a few and his slurring made him completely incomprehensible to Sheri. Fortunately, the refreshments that caused him to slur also caused him to repeat himself at least three times, which meant that Sheri managed to work out the third time what he was saying. While he talked, I watched her face to see signs of her confusion ending and her comprehension beginning. As he started telling us for the fourth time about the hostel they were all staying at and where they were going next, salvation arrived in the form of a skinny young man in a parka jacket and plimsolls.

'Hovis, I thought you were goin' tae the toilet! Leave these wummin alone, can you no' see they're eating?'

Hovis beamed and put his arm around him. 'This is Davie! Ma pal's boy. He's here wi' us fur the weekend.'

From his look of sobriety, Davie had obviously been sent along by someone in Glasgow as the responsible adult. He shepherded Hovis into the toilet then back out again past us, taking his supervisory role very seriously. He had the face of a man who knew he was spending his night rounding up 50-year-old drunks and was resigned to his fate.

By the time we had finished our food and went to sit at the bar the DJ was there. The tourists had gone and the Oban Saturday night crowd had arrived. They were just above drinking age and wearing their best outfits, and the air suddenly became about 45 per cent Lynx Africa. I wonder if provincial towns in Nigeria are full of young men on a night out wearing Scottish Heather aftershave.

Kids who had known each other since primary school were doomed to spend every Saturday night out together until they escaped for work or education in Glasgow, Inverness or offshore. Their Saturday night DJ was a wee overweight bald man with glasses and a beige and white striped polo shirt looking like a cross between a jailbird uncle and a professional karaoke singer. He played an old Ibiza anthem then a Celine Dion song, a Rod Stewart cover of the Supremes, another Ibiza rave song, then Texas.

The kids came in the door and walked anticlockwise round the bar, looking both self-conscious and anxious. They were all wearing clothes they thought they should: crisp white shirts for the males – the females in hot pants or trousers and high-heeled boots – and seemed to be trying to find their pals behind the façade of adult make-up and ill-fitting outfits. Once they found them, they stood or sat beside them in virtual silence, staring at everyone else who they knew, oversized drinks in their hands that couldn't get them buzzed quickly enough.

It was like being at the wedding of someone you don't really know, when you have been invited late as they were desperate for guests, where the best food available is a tuna mayo vol-au-vent and the bar only has warm beer or Liebfraumilch spritzers. We finished our drinks and went back up to the guesthouse sharing tales of Saturday nights of old, convinced they were the best Saturday nights anyone has ever had.

Lobster Loaves and Oysters with Whisky

The town of Oban now markets itself as the seafood capital of Scotland and it is full of seafood restaurants, fish and chip shops and more than one seafood shack. While they normally serve lobster grilled with some butter, I have put them into warm rolls. You want to use the rolls or mini breads as a bowl rather than a fancy sandwich.

If you want to continue an Oban/Mull seafood theme then you can have some oysters as an 'aperitif' – put some peaty whisky, like Ledaig, in a tiny spray bottle and spritz some on the oysters.

Serves 4

4 crispy rolls, brioches or cottage loaves
150g salted butter
2 garlic cloves, finely chopped

2 cooked lobsters, finely chopped
50ml Oban whisky
½ glass dry sherry (fino or manzanilla)
1 tablespoon chopped flat-leaf parsley
sea salt and freshly ground black pepper

Preheat the oven to 200°C/fan 180°C/gas 6 (or as hot as possible if your oven isn't great).

Cut the tops off the rolls and remove the crumbs.

Melt the butter in a saucepan on a low heat and use it to paint both sides of the bread 'lids' and the hollowed-out rolls, then put them in the oven on a baking tray for about 10 minutes.

Add the garlic to the pan and cook until lightly golden then turn the heat right down and add the lobster and the whisky.

Leave the mix to cook for a few minutes then add the sherry and parsley, and season with salt and pepper.

Remove the rolls from the oven and fill them with the hot lobster, placing the bread 'lids' on top, and serve immediately.

6

CRY FREEDOM

'O thou my muse! Guid auld Scotch drink!'
RABBIE BURNS

The train from Glasgow to Fort William is also the train to Oban. It splits on the way when the railway forks into two, so to get to Fort William from Oban the only way is by bus. It's a twice-daily modern coach, most unlike the old-fashioned eighties buses Paul Theroux must have travelled on, and the afternoon one is pretty empty. Apart from Sheri and me, the few other occupants were too young to have cars and the only other people who got on during the journey were a small group of tourists taking a quick ride from their hotel to a pub.

It's evident that to live in these places, even to go on holiday properly, you need a car. If you cannot drive, public transport is so lacking that you may not even be able to buy basic necessities; if you cannot afford the petrol, you will have to sacrifice something, either heating or food, in order to get to your work or visit a relative.

City people like me wander round for a few days, having a great time playing at countryside living. For us the downsides are the lack of anonymity and the limits of being a teenager there. But housing is proportionately as big an issue in Oban as it is in London. I met someone on a train to Oban a few months previously who worked in the homeless shelter there. He explained that the lack of council housing and the fact that most of the houses in the area were either bought or rented out as holiday homes meant that stable, affordable rented housing was in extremely short supply and families with low-paying jobs often ended up homeless. The council covers such a large geographical area that they could offer families accommodation as far away as Campbeltown, 87 miles away. But how are you supposed to then travel to your work?

We passed through various small villages and a lot of picture-postcard Scotland, and arrived at Fort William during the last light of day. With 10,000 inhabitants, it is the largest town in the Highlands; only the city of Inverness has a bigger population. As its name suggests, it was a garrison town built as a place to station soldiers who were there to subdue the local populace. Nowadays, it's overrun by hill walkers and hikers, intent on conquering emptied hills rather than suppressing Highlanders. The town is far too long and narrow, the main street pedestrianised and full of coffee bars and shops selling waterproofs and outdoor gear. Most of the hotels and big houses face Loch Linnhe, one of the biggest sea lochs in Scotland, but the main road from Glasgow runs alongside the loch so the view is a noisy experience.

I have dragged Sheri here for two things. *Braveheart* and a distillery.

Scotland doesn't have a film industry so is reliant on England or the US to tell its stories in film. *Braveheart*, a 1995 American film directed by and starring Mel Gibson, is, even today, what Scotland is most famous for apart from whisky. When I told the kids I taught in Spain where I was from they would often say, 'Sí, sí. *Braveheart!*' A Rastafarian with gold teeth and a speedboat on a small island in the Bahamas once told me that William Wallace was his hero. Almost every Scot in any far-off place in the world will get asked about *Braveheart*. An article on Scotland's first minister Nicola Sturgeon in an Italian newspaper in July 2016 had the headline 'Lady Braveheart'.

Braveheart is a western set in a medieval Scotland as realistic as Brigadoon. The goodies are the Scots with their shaggy hair and painted faces, the baddies are the English and the anglicised Scottish gentry. It is a fun film, well made and good enough to win five Oscars, but it is very much a Hollywood fantasy of Scotland.

Scottish people are still not exactly sure what to make of the film. We are slightly embarrassed at the painted faces shouting 'Freedom!', but well aware that it is what makes the world know who we are, and often the easiest thing to do is just to join in. Now Scotland rugby and football fans paint their faces blue and white and roar and scream 'Freedom!' just so everybody knows they too have seen that bit of *Braveheart*.

A few months previously I was in a friend's house and we turned the film on. The scenery in the background of some scenes was suspiciously un-Scottish. The land had perfect neat square hedgerows outlining perfect rectangular fields. Scottish hills of that size are not that orderly, so we looked it up. It was Ireland. The most famous film about Scotland of the last 30 years had been filmed partly in another country.

However, some of the film, in particular the wedding and the village scenes, had been shot in Scotland, up at Glen Nevis near Fort William. As soon as filming was finished the village was completely dismantled, but one thing had been left. A car park.

The only physical legacy of the most popular film set in Scotland in the past 30 years is a Forestry Commission sign saying 'Braveheart Car Park'. Obviously we had to go.

Ben Nevis distillery is at the far north end of Fort William. It's a utilitarian 1960s building with none of the attractive pagodas that grace older distilleries or new ones emulating the 19th century. The visitors' centre looks in such dire need of an upgrade it's almost as if the company is actively discouraging people to visit. The labelling of Ben Nevis bottles is notable for its atrocity – both the font and the oval picture of a bad artist's impression of the distillery with Scotland's highest mountain behind look like a leftover prop from *Abigail's Party*. The website's up-to-date news is from 2005, its design from earlier than that. It looks like a company that doesn't really want to sell. I wanted to know why.

The distillery is the only one in Scotland owned by a Japanese whisky company, Nikka. The company has two distilleries in Japan, Yoichi and Miyagikyo. The company was the second one set up by the founder of Japanese whisky, Masataka Taketsuru.

Taketsuru was born into a Hiroshima family which owned a long-established saké-making company that still exists today. He arrived at Glasgow University in 1918 to study organic chemistry and learn how to make whisky. He was an apprentice in malt and grain whisky distilleries, learning about whisky making and spending most of his time in Campbeltown at Hazelburn distillery. He also learned the art of blending. In 1920 he married a Scotswoman, Jessie Roberta 'Rita' Cowan, having previously been a lodger in her family home. The same year they went back to Japan to start making whisky.

Taketsuru first worked for what is now a Suntory distillery. He then moved to northern Japan in 1934 to set up and run the Yoichi distillery as an independent, in a location he picked for its similarities to Scotland. In 1940 the Nikka brand was launched. Rita provided not only financial support during difficult times – by working as an English teacher – but also moral backing during the turmoil of World War 2 when both were accused of spying for Britain, Russia and America. As a naturalised Japanese citizen, she was spared internment but became the object of abuse in their neighbourhood. After surviving World War 2, Rita died from liver disease and tuberculosis in 1961, for which her grieving husband blamed the harsh Japanese climate. He continued working in the Japanese whisky business until his own death in 1979, aged 85.

He is revered as the father of Japanese whisky and the

Japanese are very aware that their debt to him is great. His life was dramatised in a Japanese television series and it was the first time a non-Japanese actress, playing the part of Rita, had starred in an NHK Japanese-made morning show.

If you have never come across it, Japanese whisky is a great thing to seek out. It tastes quite different to Scotch; it's never peated, never smoky, and the best ones I have tried have an almost plummy taste. It is harder to find than Scotch, as they make less than 10 per cent of the amount Scotland does, and not all Scots approve of it.

I once overheard a conversation between two Scottish pensioners. The man was explaining to the woman about Japanese whisky.

'Japanese whisky? Whisky from Japan? That's just daft!' she said.

'No, Shona, I think they've been making it for over a hundred years.'

'That's ridiculous, how on earth can they know how to make whisky in Japan?'

'Some guy came over here and learned how to do it. It's supposed to be quite good. It has won some really big international whisky prizes.'

'But how can they make good whisky? They don't have our water!'

The easiest way to have solved this would have been to take Shona to a pub and give her some Japanese whisky to try. It's available in a lot of bars in Scotland; but Shona doesn't like whisky, Shona likes gin. Her nephews in Canada like whisky and whenever she visits them she takes them a nice bottle from the duty free, but she never drinks it herself. She was getting indignant and insulted by the cheek of the Japanese making a drink she doesn't like and doesn't want to try.

But not all Japanese whisky is at it seems. I met the manager of the distillery, a man well over 65, in his office and realised that, despite his modest demeanour, Colin Ross knew more about whisky in his pinkie than I ever would.

'I arrived here when the Japanese bought it [in 1989] and all the folk here told me that the whisky was rubbish, but we tried and tried mixing and blending casks and seeing what there was and then we got something good and then we started winning some prizes. It was hard work all right at the start, but we got there.'

He took me round some of the warehouses to show what he had built up.

'They take a lot of it straight off the still to Japan to mature for their own brands. You'll know that we can only call Scotch what's been made and matured here, but in Japan they can mature stuff made elsewhere.'

So, while a lot of Ben Nevis production goes to make Japanese whisky, the rest is selling pretty quickly.

'I'm bottling mostly 18-year-old and selling it as 10 at the moment as we just don't have stock,' he said. 'We can't sell it fast enough. My family keep saying I should think about retiring but why would I do that now that it's such fun? We've worked that hard for so many years, now is the time to enjoy it all.'

I went in with Sheri to try the whisky. After her hatred of Laphroaig and love of Glengoyne, she had spent the past couple of days trying Tobermory, Ledaig and Oban, becoming quite the whisky buff. She loved the Ben Nevis but her favourite had been one called McDonald's. A whisky made to taste like the old style popular whisky of the 1880s, the label looked like it was made by a provincial sign maker in a wee town in the Highlands in the 1950s, but it was heavy and sweet and had a charcoal taste. I was astonished. In three days I had managed to change her aversion to whisky to a love of a really heavy, old-fashioned dram.

I asked Colin if he would mind phoning us a taxi, as it was too far for us to walk back into town with suitcases. He asked what time our train was and got his own car out to take us. It was not any old car. Even I could tell by the smoothness, the silence and the cream leather seats that it was a good one.

The Braveheart Car Park was about a half-hour walk from the station but Colin decided that a wee afternoon outing was just the thing, so he made my dream come true and took me there in a fancy car. And I can tell you, it's a car park. Near Fort William. In Glen Nevis. There is a Forestry Commission sign saying this is the Braveheart Car Park that looks like every other Forestry Commission car park anywhere in Scotland. There is no tartan, no painted faces, not even a sign saying 'Freedom'. All I could do was stand in front of it and yell, 'Freedom!' Obviously I did. It was a long way to come and not do that. It was also quite a disappointment.

Colin remembered the filming well – some of the indoor wedding and party scenes were shot in one of the five distillery warehouses – and he showed us the glen where the village had been built. The only sign that it had once been something was a group of young Asian tourists taking photographs of an empty field.

'They couldn't keep any of it up as it was all plaster and cardboard, not stuff that was built to last. And Gibson refused to let there be any likenesses of him anywhere in the place. I don't know why. It would have been nice for folk who come here to have a photo to stand by.'

The scenery along the road was just breathtaking, one of those moments when I understood why people come from so far away to visit Scotland. It made me wonder whether, had the villages been allowed to develop instead of being burned and destroyed in the 19th century, they would have matched the scenery.

Once Colin had dropped us at the station, Sheri turned to me in delight. 'Wow, that was amazing.'

'Yeah, it's really beautiful there.'

'That was a top-of-the-range, brand-new Jaguar with its own personalised number plate we were in, Rachel.'

'Was it?'

'I never even imagined that I would be in such a car. That was special. I kept trying to take photos of it without him noticing, but look.'

She showed me all the bits that made it top of the range and the licence plate that said NIKKA1.

A few months later I met someone from Chivas who oversees almost all of their production and who had known Colin for a long time.

'Aww, they dinna want him tae go, Rachel, and I think

he's aboot 70. But he built that place up and made it what it is, so they'll do anything to keep him there. They gave him a fancy new Jaguar wi' all the extras and a private licence plate that says WHISKY1 just last year so that he wouldnae leave. God only knows what they'll come up wi' this year.'

WHISKY1 sounded even better than NIKKA1, so I didn't tell him the truth.

A sunset train journey from Fort William to Glasgow is listed in almost every travel website as one of the top 10 journeys in the world. ScotRail even uses special carriages with extra-large windows on the train so that everyone can get the maximum view. It goes through miles and miles of empty land with no houses, no villages and next to no trees. The sun was setting and the few other people in the carriage were snapping at every point they could with cameras of various sizes, mostly extra-large.

Sheri fell asleep. I looked at Scotland and marvelled at how empty so much of it was and wondered if there was ever going to be any way to put people back on these hills apart from the occasional one shooting things on them.

When we got back to Glasgow I gave Sheri the Laphroaig to try once again.

'Not my favourite,' she said. 'But you know, it's not too bad.'

Back in Barcelona, Sheri now has whisky quite often, judging from Facebook. I even saw a photo of a tasting with about seven different bottles including Ardbeg, the heavily peated Islay whisky.

Duck Stuffed with Prunes

Chicken or duck stuffed with dried fruits and pine nuts
is a really popular dish in the north of Spain over the
Christmas period, and when I spend Christmas in Spain
I still buy one ready-stuffed at the market. When I am
at home, I make this simplified version of it. Soak the
prunes overnight and, if you want, you can leave them
to macerate for two weeks and then eat as a dessert.

Serves 4

250g pitted prunes
blended whisky (enough to cover the prunes)
glug of olive oil
1 onion, chopped
3 garlic cloves, crushed
2 bay leaves
1 tablespoon pine nuts
salt and freshly ground black pepper
1 × approx. 2kg duck

Cover the prunes with the whisky the night before.

The next day, preheat the oven to 190°C/fan 170°C/
gas 5.

Put the oil in a saucepan on a medium heat and, once it
is heated, add the onion, then the garlic and bay leaves.

Once the onion and garlic are soft, add the prunes and the remaining liquid and cook for a few minutes, then add the pine nuts and season to taste.

Stuff the duck with the prune mixture – but make sure it has cooled completely if you aren't going to put the duck straight in the oven.

Pat the duck dry with kitchen towel and then rub salt and pepper into the skin. Put the duck on a rack in the oven with a roasting tin placed underneath to catch all the drips.

After 45 minutes turn the heat up to 220°C/fan 200°C/ gas 7 for 20 minutes more, until the skin is golden brown and the duck is cooked.

Remove the duck from the oven and cover with a cloth or tin foil and leave to rest for 15 minutes before carving and serving with the stuffing and veg of your choice.

7

CHEERS TO A SINGLE WHISKY

'I'm on a whisky diet. I've lost three days already.'
TOMMY COOPER

New Year in Scotland is of the utmost importance. While Catholic countries have 100 different festivals and fairs, and Yuletide/Christmas is a massive thing all round pagan northern Europe, we have Hogmanay. Before large numbers of English soldiers came up north to train during World War 2 we used to go to work on Christmas Day. Those soldiers must have been utterly bemused by our lack of interest in what is still, despite modern rampant consumerism, a really meaningful festival in England. Christmas didn't become a public holiday in Scotland until 1958.

When I was in primary school, my friend Carmela's mum and dad owned an Italian delicatessen in the East End of Glasgow and one day they had a former worker from the shop round for lunch. She had moved to a town in Oxfordshire for about a year, but it hadn't been a success. She was at the kitchen table, telling Carmela's mum all the woes of her failed move. She told her about the strangeness of the people, how she found them unapproachable, cold, distant. She had problems with her job and her housing and in the end it was too much, so she came back up the road.

'Oh but Christmas, my God, Maria, Christmas was amazing.'

Every pub, cafe or church had carol singers, the kind that we only ever saw on the telly. There were beautiful decorations in the street, every house had a holly wreath on the door and everywhere was serving mince pies. Proper homemade ones, not the cheap supermarket six-pack kind. Puddings and cakes were made three months in advance and served on every street corner (or so I remember her telling us) and people were singing in streets at all hours of the day. It sounded like a BBC Television trailer for Christmas programmes come to life.

The problem came a week later and was the final nail in the coffin of her Oxfordshire dreams.

'New Year, Maria, New Year. They all just went to their beds!'

Presbyterians, in keeping with their typically fun-loving attitude to life, didn't approve of Christmas celebrations. Well aware that they had been adapted from northern European pagan ones, they looked upon them with contempt. A man from the Isle of Lewis once told me that the first major political cause of his life was in the early 1970s, when he petitioned for a Christmas tree at home. Santa visited – his mother didn't dare banish him – but traditionally they never had a tree. After a relentless campaign, his mother gave in and even now has a small plastic one installed when he visits for Christmas. He has to bring his own Christmas cake, though; she draws the line at that.

The only excuse for anyone over the age of eight in Scotland to just 'go to their bed' at New Year is severe illness or being a key worker in the emergency services. It just doesn't happen. We stay up for the bells.

As a child it is a slightly bewildering experience. You stay up incredibly late, watching the clock tick. You are dressed up in your best clothes to sit and watch TV with various members of your family who are also all decked out in their finery. You wait and wait, get tired, crabby, snappy, and nearly fall asleep on the sofa. Then someone starts a countdown from 10 on the telly and everyone stands up with a glass of something, mostly whisky. You get an Irn-Bru or a Coke shoved in your hand and, by the time they have counted down to one, everyone shouts, 'Hurray, Happy New Year!' and hugs and kisses everyone else in the room, including you. When that's all done it's time for bed. There are no presents, no lights in the sky, no new people appear at the door. There's not even a selection box of chocolates. For a child, it all seems a bit pointless.

But now that no one marks the end of harvest with a massive party in the middle of a town, apart from the odd gala day, New Year is our big deal.

There are other New Year traditions, some of which are

slowly dying out. Customs dating back to pre-Christian times have everyone standing around a focal point, like a standing stone or a cross in the middle of the town, to see in the New Year. This still happens – just look at everyone in Edinburgh whenever the New Year celebration isn't cancelled because of bad weather – but it is not what I remember growing up.

This is one of the problems with writing about the place where you were a child, especially if you have left it. The traditions that you grew up with, the time that you grew up in, becomes *the* experience and *the* culture. I have read in several books about Scotland about the importance of public gatherings at New Year and each time I think: 'Well, it must have died out by the eighties.' It never occurs to me in my own righteous stupidity that eight-year-olds don't tend to get taken to public gatherings at midnight. Also, both of the small towns I grew up in were suburbs of Glasgow, places that evolved in the 19th century around railway stations, and neither had central market crosses to gather round.

I do remember the first thrill of being old enough to go out and about at New Year. The thing was to stay in for the bells with family, see in the New Year with *Hogmanay Live* on BBC One and leave after midnight. I was about 16 and, after meeting up with a couple of pals, we went walking round the town as a few classmates were having parties. We had dispensed with the fine clothes that had been obligatory as younger children and opted for practical warmth to wander round the streets.

A practice that hasn't changed in well over two hundred years was the post-midnight obligatory kiss of all the members of the opposite sex who crossed our paths. This sounds more of a frightening task than it was. I mean, if you had to do this in Edinburgh at New Year you'd be kissing men all night and would have frayed lips and in all likelihood more than one cold sore. But in a small suburb like Lenzie you recognise almost everyone you see from school, and they are just as excited as you are about being allowed out after the bells, like proper adults.

But in 2015 my childhood has long gone, and I am up in Scotland to spend Christmas and New Year with my mother. Since retiring she has made a load of new friends, and in September she moved to the same village as them all. This village has a centre, at least four restaurants, two of which are open at New Year. They are all within easy reach and for the first time in her life my mother has options at New Year that she can walk to. She is very excited.

My phone calls to her in November are like military strategy meetings. Clearly we will be greeting 2016 with greater planning and a clearer vision than the opening ceremony of the London Olympics.

After an in-depth study of menus and a quick look in the one dodgy pub the town has, my mother decides that we shall spend the evening at a corner cafe/restaurant/bar place that sometimes has live music and at New Year is hosting a local folk club. She hears from her pensioner pals that the tickets are like gold dust, so heads down the very hour they go on sale and gets them.

Never underestimate a retired primary school head teacher. People like my mother are used to being responsible for 300 children, staff and all the parents and carers of those children. To people like her, finding out every single option for New Year within walking distance and memorising menus, prices and drinks available is nothing. Neither is getting the tickets that are like gold dust. But if you are that chosen place, you'd better know what you've let yourself in for.

For a start, you need to have the required drink. My mother and her friends drink rosé wine. While it remains the porn among wine buffs – people who never admit to drinking it but all know what it tastes like – and hardly appears at all on wine menus in fancy restaurants, it's what they like and want to drink at New Year.

My mother and her friends have been there on various occasions and are well aware that the rosé regularly runs out. They know that the staff sort this by running out to the Tesco across the road and buying some. My mother knows that the Tesco is closing at 9pm on Hogmanay. She's a retired head teacher on a night out, of course she knows.

Preventative action was taken. We went down for a coffee a couple of days before and were served by the owner, a balding middle-aged man with a very big smile and an air of utter cluelessness. My mother explained to him that we were coming at New Year and that most of the party wanted to drink rosé wine, so could he please have extra.

'Don't you worry, love, I'll have plenty. The one thing I will have loads of at New Year is booze.'

My mother was reassured that her strategic planning and forward thinking had worked and was convinced all would be fine. I was not.

'Are you sure you don't want me to bring a couple of bottles in a bag, Mum? If they run out you can say you've brought your own and ask them to charge you corkage.'

'Oh, I think we'll be fine.'

Recently, there have been various studies into the psychological impact of retirement. People who have previously held important positions in companies and have led very structured lives full of responsibility can find the sudden loss of that life deeply traumatic. They think that having all day to play golf, go walking and take up any number of new hobbies will be fabulous, but they drastically underestimate how much they identified with their career and, all of a sudden, they find themselves unimportant, unlistened to and slightly lost. This, I have to say, is not my mother's case. She is having the time of her life. She just wants to know why no one told her retirement would be so much fun. But she still has her moments.

She has just made a simple request, within a timeframe she deems to be suitable, of someone she will be paying to provide her with a service. She now has the expectation that the task will be performed entirely to her satisfaction, just like it would have at work.

I, who am far more fluent in hospitality speak, know an accident waiting to happen when I see one. Despite having an all-day alcohol licence, this cafe has never, ever advertised its lunches with a reduced-price glass of wine, in a town – just like every other suburban town in the UK – addicted to special offers at non-peak times. I have waited 15 minutes to be served a coffee when there have been only two other people in the place and, if you order a cake, it gets served very carefully on top of a napkin. Bizarrely, one of the other restaurants in the town does this and I wonder if it's the mark of a Milngavie mafia hospitality workers' turf war that no one else is aware of.

The shelves at the back of the bar are half-empty, with oddly spaced bottles of spirits and coffee syrups. The impression is of an old bar in Communist Cuba rather than a prosperous cafe in a reasonably affluent Glaswegian suburb. No extra bottles have been put on the shelf since I arrived just before Christmas. They must all be in the fridge.

We arrive at the bar in time to get ourselves a table, a bottle of rosé and a Glengoyne. It's the only malt whisky they have, probably chosen due to the distillery's proximity. Scottish bars, even if they have a very wide range of whiskies, will almost always make sure that the local distillery takes centre stage.

Single malts like Glengoyne are produced in one distillery. What makes Glengoyne unusual is that it is made in stills located in the Highlands and matured in casks parked in the Lowlands, thanks to the distillery's location in the middle of the Highland Line.

After its foundation in 1833, Glengoyne became a small distillery producing a Highland malt. In common with Macallan whisky, sweet Golden Promise barley is used in its production. About 10 years ago, production at Glengoyne was stepped up after its acquisition by a large distillery company and now some 2 million litres are produced at its site in Dumgoyne.

Another distinguishing feature of Glengoyne is that it has a delicate and layered taste that's better than the most refined toffee apple. This is because the malt is dried with warm air, without so much as a whiff of peat being involved. It is consequently a great whisky for a bourbon drinker who thinks that all whisky is too smoky, just like Sheri thought when she tried it. The distillery sells itself as 'the most beautiful distillery in Scotland', but it would probably be a bit more truthful to say 'never thought it was so beautiful 40 minutes' drive from central Glasgow, did you?'

I drove past it recently with a friend, the distillery on the right, the warehouses on the left, separated by the Highland Line, and my friend just gasped at the view beyond.

'What a beautiful day, it's all just so clear.'

'Oh, so it is. I was just looking at all that whisky.'

But still, even if you are not a tourist you are quite right to expect that the product of your nearest distillery has pride of place at your bar, so Glengoyne is the main malt whisky available. It is also the sole malt whisky, and the bottle is only three-quarters full. The replacement must be at the back, in the store cupboard.

We have our drinks and are aware that the entertainment is about to start. There is a large table of about 12 people just to the left of the microphones and the instruments and, given their familiarity with each other, the staff and the very dressed-up kids at the bar, I assume that they are the folk club. They range in age from about 25 to 70. The other 40 or so people in attendance vary slightly less in age, from around about 63 to 70. I sip my whisky and stare.

A wee round man in his sixties with a wee round bald head stands up, grabs hold of a microphone and tells us that we are going to do some traditional Gaelic folk singing. From the blank looks around the room it's obvious that we are not exactly overrun with Gaels. It turns out he just wants us to sing a couple of sounds like 'heeee' and 'haaaaw', so we dutifully comply while remaining unconvinced that this is actually proper Gaelic. He then hands out pieces of paper with lyrics on, trying to get us to join in with a song that, confusingly, is in English.

The last time I sang this way was in primary school at *Singing Together*. The class would get a new pamphlet each season with new songs from all around the world that the nice man from the radio was teaching us. The school secretary recorded each episode on Monday morning so that five different classes could sing together on different days according to what suited each teacher. I learned a song about a yellow bird in a banana tree, something about Casey Jones in a wagon and a supposedly lazy fisherman – who seemed eminently sensible to me as he wouldn't go fishing if his candle got blown out because it was too windy, but neither would he go if it didn't flicker because it was too still. The real culprit in that song was the person who wrote it to taunt him; they must have liked work for work's sake.

We try our best to make the wee round man happy, singing his song while his face gets redder and his arms wave about ever more frantically. He looked like he was used to both a more enthusiastic and capable crowd than us. There is a table of four behind me who view having singing at a New Year folk club as an unwelcome interruption to their evening of conversation and drinking. Looking at the rest of the instruments facing us, I think they are in for a disappointing night.

I get another Glengoyne.

While most bottles of whisky no longer cost two weeks' wages, whisky is still a really big thing to have at New Year. At Christmas, supermarket shelves are lined with everything and anything that screeches excess, but by 29 December a lot of those shelves are cleared to make way for whisky. Every supermarket in Scotland, even those in very poor areas, has a selection at New Year that rivals most specialist drink shops anywhere else in the world. People still buy a good bottle to bring in the New Year. As with most customs, they may not even be exactly sure why they do it, but a decent whisky to see in the New Year is important to people. For some, it's the only time a bottle of the hard stuff crosses the threshold. In any event, it's why we have an extra bank holiday, to recover.

Even the phrases we use are peculiar to us. We see in the New Year as if midnight on 31 December needs to be observed and witnessing it happen means we will have better luck and more happiness in the year to come. In this frame of mind, we all set resolutions to start in January: this year we will lose the weight, this year we will make the extra money, this year we will write the novel. We still seem to believe in the magical power of a good New Year, as if the correct combination of good whisky, a good midnight toast and a right good time will bring upon us the luck and fortune we want for the year ahead.

Given how we ended up seeing in the New Year, I'm surprised I survived 2016 at all.

Next up is a big tall wide man with a dark stripy shirt and a beret. He sits at the keyboard and sets it to 'not quite a piano but as near as dammit'. He sounds exactly like Billy Connolly.

Now, I do not assume that all Glaswegian men sound like Billy, the way that since I have been on the radio people have assumed that Glaswegian comedian Susan Calman got less funny and more knowledgeable about food on certain programmes, but this man has almost the same inflections and intonations as the Big Yin.

It is impossible to overestimate the cultural influence of Billy Connolly on a city like Glasgow. In the 1980s, popular culture on Scottish telly involved big men in kilts singing neo-folk songs, while women sat there smiling until their faces ached at the magnificence of the men. The depiction of Scottish people on national telly was reduced to a woman from the islands twirling in a nice dress on a game show, a drunk on the soap opera *EastEnders* and English comedian Russ Abbot in an orange wig and a kilt talking incomprehensibly in a fake Scottish accent. (Russ Abbot's legacy is the See-You-Jimmy hat – the tartan caps attached to orange wigs much beloved of Scottish football fans – named after his Scottish character's catchphrase, around which an entire industry of comedic defiance was built.)

Billy told stories, about us, as one of us, on national telly. Important people like interviewer Michael Parkinson liked him. He sang daft versions of songs with a Glasgow accent, the one we all knew from a very young age was a passport to nowhere, the accent that parents with both money and aspirations would try to elocute out of us, the one we only saw when a hard man was punching someone on the telly.

Billy was clever, Billy was funny. For Glaswegians who grew up listening to him, he defined funny and he defined storytelling.

Every Glaswegian in their forties can recite from memory quotes and stories from Billy Connolly shows, the way Oxbridge dons can recite redundant Latin phrases. We all knew them and all the songs and repeated them to each other from early adolescence. I am still convinced that the sarcasm of 'aww just hold me back' actually belongs to my school friend Heather Sutherland and not Billy, even after she played me the album.

If you are a big man in your mid-forties behind an electric keyboard and a microphone, in front of a paying audience on New Year's Eve in a suburb of Glasgow, you will be aware of this. You know how much Billy means to an audience of people his age. You know how much he means to people your own age. You know that you can sing songs from Glaswegian pop groups and massacre them without too many problems, as everyone has done that at the office Christmas karaoke night out, but you have to be one brave bugger, or one exceedingly stupid one, to sing a Billy song.

When he plays the opening notes to 'One Man Went to Mow' and sings 'three men fae Carntyne went tae join the parish', I remember Heather Sutherland's album and feel something akin to relief. This must be what it is like to be held hostage and have someone hold a gun to your kneecap and fire it. However much pain you are in, the worst thing possible has happened. It's done, it's over. There is no more suspense, no tension, no doubt. You've been kneecapped. Just like yer man up there is murdering an old Billy Connolly song. It's happening, it's cruel, it's your worst nightmare. But at least there is no more tension and all doubt is gone. He sang his song, we clapped, lightly, quietly, in a somewhat perfunctory manner, but he got some applause.

He sings a couple of Simple Minds numbers and then a woman from the big table gets a tambourine. She is about five-ten and dressed head to toe in leopard print. Leopard-print boots, trousers, floaty blouse, coat and fedora. All leopard print, all slightly different. She pulls it off, she looks amazing. I want to be her.

No one and nothing on this planet does leopard print more frequently or better than Glaswegian women. I've seen leopards on safari in Sri Lanka and, I can tell you, we do leopard print better than them. If a bunch of leopards arrived in Glasgow on a Saturday night and saw the variety and panache of our women in their print, they'd turn to each other in disappointment and say, 'Fuck it, let's be panthers.'

I was once in a London restaurant and a Glaswegian friend I had not seen in over a decade came up to my table and smiled. He said he'd laughed to himself when he saw me standing up in a leopard-print skirt because it reminded him of home and how much leopard print there is around Glasgow, then he realised that it was being worn by a Glaswegian and by one he knew.

Cheers to a single whisky

I am not sure what it is about the print that we like so much, but it really should be listed as the clan tartan of the Weegie woman. Any woman who felt an affinity with Glasgow could claim it as their own. Formal occasions where men put on kilts and women a variety of dresses could be simplified by women wearing only the one pattern. Men can wear their surname, women their city. You'd know if you wanted a laugh to talk to the woman in the animal print.

This magnificent specimen of Glaswegian womanhood's sartorial choice of style and quality is sadly not reflected in her tambourine skills. While the beret man is requesting that we don't forget about him, I wish she would at least forget about the tambourine as there is neither rhythm nor reason to the banging and jangling.

He's stopped singing his Simple Minds stuff and is back to talking like Billy. She stops the tambourining.

It was nearly midnight, the stage had been cleared and BBC Two was on in the background. We were getting music and Jools Holland's *Hootenanny* party.

Hogmanay was always about us on the telly. It was the one time of the year that BBC Scotland television culture was inflicted on the entire country. Broadcast live from a hotel near Stirling to the whole of the UK, the show would feature 50-year-old men in kilts singing pseudo folk songs to their best girl, who was about 25 and with whom they were hoping to be roaming in the gloaming.

It all came to a crashing halt after New Year 1984. The BBC decided to do a live show from Gleneagles hotel and have an audience of paying hotel guests rather than a BBC

135

one. A number of these guests were distinctly unimpressed that their expensive New Year getaway was being ruined by the BBC and, after a few too many refreshments, were keen to let the camera crew know they didn't want to play ball. The pipe band were ungovernable and played as and when they liked, and veteran Scots comedian Chic Murray froze in front of a camera for almost a full minute then asked if it was on. The whole of Scotland wanted to die of embarrassment, and the BBC had to promise the rest of the UK that there would be no more tartan and pipes at New Year. Over 30 years later, BBC Scotland's New Year coverage is still prerecorded, so deep is the scar of that Hogmanay. The BBC have also kept their word to the rest of the country.

Scottish people are not the only ones superstitious about New Year. The Spanish, and other Mediterranean countries, lay out 12 grapes and at each stroke of midnight put one in their mouths. The idea is to chew and swallow them all as fast as possible for maximum luck over the coming year. I spent a New Year in a friend's house in Santander and neither of us had bought grapes, each assuming the other one would get them. We were in a blind panic as New Year with no grapes just isn't New Year. Eventually we found a packet of peanuts and reasoned that two peanuts would count as one grape. We were safe, it would all be fine. Spanish people shudder when I tell them this, and ask if that year was OK for both of us or if it was very unlucky. We were OK, we got away with it.

I went to the bar to ask for the drinks to see in the New Year. A couple of men were leaving the bar with drinks in their hands not looking very pleased. The barman looked harassed. There was no rosé wine left. Well, the others could see in the New Year with something fizzy; that was more appropriate anyway. There was no prosecco or cava and there had never been any champagne. There was one bottle of white wine that looked like it might taste of turpentine. That was it. That would have to do.

There was no Glengoyne. There was no Grant's. There was vodka or there was gin. I stared at the barman. He looked apologetic, desperately apologetic. 'People have had a lot more than we expected.' I blinked.

I wanted to scream, 'You have 80 people in your bar at New Year and you thought half a bottle of Glengoyne and two bottles of rosé wine was enough? Are you people *really* that stupid?'

I asked for a gin and tonic instead. There was ice but neither lemon nor lime.

I saw 2016 in with a glass of a drink traditionally used as a way to get rid of unwanted pregnancies mixed with a soft drink originally designed as a malaria treatment. My mother saw it in with a cheap white wine more suitable for stripping paint than drinking. I should have seen 2016 coming.

Aside from being marked by the deaths of great singers, and I do not blame myself for that – someone in Spain must have forgotten to eat their grapes – 2016 turned out to be the year that Scottish people or their descendants turned the political world on its head. Scotsmen Michael Gove and Liam Fox headed up the Brexit campaign and won the UK's June 2016 EU referendum, and son-of-a-Scotswoman Donald

Trump became the 45th president of the United States and, I promise you, had I any inkling at all that this was going to happen I would have rushed home from the New Year event and brought good whisky back with me. I would have done what I suggested to my mother and put both good whisky and pink cava in my bag before I went out.

I promise you I am never doing that again. If I spend New Year in a Mediterranean country I will carry bags of grapes around with me. I will go nowhere in Scotland on 31 December without a hip flask full of quality whisky. If I am in an airport lounge I will put 100ml in my hand luggage. This mistake will never be repeated.

Our other New Year tradition is to have steak pie for lunch on 1 January. It's a straightforward beef stew, sometimes with added sausagemeat, with a puff pastry on top. No one in their right mind would make a steak pie. Buy one; the shops are full of them, especially at New Year. If they don't sell them where you live, make a beef stew then put it in a dish and cover it with puff pastry. Once you have heated it in the oven, serve it with mashed potato, mashed turnip and steamed carrots. It is as good a hangover cure as it sounds.

If, however, you want something slightly more unusual you could make the Catalan Escudella i Carn d'Olla on the 31st and reheat it on New Year's Day. It's a dish that harks back to a time when meat was a luxury and using all different kinds for one dish was a really special treat. The idea is that the broth is served as the first course and then the meat and vegetables as the main.

Even without the addition of whisky this broth is utterly

amazing, so good in fact that it has turned at least two vegetarians back into meat-eaters. I know we need more vegetarians in this world, and creating more meat-eaters is not the superpower I would have chosen, but such is life. The whisky is added to the broth at the table. Don't put in more than one soupspoonful – you are not making a hot cocktail.

If you are ever making ramen in broth, Chinese-style soup or Italian stracciatella, then a spoonful of whisky at the end will make a great additional flavour. I used Glengoyne in this; I like the combination of a sweet whisky with the broth. You can really taste and smell the whisky when you add it at the table, so just make sure that you are not using anything too rough.

Escudella i Carn d'Olla

Serves 4

2 pig's trotters, cut in half (if you cannot get trotters or hate the idea of cooking them, then get a couple of sheets of gelatine and add them instead)
4 chicken thighs
200g pork ribs
1 beef bone
1 ham bone (you want the end of a cured Spanish ham bone from a Spanish deli; if you can't get one, just leave it out)
100g pancetta (in one piece)

1 whole *butifarra negra* (you can use Bury Black Pudding)
200g white beans, soaked overnight and drained
¼ green cabbage, shredded
4 carrots, sliced
2 parsnips, chopped
3 baby turnips, chopped
2 leeks, sliced
3 large peeled potatoes
4 soupspoons Glengoyne 10, to serve

For the meatballs
50g beef mince
50g pork mince
1 tablespoon breadcrumbs
2 garlic cloves, finely chopped
1 tablespoon chopped parsley
pinch of cinnamon
3 eggs
salt
plain flour

Place all the meat (except the black pudding) and the beans in a large stockpot and fill with water. Bring slowly to the boil and skim off any scum rising to the surface. Simmer for 1 hour then add the vegetables (except the potatoes) and cook for another hour.

Meanwhile, make the meatballs. Mix together the beef and pork mince and then add half of the breadcrumbs, the garlic, parsley, cinnamon and 2 of the eggs. Mix together, season with salt and slowly add the remaining egg and breadcrumbs until the mix is easily made into balls. Roll the balls in the flour and, once the vegetables have been in the pot for an hour, add the meatballs, potatoes and black pudding.

After 30 minutes, strain off the liquid and reserve.

Serve the soup in bowls, adding a spoonful of whisky at the table. Serve all the meat and vegetables as a second course.

8

Super blends

*'There is no bad whiskey. There are only some
whiskeys that aren't as good as others.'*
Raymond Chandler

If you look at what has been written about whisky in the past
20 years, almost all of it has been about malts and most of the
writing about whisky is catering for the specialist. Whisky
companies pay for writers and journalists to visit distilleries,
who then dutifully write up all the info about the malting
floors, the still shapes, the new-make and the ages of the different whiskies consumed.

What happens in the world of Scotch whisky is that about
90 per cent of the writing is about malt whisky, but 90 per
cent of what is drunk around the globe is a blend.

The reason that you know about whisky, the reason it is
the world's most popular spirit, often the only reason you

may have heard of a tiny wee country at the northern part of Britain that you previously thought was England, is because of blended whisky. A blended whisky is a mixture of malt whisky made in pot stills with malted barley and grain whisky made from corn, wheat or rye in continuous stills. At the moment in Scotland almost all grain whisky is made from wheat. It is produced at just seven sites.

The new-make that comes from a continuous still is very mild. But when malt whiskies are brought into the mix, grain whiskies are transformed.

The art of achieving a great taste from different casks, each with their own complexities in character, is an extraordinary skill, undervalued by the malt whisky brigade.

Blending drinks became fashionable in the second half of the 19th century, due to a combination of factors, including the development of the continuous still and the marketing nous of men like James Buchanan and John Dewar. And then there was phylloxera.

French vineyards were ravaged by this tiny sap-sucking insect which feeds on the roots and leaves of grapevines. The damaged roots make it impossible for the vines to absorb water or nutrients. Originally from America, the insect was unwittingly brought across to Europe in the 1850s by botanists who had collected samples of American vines. At home, American vines had developed a resistance to phylloxera by forming protective layers around attacked roots. European vines didn't have this ability and, in 1863, vines in the southern Rhône began to deteriorate inexplicably. By 1875 almost 40 per cent of vineyards in France had been wiped out by the phylloxera bug and, to this day, no cure has been found.

The most important product from grapevines is wine, but some of the most badly affected areas in France were in Cognac and the Charente, which devastated the cognac industry. Initially, cognac makers tried to overcome shortages by blending brandy with other drinks, with varying degrees of success. Ultimately, hard-to-find cognac reluctantly gave way in the British drinks cabinet to whisky and had even cleared the path for whisky blends.

Even today the legacy of phylloxera can be seen in France, which consumes more Scotch whisky in a month than cognac in a year and there is now a nascent French whisky-making industry, although it has a long way to go before it becomes a threat to Scotch.

However, a far more powerful force behind the spread of whisky's popularity was the expansion of the British Empire, with Scottish colonials in particular taking it wherever they went.

After extensive research over the course of writing this book I can tell you that a good blend is great, and a bad malt is bad. I have also realised that, in Scotland at least, blended whisky gets a bad rap as the generation of (almost exclusively) men who introduced themselves to malt whisky did so as malt marketing was on the rise. Whisky, along with foreign holidays and family cars, was becoming a commodity within the grasp of normal working people. No longer was it something your local pub had just one or two of, and you could have more than one type in your house. If you wanted to show how sophisticated and discerning you were, you had malts.

This is what happened to my father's generation of whisky drinkers, and the increasing snobbery about blends meant they could, by favouring malt whiskies, be different from their fathers and show how well they were doing in life by introducing them to something finer.

Humans have that deep, primal need not to be or do the same as the generation before them. I've spoken to loads of Scottish people in my research and most Scotsmen in their sixties and seventies have a favourite brand of malt whisky. They probably found them in their twenties or thirties, pleased finally to have hit on something that will prove to their fathers how well they are doing, how discerning they are and what they know. A malt whisky is an easy way to show your dad what a great guy you have grown up to be.

It also meant that in many houses there was the good whisky and the bad whisky. Up until the late 1970s, every self-respecting, middle-class suburban Scottish household had a drinks trolley that lived in the corner of the living room and, when visitors came, it was sometimes wheeled into the middle of the room for drinks to be chosen and mixed. Another custom that has almost completely died out is that of the whisky decanter. Decanters came in threes, one each for port, sherry and whisky, and the assumption was that the best whisky in the house had been put into the fancy decanter on display.

This, however, was not the case for a very old friend of my father's. Her parents were leading lights in Southside Glasgow

Catholic society and in the early seventies were well known as exemplars of elegance and entertaining. Her father was extremely welcoming and well mannered, but not a man to mess with. He put the cheapest, roughest blend he could find in his decanter; his good malt stayed in a bottle.

Whenever Eileen brought home a boy, or there was a new priest in the parish, they would be presented in the living room and the conversation would always be pretty much the same. Her father would give no indication of his opinion of either the priest or the new boyfriend in any change of manner or topic of conversation. The proof was in the drink. If they got offered whisky from the bottle everything was OK; from the decanter and the priest wouldn't last long in the parish, nor the boyfriend on Eileen's arm.

The marketing men in the 1980s did a fantastic job here convincing everyone of the superiority of malt whisky, so much so that nowadays it is a given in Scotland that a malt is better than a blend.

But the ghosts of blenders past keep reappearing. Alasdair Day, the founder of small modern distillers R&B, used a recipe book written by his grandfather Richard and compiled until 1916 to make the recently launched Tweeddale blend. Initially, he recreated it using eight casks of single malt whisky and one of grain.

The thing is, blends are the whiskies that really got the industry going; the 19th-century blends, and all the new ones made since, are what make it such a big seller. If, like me, you are searching for the spirit of whisky, tribute has to be paid to the great blenders of yore.

This is why, on a wet Sunday at the beginning of January, I ended up on an empty train at 10 o'clock in the morning on the way to Kilmarnock to meet Wullie from Saltcoats. Wullie told his pals that he wasn't going round to theirs to play the guitar because he was going to Kilmarnock to see the grave of someone he neither knew nor was related to, and to a shop that wasnae there, as a pal of his was writing a book about it.

'Ye've got a pal writing a book about graves, Wullie?'

'Naw, it's aboot whisky.'

'And yer going tae a graveyard in Kilmarnock fur that?'

'Aye.'

'Fair enough, see ye later.'

Wullie is one of the first people living in Scotland who I followed on Twitter when it was new and shiny and everyone was nice to each other. A gas fitter in his early thirties, he had originally been in the fishing industry as his father had owned a small trawler. The fishing industry on the west coast went into further decline and all that remained were some langoustine boats, so he went to work on a large trawler for a few years. He was eventually replaced on that boat by cheaper Filipino workers and ended up back in Saltcoats looking for a job for a year.

He is one of those people who could get a piece at any door. You'd welcome Wullie into your house and start off giving him the sandwich, tea, plate of food or whisky that your culture of hospitality demanded and end up wanting to give him more just for the pleasure of his easy company.

It seemed that most of Britain was flooded that January. Whitby, in North Yorkshire, had almost been cut off;

Cumbria seemed to be almost completely underwater, as were large parts of the Borders. The rivers Dee and Tay had burst their banks and flooded towns and villages along their route. Abergeldie Castle, a 450-year-old building near Balmoral beside the River Dee, was visibly shaking in its foundations due to the floodwaters.

Given climate change this may well be what happens every year from now on. My train journey south-west from Glasgow was just dreich. The sky was so dark and dull a blue that the streetlights of every town were still on. Every hill and field looked like a sodden, misshapen woollen jumper that had just been left to drip in the hope that one day it might be dry enough to wear. The trees were all bare of leaves and scraggy, leaning in directions that the wind had battered them into, and the cows were all huddled in corners of fields, dripping.

Christmas was over and New Year finished. I was on a rickety two-carriage train with one other passenger who looked like he was coming back from a night out and was trying to sleep with his jacket pulled up to his chin and his hood up. I was on my way to spend the day in a town that even the ScotRail website said was only good as the jumping-off place to go somewhere else, with only February to look forward to. And it just wouldn't stop raining.

If all of this wasn't sufficiently ominous, I wasn't far enough on in my research to know that no journey should be under-taken without supplies. Had I realised this, I would have made whisky tiffin and taken it with me.

There is a popular myth that the whole of the British Isles

runs on beer in pubs, but that is a mere fantasy of the past where everyone drank warm ale from brown jugs served by portly, whiskered men in braces. Today's Britain is fuelled almost entirely by tea, coffee and the traybake. It is not scones or Victoria sponge that keeps us going, fond as we are of thinking so. It is those pieces of flapjack, brownie, millionaire's shortbread or tiffin that are baked or cooled in a rectangular tray, cut into squares and then eaten. Walk into any bakery, supermarket or cafe anywhere in the UK and you will see that the square slice of cake is the best-selling item. Without the traybake we would descend into utter chaos; yes, it can get even worse, just imagine all the angry sugar-deprived women stomping around looking for someone to take their frustration out on.

Tiffin slides into the traybake category as a lie, since it actually requires no baking. Invented in 1900 in Troon, on the Ayrshire coast, less than 10 miles away from Kilmarnock, it's made by mixing melted chocolate, raisins, syrup and crushed rich tea biscuits. Most people nowadays use digestive biscuits instead of rich tea, but most people are faux-authentic interlopers, even if tiffin does taste better with digestives (if you use them instead, never let me know). I have even had people tell me that in their local chain cafe, tiffin has marshmallows in it and is called rocky road cake. That is something different. Tiffin is tiffin, rocky road cake is rocky road cake, and I do not think that soaking marshmallows in whisky before stirring them into melted chocolate would do much for the taste.

The Whisky Tiffin I Should Have Made to Take with Me to Kilmarnock

Makes around 12 good slices

75g raisins
4 tablespoons whisky (I've used Ballantine's or Cutty
    Sark mostly as that is the whisky I have had when I've
    been making this; use what you like but warn people
    if it is peaty, just in case)
150g dark chocolate, broken into pieces
100g salted butter
2 tablespoons golden syrup
150g rich tea biscuits, roughly broken
50g glacé cherries, chopped into small pieces

Put the raisins in a bowl and soak them in the
whisky, preferably the night before. If you forget,
just do it a couple of minutes before, and when you
are eating the finished product think how much
more you would have enjoyed your tiffin had you
remembered.

Half-fill a large saucepan with water and put on to boil.
Once it starts to boil, turn the heat right down until it
is a gentle simmer then place a smaller saucepan on top,
just above the water, and add the chocolate, butter and
syrup and let them melt, stirring occasionally.

Once the chocolate mix has melted, stir in the biscuits, cherries, raisins and whisky. Pour the melted mixture into a small square tin lined with clingfilm. Shake the tin to ensure that the tiffin has spread evenly, leave for about 30 minutes to cool then put in the fridge for a couple of hours at least, until it is cold and firm.

To serve, cut into squares.

To take on a journey, wrap a piece tightly with clingfilm and put in your jacket pocket and have the pleasure of remembering it when it becomes warm and sticky and soft and sticks to your fingers when you eat it on an empty train on a cold day.

When the train arrives at Kilmarnock, it has miraculously stopped raining and I stand outside the station opposite some closed pubs with peeling-paint doors and blacked-out windows waiting for Wullie at the appointed time.

He's not there and this is not a station in the centre of the city so there is no inside to sit in, no coffee to be had, and it all looks pretty empty. I get a Twitter message from Wullie. He's on a bus, on a Sunday service that seems to be going from Saltcoats to Kilmarnock via every single tiny village in Ayrshire, so he'll be a while, I'd best go to the bus stop and meet him.

Like most of post-industrial Scotland, modern times have been very cruel to Kilmarnock. It went from being a tiny village to a large town thanks to the Industrial Revolution and at one point had several coal mines, plus carpet and shoe factories. Some of the first trains were built in Kilmarnock, and there was all manner of other heavy engineering production in the town, almost all of which has now gone or is being run with a fraction of the staff and it has been replaced by nothing much.

I do not live in the great world of nostalgia for Scotland's industrial past. Someone I spoke to for this book told me that working in heavy industry gave men a sense of meaning. While conditions were not great and wages were not enough for a decent standard of living, they still felt they had a role in life. There is an argument that closing the industry and taking that sense of purpose from men and women in towns and cities across Scotland generated a lot of the ill health from which post-industrial Scotland suffers, especially among working-class men.

I know the stories of towns and their decline. I know of GPs who went to work in mining villages in the late 1970s expecting to become specialists in bronchial disorders but becoming HIV and AIDS experts instead, as towns lost their mines and therefore their reason for being, only to have them replaced by heroin and an outflow of people. I know of former industrial towns, much smaller than Kilmarnock, where almost no one has had a job in three generations, and children know that to do anything, even the most basic job, they will have to leave.

We Scots do love a heavy dose of sentimental nostalgia, so much so that even that is not what it used to be. But anyone spending any time reading Scottish writing of the 1930s knows that heavy industry, the working conditions, the low pay and dreadful housing conditions were seen as a great evil foisted upon a class of people who had become dispensable in the countryside, due to modern farming methods and land taken up with sheep and shooting estates, while the upper classes got even wealthier off the back of industry, trade and empire.

The ethnologist Alexander Fenton, in his book *Country Life in Scotland*, describes the movement from agriculture to industry thus:

> Centuries of farming by a population that was overwhelmingly rural up till the end of the eighteenth century must have burned such rhythms deep into their souls. It is little wonder that a sudden almost mass transition to industrial work came as such a profound shock to the system . . . It is hard, in an instant, to do away with the built-in rhythms of centuries. Change to the strict, unvarying daily routine of a factory was a mental shock.

He goes on later in the book to describe the evils of the squalor-ridden slums where most people who worked in heavy industry ended up.

But the loss of that heavy industry, particularly as working and housing conditions improved during the latter half of the 20th century, can only be unlamented if it is replaced by something better than heroin, and that never happened in the eighties.

What that kind of hardship does breed in people is humour and resilience and Killies have that in bucketloads.

Nothing is more emblematic of this than their football team anthem. In the seventies and early eighties, open hostility and violence between rival fans reached a vicious peak. Aside from the sectarian hellhole that was a Rangers and Celtic game – rival Protestant and Catholic Glasgow teams playing each other against the background of civil war in Northern Ireland – the atmosphere of almost any other league football game was ugly and threatening. The story goes, and who cares if it is 100 per cent true or not, that a fan on a supporters' bus en route to an away game was so sickened by all the hatred that after hearing the Marie Osmond song 'Paper Roses' on the radio decided that should be Kilmarnock FC's new anthem. Somehow it caught on.

You have to imagine it. The opposing team's fans are chanting and screaming and bellowing at you, calling you and your players every name under the sun. Their aim is to provoke you to equal chanting, shouting, screaming and maybe a punch-up afterwards. Your answer? Every single fan on your team waving their scarf singing a song about your love being fake like paper roses.

It's quite a sight. Even now that Scottish football is not what it was in terms of the levels of violence and hatred, watching a load of football fans waving scarves and singing a cheesy 1970s love song still brings a smile to even the sternest of faces.

It doesn't end there. In 2013 Marie Osmond was in Scotland and paid the club a special visit. Aside from having to smile a very expensive smile and say everything is wonderful as part of her profession, she really seems to be having fun on the STV News report archive. The fans watching her look overawed that the singer of their beloved anthem is actually there and going to sing for them, and one of them shows the TV cameras the Asda work contract that Marie had auto-graphed for him.

The fan who met her in Las Vegas and organised her visit has a cheaper, but just as big a smile, as Marie.

'This beats the odd win,' he told the News. 'It doesn't beat the 2012 or the '97 win, but it certainly relegates my marriage to fifth best day of my life, I can assure you.'

What the fourth best day of his life was remains a mystery to the Scottish TV-viewing public.

To get to the bus station I go down King Street, the main street of the centre of Kilmarnock. Its buildings, like most towns of its size in Scotland, are a hotchpotch of everything from foreboding, solid 18th-century Presbyterian severity, to yellow brick badly made with paper walls in the early nineties and post-World War 2 brutalist disasters. There is every chain common to places with more shopping ambition than actual cash and none of them are open.

The street itself was a victim of the Great Plague of Monoblocking that afflicted town planners of the 1990s. A mixture of misplaced infectious enthusiasm, an unused brick mountain and a desire to be seen to be doing something on the part of town councils meant that hundreds, possibly thousands, of serviceable streets that were perfectly fine and at most needed re-tarmacking were levelled off and covered in the paving that had previously only graced the driveways and back gardens of those who treated both wildlife and taste with bleak contempt.

In Kilmarnock they had the added touch of a couple of street sculptures by Shona Kinloch, but the half-torso of a swimmer coming up through monoblock has more the look of 'what the name of the wee man am I doing here?' than being full of the joy of Kilmarnock.

I walk down the road with my phone in my hand, trying to follow the map. As it's too early for the shops to be open and the street is empty apart from two guys standing about looking like a warning of the dangers of overconsumption on a Saturday night. I walk past them.

'Is that yer boyfriend yer texting?'

'No, I'm trying to get to the bus station.'

They both pull themselves up to their full height with their shoulders back. Gone are two slightly leery, slightly staggering men who should have been at home hours ago, to be replaced by two knights in shining armour ready to rescue a damsel in distress and set her on the right path away from dragons and evil and towards the great prize of Kilmarnock bus station.

'Aw hen, that's easy.' One of them walks slightly towards me and, with his left arm outstretched, 'It's just the second on the left there, round that corner and you'll see it.'

'Thanks.'

They both smile.

I find the bus station. Wullie's bus gets in at stance one. In an hour.

Salvation comes in the form of the open doors of Marks

& Spencer. You know where you are in a Marks. It's the traybake of the UK retail experience. Marks & Spencer look after you from before your first school gingham dress to your last ever nightgown which you'll wear in a nursing home in Saltcoats when you are drooling on it all day and have forgotten your own name. Before supermarkets started selling clothes far more cheaply, almost every child got their school clothes from Marks & Spencer.

Apart from reliable clothes, what sets Marks & Spencer apart is the food. Long before the lady with the sexy voice on the adverts told them that 'this was not just any ordinary lasagne', the aspirational ladies of Scotland knew. A Marks & Spencer lasagne is a pasta cut above. Any Scottish town of no great repute that has a Marks & Spencer food hall fills it with middle-aged women with proper hairdos looking proud with their baskets.

It's the Scottish working-class-done-well equivalent of the London rich getting their weekly shopping delivered in a Fortnum & Mason van.

When you get your weekend messages from Marks & Spencer, you've arrived.

When I was in my early thirties I lived in a wee village in the West of Scotland (I lasted 18 months of village life, then I moved to London) and my neighbour's mother lived two minutes up the road. We were sitting outside on the step having a drink one summer's evening when her mother's 80-year-old neighbour walked slowly past, being steadied by her daughter.

'Oh Aileen,' said the neighbour. 'I thought I'd better tell

you that I saw your mother's dog outside earlier and he looked hungry, so I just gave him some Marks & Spencer biscuits. I hope she doesn't mind.'

'That's fine, Mrs McClean. I'll tell her.'

Once Mrs McClean was out of earshot we looked at each other and burst out laughing.

'Why the hell are Marks & Spencer biscuits any different from normal ones?'

'You see,' I replied, 'with some biscuits the dog would be sick, with other ones, the dog would be deid. With Marks & Spencer's? Shiny coat and waggy tail.'

After 15 minutes in Marks & Spencer I remember how much I loathe shopping and loathe aimless window shopping even more. I know that shops are temples and museums to consumerism, and I know that there is nothing intrinsically more worthy about going round a museum looking at old objects you will never possess than there is going round shops looking at new objects you will never possess, but I like visiting museums and I hate going round shops.

I go back to the bus station and wait for Wullie in Greggs. What I have known my entire life as a pie and pasty shop has branched out into serving teas and coffees and having places to sit down. They have sandwiches mimicking their chain rival Subway and even salads now. They still have hot pasties and the woman behind the counter is determined that I am going to buy one.

'Would you like a wee hot pasty with your tea?'

'No thanks.'

'I could pop one in a wee bag for you.'

'No thanks.'

'Are you sure, pet?'

The term of endearment nearly breaks me; it turns me confessional and I abandon hope of monosyllabic introversion.

'I'm just here waiting for a friend.'

'Aww well, they just cost a pound, I could put it by for you while you wait. In fact, I could put two by for you and you could gie her one when she arrives.'

The thought of Wullie's face when discovering on arrival that his sophisticated London-living pal Rachel has been conned into buying not one, but two hot pasties from Greggs by an overeager Killie woman in a hairnet hardens my resolve.

'No thanks, I'll just have the tea.'

9

FROM SMALL BEGINNINGS ...

'There is indeed one man who can solve writer's block.
His name is Mr Johnnie Walker.'

ASHWIN SANGHI

Wullie arrives in a puff of big blue waterproofs and no desire for a pasty. We get going to find the famous blue plaque of Kilmarnock.

It's not an official round blue plaque; it's a wee rectangle put there by the council on a building that is a gold shop next to a Claire's Accessories.

It reads: 'Site of Johnnie Walker's Shop'.

This is the site of the original John Walker grocery shop where in 1820 John Walker was set up by his trustees as a minor. John Walker, founder of John Walker & Sons, producers of the world-renowned Johnnie Walker Scotch whisky, was the son of an Ayrshire farmer, Alexander Walker of Todriggs.

The most popular Scotch whisky brand in the world, a bottle of Johnnie Walker is being sold every two seconds, which amounts to more than 17 million cases annually – twice as many as Ballantine's, the next leading brand.

Its well-guarded secret blend combines grain whisky with at least 32 malt whiskies. No one, except for owner Diageo's blenders, knows for sure exactly how many, although a number of core whiskies remain a constant. Their challenge is to maintain the consistency of the brand – no mean feat given the variables in production. The blenders have faith in their nose even above their palate when it comes to making the winning mix. In all its forms it has a legion of fans.

So numerous and widespread are Johnnie Walker fans that the most reliable indicator for increased sales in any country is increasing economic activity. Buying a bottle of Johnnie Walker Red label is, almost anywhere in the developing world, such a strong sign of prestige and prosperity that without any marketing plan JW sales increase in countries which are getting more prosperous.

This empire started at the comparatively humble grocer's shop owned by John Walker on King Street, Kilmarnock. The premises were bought with the proceeds of the sale of his family's farm on the death of his father in 1819, when John was just 14 years old. Standing there, Wullie looks unimpressed. It starts raining again.

'I've never noticed this plaque before, Rachel,' he says.

'Well now ye have.'

'Aye,' he shrugs, getting wetter.

In the 19th century, while distillers made the whisky, the people who marketed and sold it were grocers and wine and tea merchants. Blending was a familiar concept already as newly imported teas were being co-mingled. But there remained a challenge for whisky blenders who had no recipe or benchmark product to match.

Grocers bought the whisky from the distillers and needed something to transport it in, so used barrels, mostly ones that had previously contained wine or sherry or port. Often they would send up their own barrels to the distillery to come back full of whisky as the distilleries themselves really had no mass system for transporting whisky. They would then mix different barrels together to make their own label. John Walker's first whisky was Walker's Kilmarnock Whisky. Lots of other now world-famous blends started in the same way.

Ballantine's was first made in a grocer's shop in Edinburgh by George Ballantine. When he extended into Glasgow in 1869, his capacity for making blended whisky boomed. George died in 1891, four years before Ballantine's whisky received a royal warrant from Queen Victoria and nearly two decades before the brand's famous 'Finest' blend was nailed.

The forebears of Matthew Gloag, who created Famous Grouse, were Perth grocers. Admittedly, theirs was a high-end business which once helped to cater for Queen Victoria and Prince Albert's visit to Scotland, in 1842. By the time

Gloag was at the helm, the business was mostly focused on wines and spirits. Famous Grouse was released onto an appreciative market in 1896. It's now owned by the Scottish-based Edrington Group, which also markets Highland Park, Cutty Sark and The Macallan whiskies.

Around the same time that Famous Grouse was being blended, a grocer's shop in Elgin was founded by James Gordon and John MacPhail. As you'll remember from Dramboree, it is still a highly respected private bottlers, wholesalers and it also owns the Benromach distillery.

Pea and Lettuce Soup

Cooking lettuce has fallen out of fashion but I think it is something that should be revived, and here is a chance. If you want a slightly richer soup then stir in some cream at the end. I don't think it needs it.

Serves 4

2 tablespoons olive oil
½ onion, finely chopped
1 garlic clove, minced
1 tablespoon Famous Grouse whisky
250g peas, fresh or frozen
½ lettuce, finely sliced
500ml hot water from the kettle
generous pinch of salt

Put the olive oil in a saucepan on a medium heat and add the onion and garlic and cook for a few minutes. Add the whisky and cook for a few more minutes.

Add the peas, lettuce and hot water and a good pinch of salt.

Cook for about 8 minutes and then purée with a hand blender or in a food processor.

Serve in bowls.

One advance in technology that really helped the whisky companies around this time was the development of the continuous still. Malt whisky has always been made in batches in pot stills. If you compare the earliest drawings of the most rudimentary stills employed by farmers to make use of their leftover barley in the 17th and 18th centuries and the stills used at Glenfiddich, which now produces about 6 million litres of malt spirit a year, the process is practically the same. Basically, a continuous still allows alcohol to be made far more quickly.

Three men are credited in various places with the invention of the continuous still: Robert Stein, Andrew Usher and Aeneas Coffey.

Stein, a distiller in Clackmannanshire, was inspired by the original development of a continuous still in Cork, Ireland, and created a column still through which the wash was pushed and alcohol collected. But Stein could never get financial backing to patent the still and make more.

That honour fell to Aeneas Coffey, an Irish excise man who was present at one of Stein's presentations and went on to further develop the continuous still until he got financial backing which enabled him to patent the Coffey still in 1830 and make and sell it all over the world.

The Coffey still is an example of fractional distillation and with this method not only does the process of extracting alcohol from a wash become far quicker, the amount of alcohol you get is greatly increased. A pot still will give you 40–50 per cent alcohol, whereas a Coffey still will produce a liquid that is 80–90 per cent alcohol and a lot faster. Cameronbridge distillery, the original location of Stein's column still, now produces 65 million litres of grain spirit a year, over 10 times the amount of Glenfiddich.

No one is a prophet in their own land and the one place where Coffey's stills were not popular was Ireland, a giant of whiskey production at the time. But where the Irish saw bland whiskey (the Irish kind is always spelled with an 'e'), the Scots saw opportunity.

To make whisky from a Coffey still you can use any grain. Most of Scotland's grain distilleries use wheat nowadays, which is then mixed with a much smaller amount of malted barley to allow for fermentation. Even now it produces a much lighter-tasting spirit than most malt distilleries and, when you consider that peat and coal were used to heat up barley when making malt and also to heat a pot still, it is little wonder that among the English gentlemen coming up to Scotland to visit the Highlands of the mid-1800s whisky had a reputation as a very strong and smoky drink.

Once grain whisky was produced, though, it could be mixed with the malted whiskies to make a softer-tasting drink which would have more appeal to the Scottish middle classes and the English traveller, coming up on the newly created railway system either as tourist or travelling merchant.

Andrew Usher, a merchant and grocer in Edinburgh, was, like Alexander Walker, the son of a successful grocer, also called Andrew, who had been blending barrels of whisky to make his own whiskies and Andrew junior saw the possibilities of grain whisky. It is he, rather than a Walker, who is known as the father of Scotch whisky. He was one of the founders of the North British distillery, a grain distillery still in Edinburgh, and was such a successful businessman that he donated £100,000 in 1896 to fund a new concert hall. Completed after his death and opened in 1914, the Usher Hall in Edinburgh has not only been named after Andrew, but if you are lucky enough to have tickets to the grand circle you walk past a bust of him in the hall. Like fellow Scot Andrew Carnegie, he was a man who gave his money away as silently as a waiter falling down a marble staircase with a tray of glasses.

Grain distilleries are not on the whisky tourist map. If you want the Johnnie Walker experience then you will be taken to the Cardhu distillery up in Moray, as Cardhu is one of the known malt whiskies used in Johnnie Walker whisky, having been purchased when Walker's was still a family firm. But malt whiskies generally make up around 15 per cent of any blended whisky, so most of what you are drinking comes from a grain distillery.

They are huge, industrial-looking places full of men in work uniforms and steel-toecapped shoes. If you ever get permission to visit one you will climb a lot of stairs and see men sitting in front of computer screens scrutinising flow charts while the radio is on in the background. Grain distilleries are mostly located in Scotland's central belt and now there are only eight of them. Between them, they produce more spirit than the over 100 malt distilleries in the rest of Scotland.

Working at a grain distillery is quite a different job; if you want to get involved in making malt whisky, you are best off getting a qualification in brewing and distilling. Grain distillers are chemical engineers who have chosen to work in the world of whisky instead of the other main options for them in Scotland – oil or water. One of the engineers at the Strathclyde distillery in Glasgow told me that fractional distillation has more in common with extracting oil than distilling malt whisky.

Old-school whisky snobs generally turn their noses up at grain whisky; they say that it is kept in inferior barrels and has next to no taste, but old casks that are then bottled can be really good quality. It doesn't taste the same as a malt whisky; it never has a peaty, smoky taste, for example, and to my mind is never as viscous, but it can still be a really enjoyable drink. Smaller whisky shops sometimes have bottles of old-style Cameron Brig available and the recently launched Haig Club and Girvan Grain are both grain whiskies rather than malt. Grain whiskies, like blends, are not things you should turn your nose up at – you may be depriving yourself of something you might enjoy.

Back to the Walkers. That John Walker's whisky didn't suffer the same fate as so many other small-time grocers' whiskies and disappear is due to his offspring. His son Alexander Walker, who had learned the art of blending tea in Glasgow, went back to Kilmarnock to help with the business. Realising its commercial cachet, he made the whisky a much more important part of it, eventually creating Walker's Old Highland Blend – the forerunner of Johnnie Walker Black and Red Labels. He also drastically increased the wholesale business, possible in part because of Kilmarnock's position as an interchange on the new Glasgow to London railway line.

Due to an increasingly competitive market, Alexander introduced the square bottle in the 1860s, partly to prevent breakages and partly to stand out from other blends on the shop shelf. Then there was the distinctive label, set at an angle of 24 degrees. Apart from allowing for more space to write, Alexander Walker felt that the slanting label would make his brand leap out from a shelf increasingly crowded with whisky bottles. He expanded his markets by enticing Glasgow's ships' captains to act as overseas agents for the blend.

With this increase in possibilities for the whisky market, Alexander Walker opened an office in London in 1880, which was run firstly by his three sons then by another Kilmarnock man, James Stevenson. It is Stevenson who is credited with the rebranding of Walker's whisky as Johnnie Walker and with the slogan 'born in 1820, still going strong'. In 1908 it was Stevenson who commissioned the cartoonist Tom Browne to draw the famous John Walker figure, basing it on a portrait of the original John, allegedly scrawled on the back of a napkin during a business lunch. Although different versions of it have been made over the decades that followed, the essence of the present striding man launched in the fifties is the same.

Johnnie Walker, now the biggest-selling blended whisky in the world – over 225 million 750cl bottles a year – started in this small shop on Kilmarnock high street.

Possibly the most eccentric Johnnie Walker story that I know concerns Israel. There are two importers of Johnnie Walker into Israel, the first of which spent money to send rabbis to Scotland to make sure that the whisky was kosher, while the second one didn't. In August 2015 the Chief Rabbi revoked the kosher certificate of the Johnnie Walker Black Label coming from the second importer, who hadn't undertaken religious vetting, saying it had been mislabelled and had to be removed from the shelves. Thus, the first importer was then the only one to provide whisky that was officially declared kosher.

It wasn't that the product was any different – a brand like Johnnie Walker needs to be consistent all over the world. It was simply that the second importer hadn't flown out rabbis to observe and certify that the product was kosher. So two identical products, one kosher, one not.

The story soon disappeared so I have no idea if some rabbis were paid to go to Scotland quickly and verify the other Johnnie Walker Black Label as kosher, but I do hope so.

Had I known all of these stories that January I do hope that Wullie would have enjoyed them and felt that his visit to a blue plaque marking a shop that wasnae there anymore was worth it. As I didn't, he just shrugged and then we went to find John Walker's grave.

As we wait to cross the main road the only other pedestrian we see walks straight past us. She has those long legs and perfectly bouncy hair that can only be achieved without great effort by a 19-year-old and she has put no effort in at all. She has a khaki-coloured coat with a hood that she isn't wearing up even in the rain and has the heavy make-up that young women desperately trying to look more grown-up than they feel wear during the day. As she walks past we both realise she is also holding the biggest cone reefer either of us has ever seen out in public. We both try not to stare.

Neither of us manages.

'I've no' seen that even in Brixton,' says Wullie.

'Not much Met-style stop and search of wee lassies in Kilmarnock I imagine,' I say.

'Naw,' agrees Wullie.

'And not a lot else to do on a Sunday afternoon.'

Wullie raises his eyebrows and looks at me hopefully. I shake my head sadly, although given the nature of the day a wee fly smoke by Johnnie Walker's grave might have been the thing to do.

We cross the road and trudge up a hill and get to the St Andrew's Glencairn Church of Scotland church, a place where All Are Welcome and there's a mother and toddler group twice a week. Where All Are Most Definitely Not Welcome is the churchyard beside the church as the gate is padlocked. My heart sinks. I have come all this way, dragged Wullie out on a Sunday-service bus to visit the grave of someone neither of us knew nor were related to and didn't think to find out if the churchyard was open.

When I told people, acquaintances and work colleagues, that I was working on a book going round bits of Scotland looking at whisky and food matching and cooking with it, the reaction went from envious side eye and, 'Oh, that sounds like an interesting project', to a big booming laugh and a shout of, 'You jammy bugger. Why the hell didn't I think to pitch that? I think I actually hate you!'

It was supposed to be an adventure that was a cross between *Brigadoon* and *Whisky Galore*. I was supposed to be constantly covered in tartan or tweed, being wooed by whisky companies in fancy hotels and trying whisky that sank with the *Titanic* or stuff that is so expensive that only me, four whisky writers and some billionaire oligarchs have tried.

I should be in a blending room, or a fancy tasting room in a distillery, one of those with soft lighting and bars lined with oak, drinking pre-mutiny Macallan. I should have brand ambassadors and distillery managers being nice to me, handing me drams and telling me stories over a log fire. This is what everyone else thinks I am doing while researching this book.

Nobody, not one single person, imagines me standing ankle-deep in muddy grass in front of a padlocked gate outside a churchyard in a post-industrial central Scottish town on a wet Sunday in January. I am clearly doing it very wrong.

I look up and see Wullie on the other side of the gates.

'Come roond, Rachel, it's open the other side!'

Thank God for that.

We get to the graveyard; it's bigger than I imagined. There're a lot of unreadable gravestones, as the elements and plants have worn them away. John Walker died in 1857, that's 159 years of stone exposure to rain, wind and lichen. We are never going to find this grave.

We decide to split up, Wullie taking the right-hand side, me the left. I can hardly decipher a thing; he's not having much more luck.

After about five minutes he shouts at me: 'Here, it's here! It's got a new stone and everything.'

I trudge through muddy grass while Wullie stands beside it, pointing.

The Argentinian comedian Enrique Pinti used to do a routine about tourists going from Argentina to Europe for the one and only time that they would be able to afford it. One of the things they would have to go and see would be the *Mona Lisa* in the Louvre. All of their friends would be telling them how amazing it was and how moved they would feel upon gazing at the painting. 'And you're standing there in front of it, thinking it's fine. I mean it's OK, it's a nice painting but I am not overwhelmed. But my God I should cry, if only for the life savings I've spent coming here, I really need to feel something!'

The Germans must have an expression for that utter lack of feeling when you finally reach the end of your pilgrimage.

Wullie stared at me. 'Well, it's the grave.'

'Aye, so it is.'

'Will we go tae the pub?' Wullie wanted to go to the Wetherspoons.

'Cheap beer, Rachel, and there is almost always a fight you can watch in that Wetherspoons – it's where everybody goes.'

Wullie, surprisingly enough, was right; all of Kilmarnock was in the Wetherspoons, a pub that was so big it was like a barn, like most Wetherspoons in Britain. This one had originally been a coaching inn and seemed to have had extra bits added onto it in the 19th century.

'This must be the place to be at the weekend.'

'Aye, although it can be a bit like a bear pit at closing time,' says Wullie. We didn't stay to see if he was right this time.

The story of Johnnie Walker in Kilmarnock ended when the bottling plant was closed down and moved elsewhere in Scotland in 2012. Although many of the workers at the plant were found alternative employment elsewhere, the town itself lost 700 jobs, and all that remains in the town to connect it with its most famous product is a plaque, a gravestone, a statue and some street names.

Yet the fact remains that without Johnnie Walker in all its hues and Ballantine's, established in 1827, the whisky industry in Scotland would collapse, leaving us with even more to be nostalgic about in pubs across Scotland.

The early history of Ballantine's mimicked that of its rival and, like Walker's, the company did appreciably better in the hands of the founder's eldest son, Archibald.

According to the company website, George Ballantine lived by the motto: 'Be yourself, be authentic, be genuine and the stories that you live will deserve to be toasted.' Clearly, he was drinking his own product when he came up with that one.

The family firm ended up in the hands of Canadian distillers Hiram Walker in 1937 and it is now part of Pernod Ricard. Ballantine's knows limitless appeal in Asia and is a big seller in other parts of the world, notably South Africa, India and Brazil, proving just how successful Scotch blends can be in finding markets overseas and how much the industry owes to those early pioneers.

Buchanan's is a blend that has fallen away from prominence in Scotland, but its popularity elsewhere in the world keeps it on the top 25 best-selling whisky lists. Just as it can be a shock to Scottish people abroad how non-Scots drink whisky, the ones they drink can also be a surprise.

The best example of this is Old Parr. If you've not heard of it, it's because it hasn't been sold in the UK and Europe since the 1980s, but in Colombia over half the sales of Scotch whisky are Old Parr. No one can tell me why, but the biggest likelihood is that it was first smuggled over from Panama and became the whisky everyone wanted. The articles and online ads describe it as 'A foreign drink with a Colombian heart'. There are special bottlings in time for regional Colombian festivals and part of the Caribbean coastal city of Barranquilla's carnival is called 'Carnaval Old Parr'.

Grand Old Parr, as it is actually called, started life in 1909 as a blended whisky made by the Greenlees brothers of London, who had been blending and selling whisky since 1871. Named after Old Tom Parr, reputedly the oldest man in Britain, the name was meant to convey the maturity of the product. In the early 1900s it was already thought that older whisky would be better. Greenlees Bros was later bought by James Calder and then in 1925 by United Distillers. Like Buchanan's, it is now owned by Diageo, and one of their Colombian staff told me they really enjoy taking non-Colombian Diageo staff to Old Parr festivals, as first they stare in disbelief and then start wondering how to get the rest of their brands integrated into festivals all over the world.

Buchanan's blend was started by James Buchanan, a Canadian-born Scot who ended up in London in 1879 at the age of 29 working as a sales agent for the whisky firm of Charles Mackinlay. By 1884 he had set up on his own as James Buchanan & Co and, aided by Glasgow blender William Lowrie, was producing his own blended whisky and after a year was supplying it to the Houses of Parliament.

In his later years Buchanan, by this time a baron, was to recall the audacity of his youthful self, on the make, determined to succeed, with a constant eye for expanding his business. To get a deal to supply the music halls of London, he contracted the accountant who was also head of the United Music Halls Company to do his own company accounts and that way got the whisky into the halls. After 18 months of trying to persuade the owner of a number of London pubs to stock Buchanan's blend, he eventually invited the man's daughters, recently bereaved of their mother, to a Burns Club Cinderella dance. After seeing his daughters have such a pleasant evening, the grieving widower, according to Buchanan, gave him the whole of his trade for all of his licensed establishments.

My favourite story of Buchanan's, and who cares whether or not it is true, is this one. After protracted negotiations with a smart London hotel in which he failed to gain a foothold, he employed 12 young, good-looking actors to go with him there for dinner. They arrived in full evening dress, complete with opera cloaks, and when the sommelier asked them what they wanted to drink they demanded Buchanan's blend. On hearing it wasn't available, all dozen well-dressed, well-mannered beautiful young actors flounced out of the hotel with a swish of their cloaks and their noses in the air.

Buchanan went on to export his whisky throughout the world, winning gold medals at exhibitions in Paris, buying some of the malt whisky distilleries used in the blend outright, and building Glentauchers distillery on Speyside, which went into production in 1898, the same year that he received a royal warrant to supply to Queen Victoria. In the early 20th century, he opened offices in New York, Buenos Aires, Hamburg and Paris and, by 1909, his was the best-selling blend in England.

By the 1930s Buchanan had let go of most of his business interests and was playing the role of English country gentleman, but his legacy to the whisky industry lives on. His insistence on the malt content of blends being both significant and well aged made him one of the pioneers in turning a rough Highland drink into both a highly respectable and aspirational one.

Gigot de la Clinique (Roast Syringed Lamb)

In 1954 Alice B. Toklas published a memoir cookbook
called *Murder in the Kitchen*. The most famous recipe
in the book is for hashish fudge and is probably the
reason why the book has never been out of print. In her
book, she says she got the gigot recipe by bribing the
cook of the French provincial surgeon who invented it.
Jonathan Meades then put it in his book, *Plagiarist in the
Kitchen*, where I came across it. The original uses cognac
but I think a whisky like Ballantine's gives it a better
flavour. You could try it with a really peaty whisky like
Octomore or Laphroaig if you wanted to throw caution
to the wind, but I am sticking to using a blend. The
French chef Yves-Marie Le Bourdonnec makes this
recipe with the Japanese malt whisky, Nikka.

Toklas' original recipe called for mutton, Meades'
uses lamb. It takes eight days to marinate the meat
properly and you need a syringe. Meades recommends a
veterinary one, I use a cake syringe.

This is the polar opposite of a bish-bosh meal in 15
minutes. It requires time, effort and expense, but is
worth it as an annual meal for a special occasion.

Serves 6–8

1 × 2.5–3kg leg of lamb
salt

For the marinade
2 bottles red wine
good glug of olive oil
4 bay leaves
30 juniper berries
20 szechuan peppercorns
2 teaspoons cumin seeds
2 teaspoons fennel seeds
400ml orange juice, strained
400ml whisky

Put all the marinade ingredients, except the whisky and orange juice, in a bowl and mix together. Put the lamb leg in a deep container and cover with the marinade – the lamb needs to be completely submerged, covered and left in a cool place, preferably a fridge. If it is too big for your fridge, put it in as cool a place as possible. I make this in early spring and keep it outside, marinating in a plastic bucket covered with a cloth in the shade and bring it in at night.

Every day for the following eight days mix 50ml orange juice (make sure the bits don't clog up your syringe) mixed with 50ml whisky. Syringe this mixture into the meat in various places. You want to inject the meat in three different places each time you syringe.

On the eighth day, preheat the oven to 200°C/fan 180°C/gas 6. Take the lamb out of the marinade (reserve this to make a gravy) and rub it with salt, then put it in the oven for 60–80 minutes or until it is cooked.

Put the reserved marinade into a saucepan, season with salt and cook on a medium heat until it has reduced by at least half.

Strain the gravy and serve it with the lamb.

10

WHISKY AND CHIPS

*'I'd much rather be someone's shot of whisky
than everyone's cup of tea.'*
CARRIE BRADSHAW

The patriarch and I were supposed to be going on holiday together. He invited me after a 15-minute explanation of why neither his wife nor his pals wanted to go with him, so he was offering to take me, and we were in the middle of getting our plans together when we had the Great Argument of 2011. The reasons are rather dull but it is a cyclical occurrence. The last time we fell out I phoned my mother full of righteous indignation, ready to launch into The Entire Story Of All The Injustices And Outrages Committed By The Patriarch To Cause Such A Calamity, and my mother said, 'When was the last time you fell out with him, again, 18 months ago? Well, you were due another fall-out so that'll be what's happened.'

This stopped me in mid-outrage and left me somewhat deflated. The aforementioned falling-out lasted far less than normal, but still too long to go on that holiday.

My father is not a lover of the Scottish countryside, or really any countryside that isn't a golf course for that matter. His idea of a trip to the countryside is a day trip to Edinburgh and a walk through Princes Street Gardens. I dug my heels in once, when I was up on a visit, and insisted we go on a country run in the car. We drove through three forests, over various hills, got rained on in a car park and ate the worst strawberry tart in Scotland in a cafe in Tighnabruaich designed to cater for bus trips.

Most distilleries are in the countryside, so if we were going to have father and daughter bonding time a proper investigation of everything the Highlands and Islands had to offer was out of the question. I needed to come up with something else, something that was more his style. And I did.

We went through the central belt to Alloa, an industrial town which still has industry left, unlike Kilmarnock. We drove round the edge of it, marvelling at town planners of the 1970s and their passion for roundabouts, and ended up lost in an industrial park. My phone was no use here, so we did the old-fashioned thing and spoke to a human being in real life, going as far as entering the reception of a window fitter's to get directions from a lady behind a desk.

It was all terribly quaint.

We managed to find Abercrombie engineers, which is where we needed to be. It's a nondescript brick building that could hold anything from locomotive engines to an online bookshop; the entrance and reception scream 1980s functionality, and there are men doing industrial work. It's just my father's kind of place. A big tall bald man with a deep booming voice comes down the stairs and asks if we're here for the tour. My dad says, 'No we're not' and turns his back to him. I say, 'Yes we are' and shake his hand. We are spending the morning with Charlie.

To distil malt whisky you need a copper still. You can use exactly the same type of malt, the same type of barrel and mature your whisky for exactly the same length of time, but if your still is a different shape you can end up with quite a different-tasting whisky. If you want consistency in taste, you need complete consistency in still shape – any repairs need to be the same, and if you are increasing your production and therefore the number of stills, you need them to be identical.

For every last detail to be the same, down to the dent on the right-hand side of the neck of your still 56 centimetres before the curve – which although you are not convinced has much influence on the taste of your whisky, you are not taking any chances with – you need someone you can trust to repair, maintain and build your stills.

In Alloa, that person is Charlie King, operations manager of Diageo Abercrombie engineers and coppersmiths.

Abercrombie started life in 1790, the year after George Washington became the first president of the United States, as the Alloa Copper Works. It's now owned by Diageo, the biggest drinks company in the world. The British-based multinational owns about 27 malt distilleries and two grain ones, as well as the Johnnie Walker brand among others.

'If it's worth drinking, Diageo probably own it,' said Charlie, 'and it's my job to make sure all the stills are in good condition.'

Up stairs covered in industrial carpet so rough that it would graze your face if you fell on it, we follow Charlie into a small conference room to see the company video and get the Official Company Chat for Visiting Journalists. My father takes a good look at Charlie with his black polo shirt, dark-blue work trousers and steel-toecapped shoes. He lowers his shoulders and relaxes; this is his kind of man.

Charlie smiles the smile of Macavity with a bowlful of fresh cream. He is spending the morning doing what is obviously one of his favourite things to do in the world – telling strangers how much he loves his job.

I look at Charlie, I look at my dad. There is a lot riding on this. A guided tour of the engineers' workshop, one of the last remnants of industrial Scotland, something not normally open to members of the public, is what my father is getting in lieu of grandchildren, a nice son-in-law and a daughter with a decent job and an affordable mortgage.

Charlie had better be good.

'Forty-four people work in this coppersmith's, with two apprentices every year,' he said. It's a promising start.

'I've been here eight years and I've taken on 16 apprentices. I've got three guys doing engineering degrees at night school, which we support them through, although I don't make it easy for them. They finish their shift then they go to college. If they want it, they'll put in the effort for it.

'I served my apprenticeship in a company called Motherwell Bridge, and then when I was 43 I did a degree in business at night school while running a factory with 220 people, Mum and Dad not well, a wife and two children, and it was the toughest thing I have ever done in my life, so I just say this to my guys, "If you want it, you're gonnae do it, but I'm no' making it easy fur ye.'"

BINGO! Charlie is a winner. I could kiss the top of his bald head.

My father left school at 16 and became an apprentice joiner at a big company near Motherwell Bridge engineers. When he started there, the staunchly Protestant owners had a contract with the Glasgow Catholic diocese, so he learned joinery as a five-year apprentice building church pews and altars. After his apprenticeship he worked as a joiner on building sites and hated it, and so he got a job in building control in the planning department in Glasgow, where he worked his way up to running one of the departments. He completed an Open University degree in his mid-thirties, and, when he took early retirement at 50, did a master's.

Paradise for my father is a place where 16-year-olds start apprenticeships and end up with degrees and even with post-graduate degrees, and where the bosses have come from the same place as the boys just starting. Boys start off with tools in their hand and finish as well-paid, highly qualified men like Charlie, with holiday homes in Florida or Spain and hobbies like golf or hill walking.

That is where his only child has led him. I have done it. I have taken him to his own personal heaven. This should get me kudos points for *years*.

When not building and repairing stills on site, the men

(and it is only men) go to distilleries to carry out checks and upgrades on about 160 stills a year in teams of two to a dozen. If you try to visit a distillery that is shut for maintenance, these are the people who are on the site preventing you from getting in.

In his travels, Charlie has visited distilleries with historical quirks. The Mortlach distillery on Speyside is a great example. When it was opened in 1823 in the wake of the Excise Act it was the first legal distillery in Dufftown. Indeed, it remained the only distillery there for more than half a century, until Glenfiddich's brewers opened for business in 1887. Initially, it was merely the way founder James Findlater chose to use his excess barley.

It has six stills that are entirely different shapes. As Charlie puts it: 'It looks like someone has gone to a car-boot sale and picked up six stills and put them there – nobody would do that now, but that is just how the business grew.'

Thanks to the growth of distilleries like these, it is imperative that Charlie and his colleagues keep traditional copper-fashioning skills alive.

'It's important in the flavour of Mortlach for those stills to have that shape now and it's my job to make sure they stay the same,' he explained.

'When I first started in this job I went to Dailuaine distillery on Speyside, which should have three massive wash stills and three smaller spirit stills. I walk in and it's got two massive wash stills and a small wash still, and then a massive spirit still and two small stills. I asked the on-site manager what that was all about and he sighed, stared at me and said,

"About 50 years ago you guys came to install a new wash and spirit still and youse got them mixed up and now that's our character."

'If you were starting to build a distillery tomorrow, you'd never do what Mortlach or Dailuaine does, but it works for those spirits.'

It's time for us to go down to the factory and, after a brief search for steel-capped shoes small enough for me, we go into the main workshop. It's the size of an airport hangar with massive bits of machinery everywhere but almost no one working. The men are all on their lunch break; this is very deliberate and part of Charlie's strategy for showing people around. When the men are all working it's just too noisy to do the tour.

If my father wasn't happy enough in the conference room, Charlie and he spend the next 20 minutes (I've got the recording, I checked) comparing notes on health and safety on construction sites and engineering workshops. If your job, like most people in the 21st century, involves sitting on a chair in front of a computer all day, health and safety often only intrudes on your life as another annoying example of the nanny state hellbent on wrapping everyone up in cotton wool like precious crystal glasses, but to these guys and anyone working in what little remains of our heavy industry, it can be a matter of life and death.

Leaning inside a still that is nearly five metres tall and trying to bang out a kink in the copper without a safety harness is a very dangerous activity, but Charlie explains that it can be a very difficult job persuading a man to use one when neither his grandfather nor his father did. My dad agreed and they both went on sharing stories about how difficult it is to get men to change their practices in order to keep safe when they had become used to unsafe ones.

I looked at them both and how they were relating to each other and all of a sudden I understood what writers and academics meant when they lamented the loss of purpose men felt when their work in heavy industry came to an end. There was a great sense of enterprise and togetherness at the coppersmith's. Charlie was proud of his job, proud to work for the company, but most of all he was proud of his guys. They were his men; he was responsible for them and he felt a sense of both ownership and loyalty towards them. He didn't sit in an office all day sending emails requesting things be done, leaving a message trail to prove he'd done his job and wasn't responsible for mess-ups. To communicate with his employees he went to the workshop to talk to them. If they were on a job in Speyside or Islay, he trusted them to do it properly and was there to support them by phone.

That type of closeness and camaraderie is also only possible with an apprenticeship system where your job requires you to be trained for it for a number of years. Soft-skills jobs, the ones that most of us now have, can take people from any background with any kind of experience; coppersmiths and engineers can't simply be trained overnight.

Listening to both my father and Charlie I realised that I have never had a job where I felt I was someone's responsibility and actually didn't know anyone else who did. People I know might work in offices in jobs they really like but would never refer to the people they manage as their 'guys'; there isn't the same sense of belonging and ownership in an office.

I had always looked at heavy industry as an evil, something that helped create slum-housing conditions, destroyed men's bodies and generated a toxic cultural myth of the Glasgow hard man. I had never seen how much it also produced a sense of belonging for men that an individualistic, competitive, post-industrial work culture has lost.

It turned out to still exist, with 44 men in a small corner of Alloa.

The next week, when I announced to my father that we were going to his hometown as there was a whisky restaurant there, he stared at me in disbelief. With his hands in his pockets, he lifted his shoulders up and leaned his head towards me.

'There's a whisky restaurant in *Wishaw*?'

My father, like his father before him, was born and bred in Wishaw, North Lanarkshire. It's one of the many central-belt towns that were built around heavy industry. There were a few coal mines nearby and Ravenscraig, a major steelworks, in the next town.

My great-grandfather, Patrick McCormack, came from Longford in Ireland to work as a clerk on the railways. Wishaw had one of Scotland's earliest lines, opened in 1844, which stretched 11 miles between collieries.

Although my father forgot to ask his father what it was like being born and growing up in Wishaw between the two world wars – and as he died when I was six years old I never had the opportunity to ask – any cursory reading of

D.H. Lawrence novels about industrial towns in the North of England, or any of Alexander Fenton's studies about the effects of heavy industrial work in Scotland on the culture of the people employed in such labour, would lead you to imagine that being born and brought up in industrial Scotland in the 1930s was anything but great. There was rampant poverty, widespread unemployment, grim housing, poor health and religious sectarianism. Even after the advent of the National Health Service, the declining industries left many workers in a poverty trap. Damian Barr's memoir, *Maggie & Me*, about growing up in nearby Newarthill, tells you that the 1980s, for many people, were just as grim.

My father enjoyed being brought up there in the 1950s and 60s so much that he left in his early twenties and, now, at the age of 70, still occasionally wakes up in a cold sweat, thinking he is back in Wishaw.

Scotland in many parts is just beautiful; even on a grey misty wet day, fields full of healthy-looking cattle with hills of every hue in the background can, and do, just take your breath away. The train from Glasgow Queen Street to Edinburgh Waverley, surely one of the least scenic rail routes in Scotland, passes through some perfectly aesthetically pleasing fields and towns.

None of them are in North Lanarkshire.

It is as if VisitScotland looked at a map and decided that North Lanarkshire would be just the place to dump almost all of the jaded, ugly bits of landscape in Scotland so that tourists could continue their journey uninterrupted by the reality of post-industrial knackeredness.

I worked in North Lanarkshire for almost a year about a decade ago and my overwhelming memory is of driving past bedraggled trees and tired-looking hedges, as if mines and steelworks and the drudge of the industrial work around them had sapped all the energy and joy out of them.

Wishaw isn't even the crown jewel in the county of North Lanarkshire. It is overshadowed by the larger town, and home to the former Ravenscraig steelworks, Motherwell. Not many places can claim to the fame of being eclipsed by Motherwell. In fact, if you have ever heard about Wishaw it will probably be because one of its butcher's shops was responsible for the largest *E. coli* breakout in the world, in 1996, which killed 21 people and made 200 ill.

Looking at the evidence, I can understand why my father greeted my announcement with some scepticism. But to give the patriarch his due, he did agree to try it – even though it involved driving 40 minutes there and back to Wishaw – on the grounds that Alloa had been great and no one puts 'Alloa' and 'great' in the same sentence unless it ends with 'to get out of'.

North Lanarkshire, like badly applied lipstick, is best seen in a low light, so a dreich day in winter is actually ideal. When you come to Scotland and are faced with nothing but rain and cloud and mist, you are told by all of us here that it really is one of the most beautiful countries in the world, if only you could see it in the sun. Nobody is referring to this place. In the rain and the mist you can think, 'Ach well, I'm sure it will look better on a clear sunny day.' Then that clear sunny day arrives and you realise it just looks worse. Every bit of ugly bedragglement, every sad field with unhappy-looking cows in it, are just highlighted in the sun. Dark, grey clouds and spitting rain suit North Lanarkshire far better, and we are quite happily trundling along the motorway on our way to visit the McCormack homeland.

Until we get to the roadworks.

I no longer have a car. The freedom that brings is immense. I normally travel by underground and am thus liberated from the many ties that cars entail – finding parking spaces, stopping at traffic lights, signalling when turning right or left or being unable to drink alcohol while out. I have also forgotten about the contemporary horror story that is the motorway roadwork.

You plan a journey on Google maps and, if you are lucky, it shows you how most of your journey will take you speeding across that great postwar construct, the modern motorway. You cruise along at a constant 70 miles an hour and arrive at your destination a full hour earlier than your grandparents would have, and when it works, as it often does, you do feel like you finally understand evolution; it is far more than mere theory and you are the pinnacle of it. All of mankind's striving and evolving has put you in the enviable position of filling a vehicle with some long-dead fossils, sitting inside it, turning on the engine and going to a far-off destination up a three-lane motorway.

But the flashing lights on the signs above you warning you to slow down sink your heart, and then you see the thing designed to instil sadness and despair into every British driver's being.

While poems have been written, songs have been sung and an entire genre of films has been made about roads, nothing memorable has been said about the orange traffic cone and there is no ode to the roadwork. No great poetry was ever commissioned to celebrate a new North Circular route round a big city.

The roadworks for the new-build A737 flyover at Paisley have certainly never been the subject of a Paolo Nutini song. But make no mistake, the orange plastic cone strikes fear and loathing into the heart of any driver who catches sight of even a flash of orange and white.

Mention the words road and trip to anyone and their hearts will jump, their eyes brighten and their tone of voice rise. Try it in the next few days; say to a friend, a work colleague or a family member, 'I am thinking about taking a road trip to ...' The destination doesn't even have to be that exciting, it can even be Wishaw, but their mood will soar at the mere idea. It's driving for driving's sake, freedom, glamour, travel. It's the total opposite of the drudgery of commuter traffic, rush-hour traffic jams or driving the children about to another party or karate class. It's Route 66, John Denver singing 'Country Roads', Thelma and Louise in a convertible; it's Jack Nicholson and Dennis Hopper on Harleys with 'Born to be Wild' in the background.

What it is not is a turquoise Nissan Micra crawling along at 10 miles per hour, beset by motorway signs flashing warnings that there are delays, inching past so many orange cones that the European orange cone mountain is now a slight bulge in a warehouse in The Hague. Nor is this the idea I had in my head three months previously, when I sat in a publisher's office saying how great a road trip round Scotland visiting distilleries and doing some cooking with whisky would be.

The culprit is Newhouse, gateway industrial estate to North Lanarkshire. There is a squillion-pound roundabout being built and some widening of the motorway. So far, all that has happened is someone has dug up an awful lot of grass verge and in its place left a load of red soil and mud, a big gaping hole and a load of cones.

To make matters even more joyous we turn off too early. I forget about the shortcut I used to take to get to work and we end up on a tour of all the cones and the roadworks and the mess of the soon-to-be roundabout, twice.

My father is displaying the patience of a rush-hour commuter and at no point does he point out that Wishaw was my bloody idea. Clearly Charlie King in Alloa has earned me extra patience points.

Eventually, we get past the hold-ups and onto the correct road and arrive in Wishaw. It looks as dark and dank as I remember. The Artisan better be good.

We walk in and get a table and, when we ask for the whisky list, are handed an entire book. Chef and proprietor Derek Mather has installed Scottish safe bets like Stornoway black pudding, haggis and mince and tatties on the menu. Moreover, the website boasts that there are over 1,300 whiskies at the Artisan and the staff are all trained whisky ambassadors. Every bit of wall in the restaurant has a shelf on it and all the shelves are full of whisky. My father looks up at it in amazement and then at me.

'Well,' he says, 'you werenae wrong about the place being full of whisky, that's for sure.'

We both sit, in shock and awe that such a place exists, while also wondering how on earth you choose a whisky to drink from among 1,300. The waitress takes our order and saves the day by explaining that the hostess trolley in front of the bar is a selection of the malts of the month. I gratefully rush up to it and see 12 open bottles, far more of a selection than most Michelin-starred restaurants in the UK would have, and all of them at the same price.

Now, if this were a road movie and I was actually Jack Nicholson with a blue saltire headscarf, a leather jacket and a Harley-Davidson, this is the point where it would all make sense. I would pick one of the malts from Derek Mather's trolley and would just get it. This would be my third act. The lighting would change, the sun would come out, Wishaw would even look good, and you the audience, a sophisticated one well versed in the language of the American road trip movie, would know that you had reached the end of my struggle. I would forget drinking expensive Edinburgh cocktails, banish all thoughts of hangovers and having aching arms from dragging suitcases up and down stairs at Euston station; I would even forget about the Newhouse roadworks.

For I would know. I would understand whisky, what it means to individuals, what it means to Scotland, what it means to my father and what it meant to his father before him.

I would understand it all, for here, in the small unprepossessing town that my great-grandparents came to as penniless Irish immigrants, would be the key to it all. The whole film would be building up to this moment and turn on it. This section would have its own song which would be the theme tune to the film; it would be a warbly ballad in which the word 'understanding' formed the main part of the chorus. Think of a ballad, like the theme tune to *Titanic* or *Frozen*; now replace the big three-word chorus 'will go on and on' or 'let it go, let it go' with 'un-der-staaaaaaaaaaaanding' and you'll get what I mean.

Sadly, this is not a Hollywood road trip movie, this is a non-fiction book, and except for the bits I made up, it's all true. Life is rarely as clear-cut and obvious as a Hollywood movie, and no big power ballad boomed out of the speakers at me as I approached the whisky trolley. I walked up and stood in front of it, chose a Highland single malt that I had not previously heard of and sat down and waited for it to be served to me. As I am a dreadfully amateur researcher, I cannot tell you which whisky it was as I didn't write the name down. It was a Glen-something; the smaller Highland whisky brands are always a Glen-something.

I have my whisky, and my father and I have both managed to stop staring at the jaw-dropping amount of whisky on display while we look through the menu.

Wishaw is not London, Paris or Barcelona. It's not even Edinburgh. To survive in a town like this you have to be able to strike a balance between what you want to serve and what your market desires. Too often, chefs who have learned their trade in bigger cities decide to take their food back to smaller hometowns and show their own people how it can be done. They tend not to ask their people if they are interested. They open restaurants certain in the knowledge that their home-town just needs somewhere decent at a reasonable price and convinced theirs will fill up with people who really under-stand that the chef is trying to bring a treasure to their area.

Sadly, this rarely happens. Being obsessed with food is a condition similar to being a Jehovah's Witness. All your friends are Jehovah's Witnesses, you all know the same songs, you all drink the same tea, you all know that this is the end of days and that you are guaranteed your place in heaven. If all the people you know and socialise with are Jehovah's Witnesses, it is very tempting to think that the whole world is with Jehovah.

Food obsessives know every restaurant within a certain radius of their house. They view the world as a series of edible experiences; when they mention on social media that they are going on a trip, all they want to know is what to eat there. They find like-minded people who also think that it is perfectly normal to escape a stag weekend for a few hours to go and eat at a restaurant alone. They take photos of all their food and post them up on social media for the world to see. They catalogue their lives as a succession of restaurant trips and food experiences. If you are on a walk in the country-side you might be interested in looking at the animals, birds and plants. The food obsessive looks at any wild animal and thinks, 'Mmm dinner.' Wild plant life is categorised as 'good to eat' or 'not worth knowing anything about'.

The food obsessive panics at the thought of going out for a meal with someone who isn't one. Social media is full of them complaining bitterly about being sent to a chain restau-rant for a family occasion; if they have chosen the restaurant they then worry about how normal people, those they avoid outside work, eat. What will they pick? Will they refuse to share? Will they know to stop talking and to take a moment to savour the food?

Like the Jehovah's Witness, the food obsessive generally only talks to people with similar views, and it is very easy to fall into the trap of assuming that everyone in the world is obsessed with food and not, as is generally the case, that you just know everyone who is obsessed.

If you live in London or Edinburgh, this is no big deal; it simply means you live a slightly narrow life as if you are a member of a cult or a sect. The problems start when you go further afield. Now in rural Scotland you'd be fine on the islands of Mull or Skye, both places with extraordinarily good restaurants; post-industrial Scotland, not so much. So you move there, open a restaurant charging half as much as its counterpart in Edinburgh and no one comes. No one gets your concept. No one wants to know. They just think that you are fancy and overpriced, and, worst of all, that you have gotten above yourself.

Talk to many chefs of restaurants in small villages in Britain and they will tell you that the locals don't come. Talk to the locals and they will tell you it's too expensive, not worth the bother, and the chef is just trying to rip people off with those prices.

To really succeed in a small, not particularly affluent town like Wishaw, you have to give people what they want. And what the people want is chips. Proper chips.

Chips used to be easy. Potatoes were peeled and cut then

deep-fried in animal fat, vegetable shortening or oil. The only labour-saving innovation was the frozen chip; the only varieties were plain or crinkle-cut. You knew where you were with a chip.

Almost every household of any class in Scotland had a chip pan with a wire basket inside it sitting on top of the cooker covered in old grease and stuck-on fat. The big change in the early 1980s was the move from lard to vegetable oil or fat. My mother started using Echo, a now defunct brand of vegetable shortening, as she was told it was far healthier than straight-forward sunflower or rapeseed oil. It was magic stuff that used to liquefy as it heated up; unlike water, it never boiled and, when sliced potatoes were added, it was an amazing sight to see the chips floating with tiny wee bubbles coming off them. The deep belch of hot oil in a chip pan expelling water released from slices of potato is the sound of a million eighties childhood teatimes. (Before I get too nostalgic, chip pan fires were a major cause of domestic house fires throughout the UK, often due to panicked people pouring water in the pan mistakenly thinking that this would douse the flames rather than enrage them. The move towards oven chips and electric deep-fat fryers is proof that not all culinary progress is bad.)

The change in chips started, as these crimes against culinary life so often do, with the importation of American fast food. Chips were all of a sudden incredibly thin and called fries; instead of being served in newspaper and with vinegar they were in cardboard containers and served with tomato ketchup. A few years later, the Tex-Mex abomination known as the potato skin crossed the Atlantic and everything went downhill from there.

Ask for a plate of chips in a cafe or restaurant anywhere in the UK nowadays and you are taking your life in your hands. You can be served ultra-thin American-style chips, a Heston Blumenthal recipe for triple-cooked chips (unlikely, but you might be lucky), identically shaped chips that have been bought in pre-prepared and frozen, and there is even a bizarre fashion for deep-frying sweet potatoes and pretending that they are chips – but none of those are the worst development in the pantheon of the deep-fried potato. The worst things are the bastard hybrid offspring of the potato skin and the American fast-food fry.

Skin-on chips are one of the worst ideas that anyone in a professional kitchen has had in the past 20 years. The attraction is obvious: it saves time peeling potatoes, but one of the major points of a chip is that the potatoes are peeled. Chips, whether skinny, fat, crunchy or soggy, are, by their very nature, refined carbohydrates with a stodgy empty taste. No one ever expects a chip to have the deep dark earthy muddy taste of a potato skin. Especially not a skin that's been deep-fried.

At the Artisan they understand this and every portion of chips I saw being served was lovingly peeled and cut into shapes as short and fat as the owner himself, presented in oval-shaped white bowls with vinegar or homemade whisky ketchup on the side.

When the chips came, my father tried the whisky ketchup. It was made with Octomore whisky, the peatiest of the Bruichladdich whiskies. He dipped a chip in it, put it in his mouth, chewed, swallowed, raised his eyebrows and put vinegar on the rest of his chips. I looked at him and laughed.

Tomato ketchup is an industrially made foodstuff; it was never supposed to be homemade and fancy. People generally only admit this in the relative privacy of a Facebook thread, but most of us don't like homemade tomato ketchup and children hate it most of all. The best make of tomato ketchup is Heinz. Your fancy deli ketchup with pips and skins that tastes of real tomatoes may well be delicious, but just as deep-fried unpeeled potatoes are not chips, that isn't really ketchup. It's a nice reduced tomato thing that may be able to moonlight as a pasta sauce.

If you are really in the mood for chips, ketchup and whisky the easiest thing to do is the following:

Peel and cut some potatoes (the best variety in the UK is Maris Piper). Either turn a deep-fat fryer full of sunflower or rapeseed oil to 160°C, or fill a deep frying pan with oil and heat it until a tiny piece of potato floats and starts to bubble in it.

Put the sliced potatoes in the hot oil and cook until golden. Lift the chips out with a wire basket or a slotted spoon and put them in a bowl lined with kitchen paper to absorb any fat.

Serve with Heinz tomato ketchup on the table and a glass of whisky in your hand.

A quick online check of chip recipes will show you that the current vogue is for twice-cooked potatoes, once in a lower-temperature oil to blanch them, after which they are left to cool, and then they are fried again at a higher temperature. Double-cooking is a better method than the one I have just given you, and if you have time and the inclination you will more than likely find yourself eating better-quality chips. Triple-cooked chips, however, should only be undertaken by a domestic cook who has a life devoid of all meaning beyond a potato, as they are best left to people who get paid to spend endless hours standing in front of hot stoves and deep-fat fryers.

We left the Artisan with my father so impressed that such a place existed in the town of his birth that he suggested we go for a walk round the rest of it instead of racing back to the car and hightailing it out of there in a trail of dust. He showed me where the two carpenter's shops my grandfather had were; the original one was now a chip shop, the second one an Indian takeaway. He showed me where his sister had trained to be a hairdresser. The butcher's where he used to get illicit discounts from the butcher's boy had turned into a bookies, and the old pool hall where he used to go instead of school was a Wetherspoons, but generally the town looked a lot more upbeat, the shops were better and there was more to do. We got in the car to go back to Glasgow with my father considering for perhaps the first time in 50 years that maybe Wishaw wasn't such a bad place after all.

While my father left Wishaw, his big sister stayed on, and in my mind Wishaw is inextricably linked to one dish. My auntie had Italian friends who taught her how to make lasagne, something my mother never cooked, and the first time I tasted it was at my auntie Rosemary's and it fast became my favourite reason for visiting her.

I have yet to meet a person who doesn't love lasagne being served at a table. Even vegans who have to make do with soya mince and tofu cheese will put up with both of those abominations to get their lasagne fix. I now make a ragù with whisky and find that it adds an edge and a depth to it which I love. Don't use a good whisky for this; use some of the cheapest stuff you have – just make sure it is proper Scotch and not a bizarre bootleg. You do get a nicer taste with better whisky, but it will be offset by the tears you will have cried into the sauce at the sight of so much good stuff being poured in.

Not My Auntie Rosemary's Lasagne

Serves 6

For the ragù
4 tablespoons olive oil
1 medium white onion, finely chopped
2 celery sticks, finely chopped
1 large carrot, finely chopped
3 large garlic cloves
500g beef mince (12% fat)
2 x 400g tins chopped tomatoes
190ml red wine
100ml whisky
2 bay leaves

2 dried red chillies
½ teaspoon dried thyme
1 teaspoon salt

For the béchamel sauce
50g butter
50g plain flour
600ml whole milk
salt and freshly ground black pepper

To assemble
about 9 sheets oven-ready lasagne
100g grated Parmesan cheese

First make the ragù. Put the oil in a heavy-based lidded saucepan on a medium-low heat and add the onion, celery and carrot. Crush the garlic and add it to the pan. Turn down the heat and leave the vegetables to sweat for 20 minutes. Add the mince and stir it all in. Leave to cook for 20 minutes, then add the remaining ingredients and cook on a low heat for 30 minutes with the lid on, then for 1 hour with the lid off.

To make the béchamel sauce, melt the butter in a medium pan over a low heat, and then whisk in the flour. Cook for a few minutes, stirring constantly, then gradually whisk in the milk, pouring it in little by little, and bring to the boil, still stirring. Season and simmer for about 5 minutes until thickened.

Preheat the oven to 180°C/fan 160°C/gas 4. Use a deep, wide ovenproof dish and put a third of the meat sauce in the bottom then top with a quarter of the béchamel and then a layer of pasta. Repeat this for two more layers, and then put the rest of the béchamel on the last layer of the pasta and sprinkle the Parmesan on top.

Cook for 35 minutes, until golden and bubbling.

My father and I were riding the crest of a family-bonding wave. I had taken him to paradise; he had discovered his hometown was doing well; we were both thoroughly enjoying each other's company. The only way was down.

A few weeks after our visit to Wishaw he wanted me to go to his whisky club at a pub round the corner from him. They had six different Springbanks – Campbeltown's main whisky which comes in five different ages, from 10 to 21 years old – to taste and no spittoons. I had hardly eaten. We both had enough whisky to forget that either of us had ever had an off switch and went on elsewhere to drink more. I was surprised the next morning to find myself in my own bed with a massive headache, my tongue stuck to the roof of my mouth and a vague recollection that something bad may have happened, but nothing so bad that it had prevented me from getting home, getting undressed and getting into bed. That I hadn't heard from my father struck me as slightly strange, but I was too busy putting myself together with Berocca and Alka-Seltzer to pay it much attention. I had arranged to meet him a few days later and I texted him about it the night before.

No answer.

I phoned him the next morning. No answer.

He phoned me back an hour later, furious.

He didn't want to talk to me after my behaviour towards him the few days before.

I said I had no idea we'd fallen out as I couldn't remember.

He said, 'Of course you can't remember – you were completely drunk.'

I didn't say, 'You were drunk too and the bugger is that you remember what happened while I don't.'

I didn't say, 'What did I do?'

I didn't say, 'I am really sorry. What I did must have been really bad if you are this angry with me.'

I didn't say any of those things, which would have been the sensible move and would have calmed the situation down and got us back on track for being friends again and doing more research together. What I did was adopt a patronising and condescending tone, saying, 'Oh well then, when you want to speak to me give me a phone' and then hung up on him.

And so ended Trips with the Patriarch.

11

HIDDEN TALENTS

'I should never have switched from Scotch to martinis.'
HUMPHREY BOGART'S LAST WORDS

Whisky at its most basic is distilled beer or ale. Those ambitious enough to start a new whisky distillery could ask any local brewers to kick off the process.

Then, if you have a small still and some know-how, whisky just isn't that hard to make. As long as you remember to remove the first quarter of it so that you don't turn people blind, it should be drinkable.

What you would have is commonly called peat reek, the Scottish equivalent of moonshine or poteen. But just because you can make it doesn't mean that you should. One of the problems you may have is that it isn't likely to have the flavour one expects from whisky.

You can get great 10- or 12-year-old malt whisky for around £35 and some decent blends for under £20, all of which have been aged for at least three years in a barrel. Your home-distilled hooch won't be as nice. In all likelihood, drinking it will be an endurance competition between your throat and your stomach, with the winner being the one that has sustained the least lasting damage.

The other reason you shouldn't distil your own whisky is that, even if you produce a fine new-make spirit and keep it for a decade in a barrel, it is illegal. Customs and excise can come and destroy your house in an effort to find your still.

It is not illegal because the state is concerned about the damage you can do to yourself and others in distilling illegal spirits. Their issue is neither public health and safety nor quality control. If you are distilling alcohol, the state wants money.

Alcohol production seems to have been taxed almost since the beginning of Scotland. The first record that there is of whisky – at the time dubbed aqua vitae or 'water of life' – has been made for the tax due. It appears in 1494 when a monk, Brother John Cor, is listed in the exchequer rolls of King James IV of Scotland as having 'eight bolls of malt to make aqua vitae'. That amounts to about 580kg. Clearly it is probably not the first time the stuff was made. Distilling is an art thought to have been brought to Scotland much earlier from Ireland by the Celts.

At the time the equipment was primitive and the scientific knowledge sparing, but distillation remained popular especially among religious communities. At first, the fiery liquid they produced – which probably bore little resemblance to the whisky we enjoy today – was appreciated for its medicinal qualities and was advocated for the relief of colic, smallpox and other ailments.

This is partly due to the lack of proper medicine. Doctors were expensive and whisky was the only painkiller available to most of the common people. There is a story in Ian R. Mitchell's *Wee Scotch Whisky Tales* of a doctor asking a countryman what happened if any of his family were ill.

'We drink fusky,' was the reply.
'And if you don't get better?'
'We drink mair fusky.'
'And if you still don't get better?'
'We dee.'

Beyond health afflictions, there's a long history of us drinking whisky, from cradle to grave in the full and certain belief of its health-giving properties. Well into the 19th century, houses in the Highlands used whisky as a base to add bitter herbs and spices to make drinks similar to those dreadful Italian digestive drinks like Cynar and Fernet Branca. Be thankful for the good sense of the men and women who stopped putting herbs and roots from the garden in your drink and gave you the wisdom of the cask-aged whisky. But if you really want to make some, don't let me stop you – here is an example below.

Highland Bitters

Orcadian folklorist and writer F. Marian McNeill
wrote *The Scots Cellar* in the mid-1950s and told all
kinds of tales of the traditions of conviviality and
drink in Scotland throughout the ages. She said this
recipe was one of the traditional bitters that were made
using whisky and drunk by old women with digestive
complaints.

Makes 1.5 litres

50g gentian root, finely chopped
30g coriander seeds
15g bitter orange peel, all pith removed
15g cloves
15g cinnamon stick
8g camomile flowers
2 bottles whisky

Put all the dry ingredients into a food processor and
roughly grind, or bash them in a mortar and pestle.
You don't want a fine powder, so take care if using a
processor. Tip into a large sterilised jar made of glass or
earthenware and pour in the whisky.

Put the lid on so that the mixture is airtight and leave
for 10 days; then strain and bottle.

Having noticed the growing popularity of whisky, in 1644 the Scottish government became the first to impose a tax on spirits, to help fund the war against the English. Needless to say, following the Union, taxes went higher still, especially as the British government needed to finance long wars against the French.

The problem with this spirit tax was the issue of collecting it. As one writer put it: 'To be engaged in illicit distillation, and to defraud the excise, was neither looked on as a crime, nor considered as a disgrace.'

The illicit whisky trade was well suited to the Highland lifestyle. In traditional farming communities, families had to work with each other to be able to grow enough to support themselves, and they turned to making whisky as it became harder to survive as farmers.

Sons would work in the Lowlands for a few months until they had earned enough for an illegal still, then they'd return home. People made deals with other local farmers to supply the barley on account; once they sold the whisky, they divided the profits with the farmer.

Small-scale whisky distilling was a traditional part of Highland life and, once the law changed, even those who enforced it saw little wrong in the practice and often turned a blind eye. In a letter used as evidence for a revenue commissioner's report in 1822, Sir George Mackenzie of Coul said: 'There is not a justice of the peace who can say, that he does not, in his own family, consume illegally made spirits.'

Justices of the peace were often local landlords, and they were well aware that illicit distilling was frequently the only thing enabling their tenants to pay rent and so normally imposed ridiculously low fines on those caught breaking the law.

I've read a story of a justice of the peace and a North-east court's embarrassment when the accused said to him, 'I havnae made a drap since yon wee keg I sent tae yersel.' And I have heard one exactly the same about a court further west.

There were, of course, some legal stills in operation. In 1778 there were eight legal stills in Edinburgh – and an estimated 400 working without payment of duty. But most of those working legally cut corners in the manufacturing process to lessen the tax obligations due on malted barley. Thus, illegally made alcohol was, at the time, better than its lawful counterpart, which was mainly drunk by the least discerning with the greatest desire to get blind drunk.

Stills were established in remote glens in the Highlands and in caves around the coast. Then the spirits had to be transported for sale and consumption, and here smugglers scaled new heights of creativity.

Women strapped metal-made belly canteens that could hold two gallons of liquid onto themselves, which made the smuggler women just look heavily pregnant. Another more elaborate container still was made to look like a passenger riding pillion on horseback.

Illegal whisky was stored in coffins, pulpits and tunnels. Excise men charged with tracking down smugglers didn't always warm to the task. But even if they were enthusiastic, law enforcers were frequently thwarted by an early-warning system operated by locals that put them at a disadvantage in the cat-and-mouse game.

At times they could only watch as smugglers rode single file through towns on their Highland ponies with empty kegs strapped to their saddles, the whisky business already completed.

Eventually, parliament saw sense, after a fashion. At the behest of the Duke of Gordon, who pointed out that distilling was a way of life in large parts of Scotland, the legal system was overhauled, resulting in an act in 1823 that radically lowered the cost of a distilling licence. According to David Daiches: 'The effect of the new Act was not immediate and illicit distilling went on, though in diminishing quantities, for some time.

'It was not in fact until the complete commercialising of whisky production and distribution by the blended whisky houses of the latter part of the nineteenth century that illicit distilling virtually disappeared.' It was Speyside man George Smith who helped shape the future for the Speyside whisky trade. He was a farmer and joiner who, in 1824, obtained a licence to make whisky legitimately at his premises in Upper Drumin by the River Livet. Local smugglers were furious at the threat this presented to their livelihood by someone they branded a 'blackleg'.

By 1839 he was producing more than 200 gallons a week and had to find land for a larger distillery, eventually producing the famous Glenlivet, which translates from Gaelic as the 'valley of the smooth-flowing one'. By the time the railway opened there in 1863, many businesses were emulating his spirit of enterprise.

By 1880 The Glenlivet was so rampantly dominant that the name was borrowed by numerous distillers to enhance their product. Legal proceedings established that only Smith's distillery could use the title in isolation, although others could include it as part of a brand.

The unforeseen consequence, at least to officials in Edinburgh and London, of successfully stamping out illicit whisky production was a population unable to make ends meet who left the area, further extending the diaspora. If you ever go on a tour of the smugglers' routes, you are taken through places that no longer exist as villages or settlements.

One of the places that suffered the most from the end of illegal distilling was an area called the Cabrach. It's a stone's throw away from Glenfiddich and was, in the early 19th century, famous for the quality of its whisky. Historian Kier German has researched the whisky trade in the area for the Cabrach Trust, a charitable group set up to bring both small-scale distilling and some employment back to the area.

I met up with him once when I was in Glasgow. 'Illegal distilling was very much a communal occupation,' Kier told me. 'There were about 1000 people living in this area before 1823 and almost all of them would be involved in one way or another in the trade.'

Often, the distilling was carried out in domestic settings by women, particularly widows, and was then smuggled out by men tying small barrels to ponies and delivered to pubs and grocers under cover of darkness. 'We have the diary of a grocer in Fyvie, a town about 30 miles away,' Kier continued. 'He was complaining that he was going to have to stay up until 2 o'clock in the morning to wait for a delivery of

Cabrach whisky, but whisky from the Cabrach was famous for its quality and highly sought after by grocers and publicans as far away as Aberdeen and Dundee.'

One of the reasons for the quality was the area's isolation. Even now it's a hard place to get to; then it was often cut off for weeks in the winter and any excise man would have been seen for miles before he arrived. This meant that people could take care in making whisky, the barley could be malted properly and the distilling could take place slowly in proper stills, as there was next to no danger of the tax man seizing them and smashing them up.

'The change in the law in 1823 meant that farmers like George Smith were able to set up distilleries which ended the communal nature of distilling,' Kier told me. 'In the Cabrach, this led to 80 men moving away in the first few years after the act was passed, as they could no longer make ends meet.'

Legal distilling was carried out at Cabrach – the ruins of Buck distillery, which was open until 1833, can still be seen on land now owned by the Forestry Commision, but it didn't last very long. 'What made the Cabrach successful at illegal distilling was its undoing after 1823,' said Kier. 'Newer, more accessible distilleries were being built closer to both the raw materials to make the stuff and the grocers and publicans who bought the whisky, so whisky from the Cabrach was no longer higher in quality but was still more expensive, meaning the legal distilleries there never made any money and quickly shut down.'

Today, instead of over 1000 inhabitants, the Cabrach has a mere 100, and while the trust has hopes of creating a new distillery, it is very much out of historical and cultural interest than a desire to compete with the big Speyside names.

A few months into researching this book, I was in a friend's pub in London chatting with a regular about the whiskies at the bar and the distilleries I was going to visit. The publican burst out laughing and said, 'Listen to you, your entire geography of Scotland is distilleries!'

I was rather taken aback but it was true. Scotland had become geographically larger to me; it was no longer the central belt and a few bits of the west coast. My expanded view was one based on stills and bottles. And whisky Scotland is a strange one, based on myth and folklore and more than a few lies.

I still hadn't been to Speyside, the area with the largest number of distilleries in Scotland. The River Spey, the fastest-flowing river in Scotland, has whisky distilleries dotted all around its banks. I had to admit that this part of North-east Scotland has always been a mystery to me. To be fair, it is a mystery to most people from the West of Scotland, known only as the place where *Sunset Song* is set, the first book in the *Scots Quair* trilogy which became the scourge of every Scottish teenager forced at school to read about the trials and tribulations of Chris Guthrie's life on an Aberdeenshire farm in the early part of the 20th century. Lewis Grassic Gibbon's first book about Chris, her marriage, management of the farm alone when her husband went to fight in the Great War, his changed behaviour when home on leave and eventual death in the war still regularly tops the polls of favourite Scottish books, and I am never sure if this is misplaced nostalgia for a rural past most of Scotland has never known, or a more personal one for a lost adolescence. The novel is good but I find it hard to believe that nothing better has been written in Scottish literature since it was published in 1932.

I had only been in that direction once, when I was 20 and on a week-long road trip right round Scotland, going across to St Andrews, up to Aberdeen and then back across west. Mostly I remember Aberdeen being very cold, windy and grey, and a lot of the surrounding scenery being very flat. That scenery provides the basis for excellent growing conditions for barley and is one of the reasons why the area has so many distilleries.

The names of the towns and villages in the area are well known to the international whisky fan. I once listened to a Mexican podcast about whisky. It was, I have to say, one of the best podcasts on whisky I've heard – although making a whisky podcast that's better than most of the stuff that's out there is not a particularly difficult task. Anyway, one man is explaining all about Scotch whisky, what makes it Scotch, what blends and malts are and then starts to tell the delighted pair about the different whisky regions.

'There is this river,' he says. 'This river where most whisky is made. They have over 80 distilleries there [tell me about it, pal, I'm thinking, far too many to name] ... hmmm, I can't remember the name of the river right now.'

'Never mind,' says a woman next to him. 'We have learned so much today from you, Antonio, it has been marvellous.'

Spanish speakers like superlatives almost as much as Californians. The thing is, it doesn't sound so deeply weird in another language.

Shrieking '*Fantástico, fenomenal, maravilloso!*' for something that's just 'no' bad' is fine in Spanish. It's just what they do; everything is always amazing in Spanish.

Then Marvellous Antonio pipes up: 'Hold on, I've remembered! The river, it's the river ... It's the River Glen! That's it, El Río Glen. That's why so many whiskies have got the name "Glen" in them. They're named after the river.'

As you can imagine, by this time I am bending over my speaker and flapping my arms out to the side, screaming: 'It's the SPEY Antonio!!! El Río Spey! Glen is the Scottish word for valley. Spey is the name of the river. SPEY SPEY SPEY!'

As you can also imagine, my shouting at a podcast recorded a year previously had no dramatic effect on Marvellous Antonio who is no clearer today about what is a river and what is a valley in Scots.

The reassuring thing about this is that the next time you read or hear some nonsense about Mexican food written or spoken in English, rather than getting angry at the writer's ignorance, you can just smile ironically and think of the Río Glen.

The Putney

My friend the food writer Kay Plunkett-Hogge, apart from knowing everything there is to know about Thai food and having the best Thai mariachi dwarf story in existence, is a dab hand at cocktails.

This is her version of a Manhattan which she makes with her half-Jamaican husband's favourite whisky, Balvenie rum cask finish.

I've called it The Putney, as that is the west London area where they live.

Serves 1

60ml Balvenie rum cask
15ml Belsazar red vermouth
ice
a few dashes of pimento bitters
orange wedge, to decorate

To make the drink, pour the whisky and vermouth into an ice-filled shaker or stirring glass, and stir until it's really cold. Pour out into a cocktail glass. Add a good dash of bitters and decorate with the orange wedge.

As luck would have it, I was invited to the heart of distillery land in Speyside. A relatively small area, it has around 50 distilleries and is a distinct whisky region. Big names like Glenfiddich, Macallan, Balvenie and, of course, The Glenlivet are Speyside whiskies.

Twenty-first-century Speyside has 50 distilleries, and landed estates where you can work organising fishing trips or shooting parties. The biggest town in Speyside is Keith, with a population of 5,000; the other big one is Grantown, which has just over 2,000 inhabitants. Everyone in Speyside knows about whisky and almost as many know about salmon fishing, almost all of the jobs here are connected in one way or another. As you travel through Speyside on the Inverness to Aberdeen trainline, you see how emptied it is of almost anything but distilleries and estates.

I was on a two-day industry jolly, having been invited by the public relations company at the very last minute. I have no idea who dropped out but I was not too proud to take their place and go to Aberlour. It wasn't a press trip; I had not much idea what it was beyond a round trip on the train up via Inverness and back down via Aberdeen, and two days and one night to talk about whisky.

I arrived to find two bar owners, a buyer for a big drinks website, a French journalist, and some Taiwanese whisky enthusiasts.

When I say bar owners it would be doing Sean Kenyon and Ryan Chetiyawardana a disservice if you were thinking of the kind of people who own the pub round the corner from your house. Both of them are five-star Michelin chefs of the bar world. Kenyon comes from a family of American bartenders and owns and runs two bars in Denver, Colorado. He won Best Bartender in America in 2014 and one of his bars won Best American Bar in 2015. A philosophy graduate, Chetiyawardana is the Ferran Adria and David Lynch of the spirit world. No one is as thoughtful or as innovative as him in the drinks arena. When he launched his brand, Mr Lyan, he had a cocktail of Talisker and oak leaf maturing in a salt-baked cask that he poured straight from the barrel into a glass. He has won every prize and every accolade the drinks world can give him; mention his name to people in the drinks business and all they have are kind words and admiration.

I spent two and a half days with them, doing whisky blending, having dinner, a round-table discussion – and they did not stop talking about drink. I am not entirely sure that either of them even drew breath during that time. The two of them live and breathe booze and bars. I have spent weekends with chefs talking about food, covering everything from restaurant gossip and new dishes that are becoming popular, to food books and every single YouTube video that Heston Blumenthal is in, but I have never seen anything quite so focused as the two of them. The Dramboree people and their whisky obsession were as nothing compared to Sean and Ryan.

We were there to learn about an Aberlour special bottling. Like a lot of distilleries, Aberlour created a special edition to hark back to the original style of the whisky. Called A'bunadh, it's a no-age-statement whisky that hasn't been chill-filtered and is blended using what the blenders decided were the best-quality casks in the warehouse.

If you have just been staring at the word 'blended' and wondering what the fuss is about, let me explain.

A single malt whisky with an age statement on it means that all the whisky in the bottle comes from the same malt distillery and the youngest whisky in the barrel is the age on the bottle. A Highland Park 10 only has whisky from Highland Park distillery in it and the youngest whisky in the bottle will be 10 years old. Water is often added to the whisky before bottling to reduce the strength. Cask strength means the whisky is the strength it was when it came out of the cask and a single-cask whisky is just that – all the whisky in the bottle has come from the one cask. A malt whisky with no age statement on it has been blended for a specific taste and there is no way of knowing the age of the whisky that went into the bottle.

If any of this is news to you then go to a shop, look at a couple of bottles of whisky, and you'll quickly and easily see what is going on with each bottle.

At Aberlour we had an opportunity to blend our own version of A'bunadh with six different casks being poured into bottles of 250ml for us to blend. Professional blenders blend up to 30 different casks and so I reckoned that five would be easy. I am a competent cook, good with flavours and good at mixing them.

I proudly made my blend, thought I was fantastic and took it home with me along with a bottle of A'bunadh as a present. Mine was awful in comparison. It tasted of wood and sawdust and I ended up hiding it away along with my shame. I have since attempted to blend whisky on two other occasions and the only time it was any good was when a master blender stood over me and told me what to do. Respect a blender; they have a skill that seems simple to the eye, but it is not something for the hobbyist.

I left the two days at Aberlour slightly bewildered about what we had been there for. Apart from the blending, we had dinner in tartan and kilts and then a free-ranging discussion the next day about the things that A'bunadh could be served with and how to serve it in a bar. As A'bunadh is matured in sherry casks and has quite a sweet taste, I suggested Spanish ham, which everyone agreed was a good idea, even the Taiwanese as cured Spanish ham is becoming popular there.

In the end I wondered if the main point of the trip was to keep Aberlour in general and A'bunadh in particular in people's minds. To be fair, that has worked with me, but I do not spend my life in bars devising drinks and serving them to customers or going to whisky tastings like the Taiwanese, so I am not sure how well it will have worked with the others. As I got back on the train to Keith I wasn't convinced that Speyside distilleries and industry jollies held the key to the spirit of whisky either. But it was great to see the historic home of legal whisky manufacture.

Nowadays, aside from a few bottles that you might get handed to you under a table at a whisky festival which may possibly be a home blend mixed from shop-bought spirits, illegal whisky production is pretty much consigned to folklore. But there is the odd rumour of a more modern take on that ancient heritage.

In 1992 Scottish journalist Tom Morton wrote *Spirit of Adventure: A Journey Beyond the Whisky Trails*, and in it he mentions bravely asking about peat reek in pubs in tiny villages near distilleries. He also signposts a story that appeared in the *West Highland Free Press* in 1987 by journalist Torcuil Crichton as probably the last-known raid by customs and excise in search of a still.

As Scotland is very small, I know Torcuil. He is no longer at the *West Highland Free Press*, but is the Westminster correspondent for the *Scottish Daily Record* and one of two London-based Scottish journalists I know. He was astonished when I asked him about this story and was happy to give me more details; and, after passing on to me the unverifiable rumour that the Stornoway karate club on the Isle of Lewis made their own peat reek in the 1980s, he told the tale of the last raid for an illegal still.

'This all happened in 1987 when I was working at the *West Highland Free Press*. It was at Gairloch which was the real back of beyond. If you were passing through you were either on your way to the moon, or on your way to Lewis. Kay Matheson, one of the women who had stolen the Stone of Destiny from Westminster Abbey in 1950, phoned the office. She had gone back up to teach in Wester Ross and had retired many years previously. She died a few years ago, so I don't mind revealing her as the source of the story.

'She phoned full of mischief to tell me that there had been this raid by customs and excise in Redpoint. She said that the customs and excise men had swooped down on the peninsula and raided houses looking for whisky stills and found nothing because the stilling had stopped just a few weeks before.

'She gave me the names of two men to talk to about it and that is when the story started falling apart. In those days the way you phoned people up was to look up their names in the phone book, and there were two John A. McCleods. The first one I spoke to said he knew nothing about it but luckily I had got the wrong one. The second one did tell me the story, but wouldn't go on record and only acknowledged the bare-bones facts. Basically, he didn't want any more trouble.

'The story then hung in the balance as she didn't want to be a source and he didn't want to be a source. So we contacted the customs and excise department and they said, yeah, they did raid the place.

'The problem was that the dates customs and excise gave us were quite different to what we'd been told and the raid had happened weeks ago, but it's not news until it's told, so we just wrote it up and, bingo, that is the story of the last customs and excise raid looking for an illegal still.'

Tom Morton tells it like this (Torcuil obviously still remembered it as occurring at Gairloch):

On 9th December 1987, at 8am, fourteen customs and excise officers arrived on the remote Wester Ross peninsula with three local policemen, and proceeded to raid seven houses and out-buildings which included, according to Torcuil Crichton's report in the *FP*, 'digging up floorboards and searching babies' cribs'. A Mr Kenneth MacKenzie of North Erradale was detained for four hours and questioned about the half-bottle of home-made spirit discovered in his house, which he claimed was a sentimental reminder of long abandoned activities. 'It might have been an embarrassment for the customs officers to find only one half-bottle but it was a bigger embarrassment for the people whose homes were raided,' said Mr MacKenzie. 'People around here are generally law-abiding – the way the customs officers behaved you would think we were making whisky whole-sale and exporting it worldwide. We don't make a habit of drinking whisky here. I've still got the bottle from last New Year in the cupboard.' The customs officers were unrepent-ant. 'Clearly something is going on,' said Brian Scott, an Aberdeen customs official. 'We acted on suspicion of illegal distillation and a quantity of spirit was found.'

And it was. There was more than just Mr MacKenzie's half-bottle. One and a half litres in total, although in the end the whole incident was allowed to pass into oblivion without charges being brought or the raids repeated. Perhaps the phantom distillers went quietly underground. Or perhaps they never existed. Fifty-one years previously, though, they most certainly had. In 1936 six Melvaig men were sent to prison for illicit distilling, and one of them was Mr MacKenzie's grandfather. This was all reported in the Christmas Day 1987 edition of the *Free Press*. The following week's paper had to carry an apology to a Mr Kenneth MacKenzie of Gairloch, whose telephone number was one digit removed from that of the North Erradale Kenneth MacKenzie and who had been inadvertently credited by the paper as being the man with the illicit half-bottle. 'He has been inundated with telephone calls requesting New Year orders of the famous dram,' read a paragraph. 'We apologise for the inconvenience caused, Mr MacKenzie: *bliadhna mhath ur* [happy New Year] to you both!'

After Torcuil had told me what he remembered, I handed him Tom's account. While reading it, he smiled and nodded at all the phrases that he had forgotten, then got a wistful look on his face at the memory. 'God, we used to have fun,' he said.

Being a young man based on Skye and reporting on the goings-on in the Highlands and Islands must be preferable to being 50 and getting unsubstantiated, unreportable gossip from Scottish MPs in Westminster.

12

A TAXING EXISTENCE

*'My God, so much I like to drink Scotch that sometimes I
think my name is Igor Stra-whiskey.'*
IGOR STRAVINSKY

The Hebridean islands are all part of the whisky myth even if
for years there has been almost no legal distilling happening
on many of them. Islands like Lewis and North and South
Uist have all had very strong associations with whisky, but as
they were so isolated they were never places that developed
big legal distilleries – their distilling was mostly small-scale
and away from the eyes of the taxman.

The very name whisky is a corruption of the Gaelic *uisge
beatha* which, given its widespread use, must make it the most
successful Gaelic word of all time.

My Mother's Roadside Chicken

I was watching Gaelic TV recently and two men from Skye were talking about the strange Lowland habit of climbing mountains as a pastime, something they would only do if a sheep was trapped at the top of one. It made me wonder if there was a Gaelic insult along the lines of 'daft enough to climb a sheepless mountain'.

My mother was an avid hill walker and mountain climber for many years and she grew frustrated by not being able to find anywhere to eat nearby after a long hike. So she started taking her own food and, being my mother, it was never ready-made supermarket sandwiches. Soon she had a fold-up table, fold-up chairs, a cool box, a gas camping stove, pot, chopping board, and matching melamine cutlery in almost permanent residence in the back of her car.

This is one of the dishes that she would regularly make in the summer in the open air when she had come off a mountain with no sheep.

Serves 2

glug of olive oil
1 onion, sliced
2 garlic cloves, finely chopped
1 red pepper, sliced
200g mushrooms, sliced
350g chicken fillets

salt and freshly ground black pepper
30ml Talisker whisky
1 tablespoon crème fraîche

Put the oil in a saucepan or frying pan on a high heat
and then add the onion, garlic, pepper and mushrooms.

After a couple of minutes add the chicken fillets, season
and keep stirring.

Once the outside of the chicken has turned white add
the whisky and cook for a few more minutes until the
chicken is cooked through (with no pink meat left).

Stir in the crème fraîche then take the pan off the heat
and serve.

There are a couple of new distilleries recently built in the
Outer Hebrides: the Abhainn Dearg distillery on the Isle of
Lewis, which will sell its first 10-year-old whisky in 2018,
and the Harris distillery, which distilled its first whisky in
January 2016. The Harris distillery is a social enterprise that
received government funding and was deliberately set up to
create jobs on the island.

A distillery creating 30 jobs may not sound like a lot if
you live in a city, but these are islands with massive issues of
population decline. Thirty jobs keep a shop open, an extra
teacher in the classroom, a doctor. Thirty jobs can make your
community thrive.

In the summer of 2014 I went to visit a friend on North Uist. Her husband had recently taken up the post of doctor there and they were living in a 1960s house that had been a convent until both nuns retired and went to live on the mainland. I had only known Fiona virtually, but, as happens a lot these days, I had been in contact with her on social media for so long that it didn't seem to matter that I would have walked past her in the street and not had a clue that it was her.

I had come up straight from London and was immediately quite lost in such an empty landscape. The thing I found the most disconcerting was my complete illiteracy when it came to the land and nature around me. I move in a world that I can read. I understand Tube maps. I know how to use my smartphone to tell me how to get from place to place. I know what restaurants mean in the pecking order of London and I know exactly how to judge you by the restaurants you would like to go to.

My area of London also has its own language. I can measure and appreciate its subtext. If a native Uibhisteach, someone from Uist, came to visit they would just see various kebab shops, takeaways and cafes. They would all look the same to her. I know they are not. A Uibhisteach wouldn't know which one makes their own cakes, which buys them from somewhere good, which cafes make regular visits to Costco.

I have counted the number of pubs which have been refurbished and turned into gastro-pubs in the past three years. I know that none of them are worth the bother eating in. I know what to think of people who disagree with me on this. All of this I know.

But I am speechless when confronted by nature as I have no clue what to do. I do not understand what to do with birds, sea, sand, hills. The only owls I've seen were in the Brownies; I have no idea which seabird it is I am looking at unless it's a common herring gull, and wheat, barley and wild grass all look the same to me.

I spent two days on the beach with Fiona's dog, across an empty golf course that closed in the winter to be used as grazing for cows, past tiny fields of grass and barley guarded by scarecrows with shimmering DVDs tied to them to scare away birds.

I was always, even in July, entirely alone. I'd come back excited about seeing wee black and white birds, medium-sized white and black birds and big white ones with black crests. Fiona's husband would patiently ask me a few more questions and tell me I had seen sanderlings, black-tailed godwits or sandpipers, but it was no use. It was like talking about whisky-cask finishes to someone who had never drunk alcohol. They were just words that made no sense to me.

The south end of South Uist looks onto the island of Eriskay, famous as the place where the SS *Politician* foundered in 1941. It was an 8,000-ton cargo ship which left Liverpool with, among other things, 260,000 bottles of whisky due to be sold in the US – so no duty had been paid on it.

The ship ran aground in a storm in the bay between Eriskay and South Uist and, after the islanders had rescued the crew, they set about rescuing the whisky. People from all over the Outer Hebrides came to get the whisky, viewing it as a perfectly moral thing to do as it was part of the bounty of the sea.

Unsurprisingly, Charles McColl, the local customs officer, incensed that the taxman hadn't been paid for the whisky, didn't take the same view. In true customs and excise style, officials raided villages and crofts, turning everything upside down with the aim of retrieving the whisky and punishing the errant islanders. The police, mostly islanders themselves, weren't particularly interested in persecuting the whisky rescuers, but McColl was not to be beaten and he managed to get some of the islanders jailed in Inverness and Peterhead for up to six weeks.

Meanwhile, the salvage attempts on the SS *Politician* were abandoned, and to ensure that none of the whisky that remained could be 'rescued', McColl got permission to dynamite the hull and so destroyed the remaining bottles. An islander, Angus John Campbell, reputedly commented, 'Dynamiting whisky. You wouldn't think there'd be men in the world so crazy as that!'

If this story is in any way familiar to you, it's because it formed the basis of Compton Mackenzie's comic novel *Whisky Galore*. He went on to write the screenplay for the 1949 film, and since then it has become a radio play, there have been several theatre productions, a musical and most recently a remake of the film.

Mackenzie was born in County Durham but had traced his ancestors to Scotland and decided that he was Scottish. So Scottish that he was one of the founders of the Scottish National Party in 1928. He built a house on the island of Barra in the early 1930s and, although in his later years lived in Edinburgh, was buried there in 1972.

An activist and a serious writer, Mackenzie was a great champion of the rights of the Hebridean fishermen in the immediate postwar period, and he also founded and ran the classical magazine, *Gramophone*, but he is best remembered for *Whisky Galore* and another comic novel, *The Monarch of the Glen*, which was turned into a long-running BBC TV series in the early 2000s.

Whisky Galore the novel is a work of comic genius. Mackenzie properly understood the tensions of class and rank between neo-colonialist upper-middle-class outsiders either from England or mainland Scotland and the ways of islanders. In his story, the islands of Great Toddy and Little Toddy (South Uist and Eriskay) have no whisky on them at all due to the privations of World War 2. One of the most famous lines in the 1949 film, one often repeated in dreadful mock Hebridean accents (often by me, but never in front of a Gael), is by a boy at school reading out his composition: 'There was no whisky on the island and we were all very sad.'

What the films, the radio play and the theatre productions fail to show effectively is what having no whisky meant to islanders.

Mackenzie, an outsider, was adored on Barra. He made the place and the people his home and his house was as likely to be filled with fishermen and crofters as visiting dignitaries. He knew that for islanders whisky was more than a drink; it signified hospitality, bonding and social cohesion. A beer without a wee half-chaser of whisky in the pub was a deprivation, but to have to offer a guest at home ale, ginger beer or tea instead of whisky was a tragedy. The point is not that the guest will say yes, the point is that it is there to be offered.

When Prunella Scales and Timothy West made one of their *Great Canal Journeys* through the Forth and Clyde canal during their television series, the Scotsman they were travelling with ended the journey by producing a bottle of whisky and saying, 'You'll take a wee dram.' He wasn't asking them if they would like a drink and if they'd prefer a gin and tonic or a glass of wine. He was offering hospitality in the form of whisky, a chance to share and contemplate the day over a common drink.

I asked someone who is from an Aberdeenshire farming family about this idea of whisky being hospitality and he told me his grandfather automatically handed a small glass of whisky to anyone who came to his door in the evening as soon as he could afford to keep a regular bottle in the house. In the same way that it defies the laws of physics to be inside a Nigerian's house for more than 15 minutes and not be handed a full plate of food, or any Spanish household without being immediately presented with olives, ham and wine, Scottish people have traditionally offered guests whisky as a way of being hospitable.

Back at Fiona's house on South Uist, after dinner the first night her husband produced a dazzling assortment of whisky. I found this quite strange as neither of them are really whisky drinkers. They would drink a dram to avoid causing offence but they'd much rather have wine and brandy or gin.

The whisky, it turned out, had all been given as presents from grateful patients, most of whom were crofters way past official retirement age. Tall thin bachelors with deep-blue eyes, DNA evidence of the last Viking settlers, grateful to the doctor for sorting out their 80-year-old backs – what better way to show appreciation than a bottle of whisky?

I looked at the assortment. Some of it was from the West Highlands, all of it was peated, most of it was from the island of Islay.

Crofters are subsistence farmers who survived the infamous Clearances from the Highlands and Islands in the 18th and 19th centuries. According to political theorist Karl Marx, it was 'the robbery of the common lands'. In fact, the Clearances are far more complex than sanctioned land-grabs. Politically, it is starkly apparent that both the English and the Scottish Lowlanders wanted to subdue problematic Highlanders after the Jacobite rebellion in 1745. Legislation helped to disable the clan system that had previously given some measure of protection to society's most vulnerable, albeit in a feudal structure, and landlords went from seeing themselves as custodians of their people to new ones simply looking to profit from the land, mostly to keep their lavish Edinburgh or London houses and lifestyles intact.

The money in the late 18th and 19th centuries was in sheep. Meat was needed in the fast-growing industrial cities and wool required for the textile factories.

Huge flocks requiring few shepherds were imposed on land that once supported dozens of families. It was the cruelty with which these families were evicted that's recalled with such bitterness. It all resulted in the Scottish diaspora, leaving vast swathes of the Highlands depopulated. The homes that weren't burned down by fixers acting for greedy landlords were soon swallowed up by the landscape on which they had originally been built. People were shoved off land and left to survive on barren land by the coast or put on overcrowded boats and sent to Canada or Australia, often arriving in pitiful states.

The most notorious Clearance landlord of all was the Duke (although it was mostly the Duchess who was responsible) of Sutherland. Their treatment of their tenants was regarded as brutal even by the contemporary London press, and the vast emptiness of Scotland further north of Inverness is mostly their legacy. The Duke also built Clynelish distillery (now owned by Diageo) as another money-making scheme in 1819, using former evicted tenants as labour and paying them with coins that they could only use in his shops.

There have been many books written about these shameful and sorrowful events, and ten minutes talking to people involved today with community land ownership and land reform is all it takes to realise what a devastating legacy of barrenness this has left the Highlands of Scotland. Looking at a map of whisky distilleries and seeing almost none in the far north west tells the same story. The tiny number of small-scale crofters resisted the changes, and have survived two world wars and further depopulation in the 1960s and 70s. One hopes that they will also survive the present turbulent times.

If you ever find yourself drinking with an old crofter from the Hebrides or Highlands, please ignore everything this book tells you. Cocktails made with whisky, especially malt, are not OK; never add green tea, coconut water or anything else but water to your whisky, and even then only if your drinking companion thinks it is OK. Do Not Use Ice. Don't even mention that you have ever thought of having whisky and food together, much less using it in cooking. For a traditional crofter, everything that isn't boiled in water is baked in an oven and whisky is never added. To suggest that blue cheese goes really well with one of his peaty malts and a splash of it in his broth might be a good idea would be akin to standing up in the middle of a meeting of the WI or a quilting circle and explaining in great detail exactly how your dogging session went the night before. Whisky is a crofter's heritage; he doesn't need to know what you are doing with it.

The only thing that you could tell your crofter about is cranachan. It's an old Scottish dessert where toasted oats, fresh thick cream and fruit were put together in a bowl. Nowadays, the cream is whipped with whisky and the oats, cream and fruit are served in layers in a glass.

You have almost certainly heard of cranachan – it's the dessert that gets rolled out every January on Burns Night, the one night of the year when the whole world turns Scottish as a way to end the misery of a dark January detox. There are other Scottish desserts but this is the one that restaurants all seem to opt for.

It is really easy to make at home and is one of those where the quality of the whisky really does make a difference to the taste. As you are using red fruits, a heavily peated Islay isn't really a good idea for this dish, but you could use a lighter peat like Highland Park. My favourites with cranachan are Tomatin, Glenkinchie or Auchentoshan.

Cranachan

Serves 4

80g porridge oats
550ml double cream
7 tablespoons whisky
2 tablespoons honey
400g fresh raspberries

Toast the oats in a frying pan for a few minutes, taking care not to burn them.

Lightly whip the cream until it reaches the soft peak stage, then fold in the whisky and honey.

Layer the cream then the oats and the raspberries in dessert glasses and serve.

Even a crofter would be happy with you using his good whisky for this.

13

COCKTAILS AND KILTS

'We borrowed golf from Scotland as we borrowed whiskey.
Not because it is Scottish, but because it is good.'
HORACE HUTCHINSON

Whatever kind of work you do in this world, it's nice to be recognised. Whether it be charitable work of such public renown that the monarchy declares you a person of note within the British Empire, or you give the governing party of the United Kingdom so much money that they make you a lord, rewards and recognition are a thing that people like.

In the Scotch whisky industry you get given a quaich to keep. A quaich is a shallow two-handled cup, the origins of which are surrounded in more bad stories and good lies than the Loch Ness monster herself. The boring facts are that they were popular in the late 17th century in Edinburgh, and quite possibly the shape of them originated from bleeding vessels used medicinally at the time in England and the Netherlands. Or a scallop shell.

However, the name quaich comes from the Gaelic for cup, so it obviously has some great Highland significance that is shrouded in mystery and myth. Nowadays, quaichs are mostly pewter and are very popular as engagement presents. Someone somewhere came up with the idea that the bride and groom should share a dram out of a quaich as a sign of betrothal and then the same quaich be used as the baptismal cup for any babies born of the union.

I have no idea who told me that story, I may possibly have made bits of it up myself, but it sounds good and, even if it's not true, it should be. I buy quaichs for couples I know who get engaged and thrill them with a story they also pretend to believe.

The Scotch whisky industry, full of people who know a good lie when they see one, decided a number of years ago to award people within the business by making them Keepers of the Quaich in a secret ceremony, with a good knees-up afterwards. Exactly when they started doing this they don't really like to say, as the ceremony should be as old as it is secret, but at the banquet afterwards an old man got up and explained in a speech that he had started it 30 years ago after seeing the Confrérie des Chevaliers du Tastevin in Burgundy. Literally, the Fraternity of Knights of the Wine Tasting Cup, the order was started in 1703 as the Ordre de la Boisson, the Order of the Drink, and revived in 1934, and now lots of wine regions have an 'order'.

Do a lot for the Spanish wine industry in the UK and

they will make you a Knight of the Grand Order of Wine. You go to a dinner wearing a robe that looks like a cardinal's Saturday afternoon attire crossed with a medieval Spanish jester and someone waves a sword over you in a regal manner. In cava country, they invite you to be a Lady or Gentleman of Honour in Cava. It all gets a bit Monty Python and the Knights of Ni, but it also shows that the industry as a whole appreciates the efforts you have made in promoting their product, and you haven't had to donate nearly a million quid to a political party in order to be crossed with a sword.

The Scotch industry decided that if they were going to do this kind of thing, there were two non-negotiable points. The first was that the entire industry was going to be part of it, not just one or two brands or big companies; the second, that it was going to have to be better than anything anyone else did.

We cannot just randomly assign peerages in the United Kingdom, and even after devolution, Scotland has no honours system of its own, so the honour bestowed on you is to be made a Keeper of the Quaich in a secret ceremony in a faux-medieval Victorian castle in the countryside in Scotland.

Reader, they invited me to the event.

I have no idea what went on in the actual ceremony, but all the new Keepers looked really happy afterwards with their Keeper badges and special wee quaichs. Maybe they all drank some secret elixir known only to the inhabitants of Blair Castle and the Loch Ness monster and now hold the key to eternal life, but as they aren't allowed to tell anyone no non-Keeper knows. I got invited to the banquet after-wards and to stay two nights at the Gleneagles hotel, one of Scotland's most iconic, for the event.

It had to be better than a graveyard in Kilmarnock, being chatted up in Oban by a man with his name tattooed on his knuckles or even eating chips in Wishaw with my father, so I said yes and went shopping for a cut-price formal dress suitable for such an occasion.

I got dropped off at Gleneagles and put in a room at the very back of the hotel with a view onto a car park. The room was nearly twice the size of my studio flat in London, with a carpet so deep it nearly covered my ankles, and towels and robes so fluffy they felt like falling into warm snow. I imme-diately did what any sensible middle-aged woman does when faced with such levels of unaccustomed luxury. I FaceTimed my mother, showing her the whole place while screaming, 'Can you believe how fabulous this is??!', then posted at least half a dozen photos on Facebook.

I composed myself and went down to dinner. There I met a variety of people in the industry, a couple of whom were being made Keepers at the end of long careers in whisky, a number of whom went to the Keepers Banquet twice a year as part of their jobs and some other people either invited to the banquet or also being made Keepers.

After welcoming speeches and a buffet dinner, the time came for the desserts. There were about 50 of us and various cold cakes and cream desserts and cheese were put out on the buffet table. One of the waiting staff stood behind a gas burner and announced he would be making flambé banana crêpes. Claudia, the lady who organised the stay at the hotel, smiled. 'That was my idea. I told them, do anything you want for dinner but we have to have some flambé for dessert.'

'Isn't that a bit old-fashioned?' I may have used a slightly patronising 'I know all about food trends, dear, and this isn't one of them' tone in my remark.

She leaned towards me and touched my arm, 'Darling, *everybody* loves flambé.'

If you find yourself in charge of organising a large meal for work colleagues and you want to see your boss stand obediently in a queue, wide-eyed and smiling like a tiny child waiting to go and see Santa at a shopping centre, ask the venue you are eating at to do a flambé dessert. Your colleagues will do everything they can to contain their squeals of delight and will discuss the last time they were in a place that did flambé, how long ago that was, where exactly they were in the world, and why it is a pity that so few restaurants offer them. The woman in your office who runs up mountains at the weekend as a hobby and only eats raw fish and steel will go misty-eyed at the sight of a blue flame on a crêpe suzette. The man in middle management, who has been told by his doctor that he is two steps away from a major heart attack and has given up everything but steamed vegetables and egg whites, will decide that a treat just this once is OK. You will become the most popular person in your workplace for at least a fortnight, as you will have fulfilled a heart's desire your colleagues didn't even know they had, because believe me, darling, as I can bear witness, *everybody* loves flambé.

Everybody Loves Flambé Bananas

This is a really impressive thing to do if you have guests
who are in your kitchen, and is really quick to make.
Just make sure that you control your flames properly –
please don't burn your kitchen down.

Serves 4

4 large ripe (but not completely black) bananas
50g butter
2 tablespoons demerara sugar
40ml whisky (unpeated if you use a malt, ideally a
    Speyside, or use a soft blend)

Cut the bananas in half lengthwise then in half across.

Melt the butter in a large frying pan and, when it starts
to foam, add the bananas and sprinkle over the sugar.

Fry the bananas on both sides, coating them with the
butter and sugar until they start to caramelise.

Put the whisky in a ladle or a jug and pour onto the
pan – stand back as you wait for the flame to die down.

Serve with ice cream or cream, or with crêpes if you
like.

We adjourned to the bar and I met a man who was about to be made a Keeper and tried not to swoon like a fangirl. It was Alessandro Palazzi, the chief bartender at Dukes Bar in London. Alessandro has been in the industry for over 40 years, having moved from his native Ancona in northern Italy to work in London in legendary bars the names of which bring tears to a barfly's eyes both for the drunken stories of the Great and the Glamorous and for the calibre of the cocktails available. Dukes Bar, where Alessandro reigns supreme, is a place of old money (or nonchalant no money when I am there), quality tweed rather than diamond bling, quiet New Englanders rather than brazen Texans. The gin martinis, their biggest-selling drink, are made in front of you from a drinks trolley by a bartender in a white jacket and black bow tie. They are very large and very dry. The story is that they will never serve a customer more than two. A couple of people I know claim to have been served three. I am not sure if I believe them, but I will never say that to their face or ask Alessandro. Everyone needs myth in their life and 'Alessandro served me three' is a pretty good one.

Being made a Keeper, he told me, was one of the proudest moments in his career.

'But you must be a member of every drinks guild and booze industry body going?'

'Oh yeah,' he said, 'but Keepers is special. This is the Scotch industry. It's bigger than any other one and it is much harder to be made a Keeper. This is many people in whisky over many years saying they believe that I have done something for the industry that has made a difference. It is an amazing feeling.'

Joining him for the ceremony was his second-in-command at Dukes, Mauricio. A young Italian, he had the look of a surprised deer who had just been discovered in a thicket by unsuspecting walkers. He played the role of dutiful and loyal apprentice to Alessandro's magician on a night out perfectly.

Alessandro wouldn't be happy at being described as a sorcerer; he has no time for the increasingly popular magic, mixology and alchemy in the cocktail world. At Dukes you are as likely to get a green cocktail overflowing with liquid nitrogen smoke as you are a line-up of Jägerbomb shots. What he does is make some of the best old-style cocktails you have ever tried using the best ingredients that match. No one mixes a better drink than Alessandro and he is one of the foundations on which London cocktail society is built.

Every time I spoke to him during those two days I made a list in my head of all the London pals I could impress with a 'We must go to Dukes, I've not seen Alessandro in ages . . . Oh yes, I met him in Scotland, we had a great time together.' It was a big list.

So busy was I mentally making a lot of people envious and sealing my own myth as a woman about town in my imagination that, a couple of months later, I had to ask him for a cocktail recipe for you as I forgot at the time.

When I did ask, he kindly phoned me and told me exactly how to make an old-fashioned. He repeatedly said that there were two secrets to it – patience and good ingredients. I've had old-fashioneds consisting of bitters, a cheap blend and some orange juice from a carton; I've mostly made them myself. Alessandro's old-fashioned bears no resemblance to that at all. He was very precise in his recommendations: the oranges need to be organic so that you can extract the oil from the peel; don't use cheap glacé maraschino cherries from the supermarket. He wants you to use Griottines, French morello cherries that have been macerated in kirsch. He uses Caol Ila Distillers Edition from Islay for his Scotch old-fashioneds, but would normally use Maker's Mark bourbon. Yes, bourbon.

If you have been paying attention, you'll realise that there are few references to that drink in this book. It has not slipped under my radar unnoticed; there has been no sneaky, underhand bourbon slide. I hold Alessandro Palazzi in such high regard that I have allowed him to tell you that his preferred choice for making an old-fashioned is Maker's Mark, the Kentucky bourbon that comes in a square bottle sealed with red wax. Bourbon is predominantly made with corn, although there is a smidgen of malted barley in there too, so it doesn't enjoy the same qualities as Scotch. At all.

So much respect do I have for Alessandro that I am not suggesting that any whisky other than double-matured Caol Ila (pronounced Cull Eela) Distillers Edition from Islay should be used for this. I will not mention that I find old-fashioneds made from Aberlour A'bunadh magnificent. He says that the best Scotch for an old-fashioned is a strong, peaty Islay malt, and if Alessandro says it, it must be true.

Alessandro Palazzi's Old-Fashioned

Serves 1

1 sugar lump (or ½ teaspoon)
a few drops of Angostura bitters
1 teaspoon soda water
ice (make sure it is ice from a plastic tray, not from the
    supermarket or the garage; you want good-shaped
    proper cubes)
60ml Caol Ila Distillers Edition whisky
3 Griottines (morello cherries in kirsch)
peel of 1 organic orange

Take an old-fashioned glass or a good square tumbler,
add the sugar, 3–4 drops of Angostura bitters and the
soda water and stir. Add a cube of ice and about a third
of the whisky and stir; add another ice cube and another
third of the whisky and stir. Add another ice cube, the
cherries and a teaspoon of the kirsch and stir. Lastly,
add one more ice cube, the remaining whisky, and rub
the orange peel round the side of the glass to get the oil
from the skin into the drink. Cut a piece of the peel,
place it into the glass and serve.

Early the next evening I was on a bus with women in formal
dresses of various types, my dress being by far the cheapest
as it had cost me less than the price of a cocktail from the

night before, and men in kilts. We were off to Blair Castle, the ancestral home of the Duke of Atholl, the only man in Europe with his own private army.

The duke himself wasn't there for the occasion. He is a South African who runs a print shop in Cape Town and has a wife called Charmaine. The complicated succession rules for dukes meant that he became the duke most unexpectedly to him and now regularly travels to Scotland to perform the required ceremonial duties. The previous duke's sister runs things, with all the family assets, like most Scottish gentry, being in a trust, thus avoiding the need to pay tax or death duties.

The army is ceremonial, consisting mostly of bagpipers and drummers, and on arriving at the castle for the banquet everyone walked individually up a red carpet through a gauntlet of the duke's best soldiers. After formal photos had been taken in the entrance of the hall, banquet guests were free to go upstairs to a reception room and have some whisky and some canapés while the new Keepers were being sworn in. It gave me a chance to wander round and look at who was there and what they were wearing.

Almost all the women were in long formal dresses, and the men were mostly in kilts. The crimes against tartan that evening were many and varied. As most Keepers aren't Scottish many don't know how to wear kilts. The French, in particular, can wear them on their hips instead of their waist and have the pleats to the front instead of the back. The Mexicans were thoroughly enjoying the kilt experience but had no idea how to walk, sit or stand in them and kept observing older Scottish men in the hope of picking up tips. A few of the older Scotsmen had overindulged in a blinding combination of tartan.

Acceptable formal kilt outfits consist of cream woollen socks, with an optional small dagger tucked into one; a kilt in either your clan tartan or someone else's; a belt and a buckle; a sporran, which is a small pouch that hangs from the waist to compensate for a lack of pockets; and a bow tie and formal white shirt and black jacket. What is not acceptable to any reasonable person is matching (or not in two cases) tartan socks and a tartan waistcoat just to prove you know your tartan. Before any festivities begin, people want to reach for their sunglasses when talking to men in such attire who, after a few refreshments, are likely to induce premature dizziness, which breaks both the rules of good manners and courtesy.

The other outfit for men was tartan trousers, formal dinner jacket and black bow tie, a look that could best be described as 18th-century soldier in search of a bear hat and a musket. The three most senior members of the Scottish aristocracy in attendance wore very different outfits and looked like Bonnie Prince Charlie, Lord Byron and an Irish leprechaun in a rather fetching trio.

There is only one person to blame for the bagpipes, the tartan and the Victorian medieval banqueting hall. The man who created the ideals that launched the images on a million shortbread tins, the man with the biggest monument ever built for a writer – one that literary critic Stuart Kelly says looks like 'a steam punk version of Thunderbird 3' – the man

who inspired years of dreadful BBC Scotland tartan tat programmes, the 19th-century poet, novelist and self-important
busybody Sir Walter Scott.

Generally, Sir Walter Scott's novels have not fared well
in the popular public consciousness. Still, there is a Walter
Scott society in Edinburgh where I imagine a few men in
three-piece tweed suits, all bearing an uncanny resemblance
to the actor James Robertson Justice, convince themselves
he is still good. But the heroic stories of Highland chivalry,
written by a Lowlander with no knowledge of Gaelic, are
mostly unreadable to a modern audience. I know one person
who says that they are bearable once you get past the first
158 pages, but he is passionate about Scottish property and
conveyancing law so may find Sir Walter light relief.

Scott's most enduring contribution to Scotland and Scottish
cultural life, inventing Highland regalia, clan tartans and
making bagpipes and myths our national symbols, started with
an all-too-common problem. What do you do with a useless
member of the English upper classes to make sure they can't
cause too much trouble?

King George IV was such a man. Selfish, irresponsible,
vain, profligate, his behaviour had become a major headache
for contemporary London's political establishment, much of
whose time was taken up with damage limitation and control.

In 1822, the leaders of many European countries were
meeting in Verona for an international conference to discuss
diplomatic and international affairs. One thing British dip-
lomats did not want, under any circumstances, was George
IV to be there. In the later 19th century George would have

been packed off to India to host parties for colonists and shoot things. In the 20th he would have been sent, like the Duke of Windsor, to play at ruling a small Caribbean island. In 1822 the headache was solved by sending him to Scotland.

No monarch had been to Scotland for 170 years and, having already visited Ireland, it was impressed upon the king that he needed to travel north. Edinburgh city council found itself with two weeks to organise the royal visit and appointed Sir Walter Scott as chief consultant. Sir Walter's lasting legacy was to create for the king's visit such a fantasy of bagpipes and tartan parades that they still endure today as symbols of true Scotland and the real authentic Highlands.

There are libraries full of chronicles, tales and accounts of Walter Scott and his creation of the romantic idea of Scotland. Some of them are completely historically accurate, many more are entirely serious, but the most entertaining one is a radio play by Mike Harris called *Inventing Scotland: The more or less true story of how one man's need for cash created a national myth and saved the Union.*

Harris's fictionalised account of the regal visit and Scott's role in it gives the event the treatment it deserves, and presents it as an entertaining farce. The novelist John Gibson Lockhart, Scott's son-in-law, is the narrator of the tale and describes the visit as a 'Caledonian circus where the king is the elephant and Scott the tamer', while Scott's enthusiasm leads him to arrange for a textile mill to produce 'quantities of plaid in various traditional clan tartans devised specially for the occasion'.

The king arrives, fatter than anyone ever imagined, drinks

copious amounts of cherry brandy, and is presented to various groups of 'traditionally' dressed ladies, gentlemen and 'soldiers'. Harris's play emphasises how much of this tradition was invented about 10 days prior to the arrival of George IV, and how Lowland society was happy to go along with the farce, with the king playing the head chieftain of entirely made-up clans.

Scott's hastily arranged pageant is the ongoing subject of ridicule in many sections of Scottish society. I distinctly remember, in my early twenties, boring Spanish people who wanted stories of clan tartans and Highland chivalry with rants about a jumped-up, hypocritical Lowlander making it all up to impress a useless, obese monarch and then Scotland's capital having the stupidity to build a statue of the king with a fantasy post-Weight Watchers figure. But no one could dispute the effectiveness of the visit in creating an idea of Scotland that has endured to this day, as well as establishing the monarchy as pro-Scottish and pro-Highland, leading to the construction of Balmoral and a million Victorian Highland fantasies.

As well as his beloved cherry brandy, portly George drank Glenlivet made illegally in Ballindalloch during the visit, which only served to heighten his popularity and add fuel to the whisky myth. Scott asked if he could keep the glass as a memento, but it shattered after he sat on it later the same day.

The king wore a kilt just once during his visit, to greet visitors at Holyroodhouse. The story goes that, as everyone in Edinburgh had underestimated the sheer size of his girth, his kilt was too short and, to save Edinburgh society ladies' blushes from the sight of far more of the royal personage than they had bargained for, his legs were covered with salmon pink stockings. The kilted king is the official image that looms large from the era, not least thanks to a flattering portrait by artist David Wilkie, who tactfully reduced the size of his waist and made the extraordinary tights vanish altogether. However, the tartan was included and a trend was set. A ban on Highland dress instituted after the Jacobite rebellion was now long forgotten, and the recently invented one declared authentic. Thereafter, everything Scottish had tartan in it.

Fake Highland dress and a fake Oriental pavilion in Brighton are probably George IV's best-known legacies to his subjects; the popular use of tartan and bagpipes are most certainly Scott's.

No country in the world is so closely associated with a pattern on a cloth as Scotland is with tartan. The kilt was adopted as the official dress for many of the Scottish regiments in the armed forces – the last soldier to wear a kilt for anything other than ceremonial purposes was in Dunkirk in 1940 – and where small towns and villages in the North of England have brass bands, comparable places in Scotland have bagpipe bands and a uniform involving a kilt.

Kilts are seen as suitable for men to wear on celebratory occasions, be it weddings, special church festivals and formal dinners and events. They are not, however, suitable for funerals. Scott may have wanted to keep us as happy as the spiritual descendants of John Knox – founder of the

Presbyterian Church – could be when wearing our made-up national dress.

Please do not think the previous paragraphs are a case for abandoning kilts and tartan and bagpipes as symbols of Scottishness. I am a fan of made-up traditions. I have been to many a 'traditional' food or wine festival in Spain and later discovered it only started in the 1980s, and I have not enjoyed them any less because of their relative youth. I am very much in favour of a new tradition in Scottish cooking involving adding whisky, and am the last person to criticise anyone for inventing tradition. A true Highland tradition of the period would have to involve setting fire to the dwelling of a recently evicted tenant farmer; having fun wearing a tartan kilt or trousers is a lot more civilised.

If Sir Walter Scott were to come back from the dead and visit the Keepers of the Quaich banquet he could be no happier than if he had ascended directly to heaven on a tartan carpet, serenaded by bagpiping angels. I doubt there is a better organised and executed or more fun banquet of its kind in the whole of Scotland. The speeches are perfectly timed to be not too long or boring, the food arrives simultaneously for over three hundred people and is still hot, the entertainment is an orgy of Scottish music, tartan and bagpipes. Other industries may hand out rewards and thank yous, but I doubt any industry will put on an event better than this.

It's the details that show you how well things are done. As anyone who has ever been to a banquet or a large wedding will know, getting food that hasn't gone cold or taken an eternity is a rare and precious thing. All of our food was hot. Waiting staff stood behind each guest until a man with an earpiece came and nodded his head so a whole table was served at the same time. No plate was cleared until the last person had finished and when the waiting staff talked to any of the guests they used their first name from looking at their place card rather than 'sir' or 'madam'. This is one of the most formal events and venues it is possible to go to in Scotland and even then everything is being done to make it informal and fun.

Despite being about as far away as you can possibly be from Scotland, Thais love Scotch whisky. The term whisky in Thailand is freely used for rum. Several of them were at the banquet with me as Thai Beverages owns the Inver House group, which has about five malt distilleries and a number of brands of blended whisky.

My friend who gave me the Speyside Putney recipe, food writer Kay Plunkett-Hogge, was born and brought up in Thailand, and she gave me this Thai recipe for whisky with beef.

Do not mess with this recipe. Do what it says. I have replaced ingredients, changed amounts and done all kinds of things with it and it has never been as good as just following Kay's instructions.

If you feel the need to emphasise the Thai connection then one of the blends from the Inver House group would be great to use, otherwise just use the everyday whisky you have at hand.

Have it with a long whisky and soda and pretend you are in a hot tropical climate.

Seua Long Hai (Grilled Beef with a Spicy Dipping Sauce)

This recipe's name translates as 'crying tiger', the story being that a tiger stole some from a local village and it was so spicy he cried.

Serves 2 as a main or 4 as a starter

400g sirloin steak
½ tablespoon whisky
½ tablespoon soy sauce
dash of vegetable oil

For the nam jim jao
3 tablespoons nam pla (fish sauce)
3 tablespoons lime juice
2 tablespoons ground chilli powder
1 tablespoon finely chopped coriander
2 small Thai shallots or 1 larger shallot, very finely
    sliced

Marinate the steak in the whisky, soy sauce and vegetable oil for 30 minutes or so.

Heat a grill pan until you can feel the heat rising onto your hand when you hold it 10cm above – we want it HOT!

Pop the steak on the grill and cook it to your liking –
about 8 minutes all in for medium. Set it aside to rest for
5–10 minutes.

Meanwhile, mix together the ingredients for the nam
jim jao dipping sauce.

Slice the steak thinly and serve on a plate with the
dipping sauce on the side.

14

OLD WAYS AND GOOD DAYS

'I wish to live to 150 years old, but the day I die,
I wish it to be with a cigarette in one hand
and a glass of whiskey in the other.'

AVA GARDNER

'I'll come with you, if you go to Campbeltown' is not the
reaction I was expecting from anyone, never mind a friend
born and brought up in Kent whose entire family are from
Wales. Everyone wants to go to an island, the Highlands, or
even to visit as many distilleries as is possible in three days,
but Campbeltown?

It's right at the bottom of the Kintyre peninsula. Its most
recent claim to fame is that ex-Beatle Paul McCartney had a
farm there to which he retreated after the Beatles broke up.
'Mull of Kintyre', the song McCartney wrote and performed
with the band Wings, was written at High Park farm and the

bagpipes on the record were played by the Campbeltown Pipe Band. It was the Christmas number one in 1977 and became the best-selling single of the seventies.

My friend Sam is not a Beatles fan, so a pilgrimage for Paul couldn't have been her reason for wanting to go there. She was a vegetarian for years, but no one likes the Linda McCartney range of rehydrated textured soy sausages enough to go all the way to Campbeltown to sit in Lady McCartney's memorial garden and eat a soy sausage.

Campbeltown has a very long association with whisky. During the boom in production of the 19th century Campbeltown's whisky was big business. Its position, way down at the bottom of a nearly empty peninsula, looks isolated now. But when the sea was the main mode of transport, Campbeltown, built around a deep-water natural harbour, was perfectly placed to send whisky directly across the ocean to the United States or up the River Clyde to Glasgow for transport further afield. The abundance of local peat, a small seam of local coal and the surrounding farmland which could grow great quantities of barley in a climate assisted by the Gulf Stream made it an ideal place for whisky production. So prolific was its trade that Campbeltown was dubbed a 'whisky metropolis'.

The first recorded evidence of whisky distilling in Campbeltown was around the mid-1600s but by 1814 there were 22 distilleries, which eventually rose to 33. With a population of less than 10,000 even at the height of its whisky production, Campbeltown was made by whisky.

If you are scratching your head trying to think of more

than one whisky from Campbeltown, and wondering what the other 30 distilleries that you have never heard of might be, you will realise that somewhere it all went wrong. Campbeltown's whisky decline is a booze morality tale of changing tastes, technological advance, business shortcuts and the vagaries of international trade.

One of the first challenges Campbeltown's distilleries came up against was changing tastes. The whisky they made was almost all bought by blenders who found their customers were demanding a lighter, less peaty style of whisky. One of the ways the distillers could make a lighter-tasting malt was to use a mix of coal and peat in the kiln and exclusively coal to heat the stills, but they were facing competition from the other side of the country.

It cannot be underestimated how much of a revolution the railway was to the whole of mainland Britain. If you consider how much life has changed since smartphone technology and the internet, railways changed society even more. With modern technology we can find out what has happened so much more quickly, but railways got people and things to towns and cities in far less time than it had previously taken. Goods that had been hard to transport could reach their destination on the same day. Fresh food could arrive in cities for same-day distribution, with the result that places within travelling distance of London changed their entire crops to meet the demand of the capital. There is still a heritage train line in Hampshire in southern England called the 'Watercress Line', which was originally used to transport watercress to London every morning of the growing season. Boats and horse and carriages risked becoming obsolete.

In Scotland not only did the railway create a nationwide tourist industry, it also opened up access to the whisky of Speyside in Aberdeenshire and Moray, leaving the Campbeltown distillers facing stiff competition. New distilleries in Speyside were built right beside railways to enable ease of transit, while older ones found that transporting from the nearest station vastly reduced the time it took to reach big population centres.

Campbeltown did have its own narrow-gauge railway from the 1870s, which itself replaced a canal, but it didn't survive the town's changing fortunes and closed around 1930.

Thirdly, there was a quality issue. As they faced more competition they started to cut corners. Distillers were putting too much foreshot or feints with the whisky; they weren't taking enough care with the upkeep and cleaning of the stills, or paying enough attention to the quality of the barley they were malting, and so started to get a bad reputation among blenders, who then went for whisky from other areas, which was now just as easy to get hold of as Campbeltown whisky.

Lastly, whisky had to contend with two major events that affected the entire industry. The Great War of 1914–1918 and US Prohibition. In the case of war, farmers and distillers understood that, in a time of national crisis, barley was needed elsewhere, to feed people throughout the conflict.

Prohibition was a different story. Although it wasn't enacted nationally in America until 1920, no fewer than 26 states had brought in alcohol bans beforehand, reflecting the success of the temperance movement. Those who campaigned against alcohol were convinced it compromised both the health and character of America. Surely other products like milk would boom when they became a viable alternative to booze?

That's not what happened. Health deteriorated – and people died – after drinking dangerous, illegally made moonshine. The Government lost $11 billion from the lack of drinks levies and high costs incurred in enforcing the ban. Crime did not fall away as predicted by the optimistic non-drinkers. Instead, organised crime boomed.

It was not illegal to drink alcohol, only to make and sell it, so there were opportunities for Scottish distillers to trade legally with Canada, where demand for drink rose thanks to its porous border with the USA. But Campbeltown felt the pinch after previously cashing in on a geographic position that made it ideal for exporting to the US. Those trade routes weren't opened again until 1933 when a constitutional act repealed the restrictions on alcohol.

The final nail in the coffin was the drying-up of a local coal seam in 1923, which meant that distillery fuel costs increased.

Although almost all of the former distilleries have been demolished, Campbeltown still occupies a very important place in the history of Scotch whisky, so I could understand why a whisky buff would want to go there. But Sam likes gin and an occasional rye whisky; she doesn't like Scotch at all, so she couldn't want to go and see what the whisky metropolis of the 19th century is like in the early 21st.

'I've wanted to go to Campbeltown for about five years,'

she told me over dinner. 'My grandfather died in a plane accident in Argyle during the Second World War and his memorial stone is there. None of the family have ever been to see it and I want to go, so I'll come with you if you go there for a whisky trip.'

At the end of July 2016 we were sitting on a bus from Glasgow to Campbeltown, armed with a packed lunch of flatbread and cheese with the lettuce and tomato wrapped separately in clingfilm so that the sandwiches wouldn't get soggy.

I realised the first reason that almost no one goes to Campbeltown. As the crow flies, from Glasgow to Campbeltown is 60 miles. But Scotland is full of lochs, inlets and tiny archipelagos. To get there from Glasgow the road goes up past the whole of Loch Lomond, across Loch Fyne and down past Inveraray just to get to the top of the Kintyre peninsula. It's an overdose of Scotland, going past four lochs, three baronial castles and a load of hills before you even get to Inveraray. Then you have a three-hour drive down the entire peninsula. It takes almost the same length of time to get to Campbeltown from Glasgow as it does from Glasgow to London on the train, and London has far better restaurants.

The other reason no one goes to Campbeltown is its present reputation. The town that lost its whisky industry was left with herring – but herring stocks collapsed a long time ago and the fishing industry that remained went into steady decline, so it's not known as a great place to visit.

Halfway down the peninsula we stopped at Tarbert, and Sam's face lit up. There are nearly half a dozen places in

Scotland called Tarbert. The name comes from the Gaelic *tairbeart*, which means 'to carry across'. These towns are built on isthmuses, tiny bits of land between expanses of water, and often goods and even boats were carried across the land to save time sailing all the way round. According to the history books, this Tarbert's place is where, in 1028, Magnus the Barefoot, King of Norway, carried his longboat across the isthmus to emphasise his ownership of the Western Isles. I have a memory of being told this when I was 10 years old in primary six by my teacher Mrs Chillas.

Every time I see a map of Scotland, especially the BBC Scotland logo, with the Kintyre peninsula jutting down on the left-hand side, I have thought, 'A king once got his men to carry a boat across that so that he could own it.' Every time I have been to the Viking fish and chip shop in the seaside town of Largs and walked past the cartoon Viking statue, I have thought, 'They once walked over the entire Kintyre peninsula while carrying a boat. I mean, they were something else.'

It turns out that the shoeless king got his men to walk a mile across the land with their boat at Tarbert and that is a far less interesting feat than the nearly nine miles across that I have spent more than 30 years assuming it was. Adulthood is such a disappointment.

Today, Tarbert is an attractive harbour village with a relatively large marina and a row of craft shops and restaurants designed for the middle-class holidaymaker. On a sunny summer's day it looks like a Scottish version of Honfleur, in Normandy, France, the natural home of a generation of painters. It is all picturesque boats, tablecloths for glasses of white wine and langoustines served with freshly made garlic mayonnaise.

'This looks lovely,' said Sam.

'Yeah, Campbeltown isn't meant to be like this.'

She looked at my face and laughed. 'Is it not? Will it be really awful?'

'I hope not.'

My vague memories of Campbeltown consist of it always being the place last on the list of route confirmation signs on the road up towards Loch Lomond. It says 124 miles on the road sign as you drive out of Glasgow and it always seemed as far away as that other mythical place in the opposite direction – Carlisle.

Before I knew it had been the whisky metropolis, it was that place at the very end of the road that I never managed to get to, as I would always turn around somewhere just after Inveraray. The bottom half of the peninsula was too far away for a Sunday run in the car from Glasgow, so we never went.

Everyone's faces twisted into a grimace when I mentioned Campbeltown.

'I went about 10 years ago and it was like Glasgow in the seventies, and not in a good way.'

'I have never seen anything like it in Campbeltown, Rachel, never. Any drugs you want just passed over the bar bold as brass, in front of anyone. It might have got better in the 15 years since I was there. I mean, it could hardly get worse.'

My only other guide for Campbeltown was a trio of crime novels set in a fictional town called Kinloch. *Whisky from Small Glasses*, the first in the series by Denzil Meyrick, has DCI Jim Daley being sent off from relative comfort in big-town Scotland to a thinly disguised Campbeltown to solve a murder. When the police pathologist finds out where Daley is going, he says: 'Wonderful place, Kinloch. An old friend of mine lives down there: great fishing, golf, fantastic scenery.' He had a faraway look. 'People are as mad as fuck, though.'

Daley then tells another colleague who says: 'Mind you met my brother, Willie, at the fitba'?' Daley grunted in the affirmative. 'Aye, well, I'd forgotten he wiz doon there workin' aboot three years ago. He's a sparky, mind?'

'I remember he swears more than you. I didn't think that was possible. Anyway, how did he like Kinloch?'

'Fuck me, we had tae wring his liver oot wi' a mangle when he came back. He says they're a' near daft doon there. The wife reminded me last night, you know, when I says I might be goin' doon for a while. A' mad wi' the drink, fightin' their ain shadows, an' close-knit tae. I'm thinking yer in fir a fuckin' hard time wi' that mob, for sure.'

Meyrick's ear for conversation between men and re-creation of the atmosphere of the town are really impressive. Excluding the gruesome murders and corruption, there probably isn't a better description of what modern-day Campbeltown looks like or how the men there speak. I reread the books after my trip and realised that we had stayed in the same hotel as Daley does and, although our rooms had been refurbished, the entrance hall and stairs looked and smelled exactly as Meyrick described.

As for the sanity or otherwise of Campbeltonians, that is not for me to say.

As the bus headed south from Tarbert the two things most striking about Kintyre were how flat it was and how empty. I am used to emptiness. Most of Scotland is empty. People have either been cleared off or gone of their own accord because there is nothing to do. Places like Mull have become retirement villages for pensioners from Surrey or the central belt. The villages that exist in Kintyre are no exception – full of pensioners, with the odd row of holiday homes. We drove past a couple of caravan parks full of camper vans from northern Europe, and further on saw an isolated log cabin with peeling paint. It was facing the sea and covered in satellite dishes and TV aerials, its occupant intricately connected to the world and deeply isolated from it.

The emptiness here felt foreign to the Scotland that I knew. The green was too lush, the hills too low to be familiar. And much like the North-east and the *Scots Quair* trilogy, it suffers from not being a Scotland that exists much in the imagination beyond the best-selling British single of the 1970s.

When we arrived at the town and drove past several blocks of run-down-looking council flats, I hoped to God there was more to the place than that. Sam looked at me, a bit concerned, but we walked down the street to the waterside and saw a perfectly pretty, functioning, old-fashioned town with solid Scottish brick buildings looking out onto a bay with low hills behind the houses. Unlike Oban, there was virtually nothing newly built beyond the postwar council flats, but a sunny day, a glittering sea and a small marina make anywhere look stunning, so with some relief we set off to find Sam's grandfather.

She tells this story much better than I do:

'I never knew my grandfather. I knew that he had died in the war while my grandmother was pregnant with my mother. I had always heard that he was a fun and popular man, but knew very little about him other than that. The circumstances surrounding his death were always muddied.

'I happened to meet a wing commander in the RAF at an event a few years ago. He was very dashing – and my grandfather had been a wing commander. I thought that wing commanders flew planes but it turns out that they don't, it's just a title, like managing director or stationery manager, so that was quite a disappointment. But we got on well, so I asked him if he'd help me find out about my grandfather and he did.

'He came back to me with a huge amount of information that had taken him quite a long time to find. My grandfather's name was Benjamin Jones and it turns out there were a lot of those in the RAF who died in the war. But a close family friend told me that he'd been shot down in a captured German airplane, the only bit of useful information that I had.

'There was enough truth in that for this wing commander to find out what happened.

'My grandfather, being 35, had been far too old to go to war himself so he was up in the Hebrides training 19-year-olds to fly planes. A whole group of them went down in an old German aircraft that had been requisitioned and reworked and everyone on board had been killed. They had crashed into the sea near Tarbert on 3 July 1943, so it was decided to place their memorial stones in the Kilkerran cemetery at Campbeltown.

'The wing commander almost didn't want to tell me that because it wasn't a "hero's death" and if I had been much more direct family he'd have couched it in much softer terms.

'I don't know how you really could have; it just wasn't a hero's death. My mother never really talked about her father and I didn't know why. When I told her I was coming here to see his memorial stone, she told me something that the wing commander hadn't. I don't know how much of this is actually true, but there is a possibility that it was my grandfather's fault the plane went down, because perhaps he and a mate had been the ones who'd rebuilt the plane.

'If this is true, that would make for even more reason for it all to be hushed up. She actually said that there was a possibility that if he'd survived, they could have been court-martialled. Clearly, that's why my family would not have talked about it and why it has taken me all this time to find out the truth. It is a family embarrassment.'

Armed with a photo of Benjamin in his uniform, an old photo of Campbeltown and the position number of the grave, we went off to the cemetery on the outskirts of the town to find the stone.

Just as we need to show our parents how well we are doing, we also have a deep need to know where we came from. It is profoundly human to respect and give thanks to ancestors for giving us a life that we never asked for and may not want.

Everyone finds it natural that an adopted child should want to find their birth parents. People who live in the New World declare, 'We are Italian, we are Irish', even though they never have or will visit those countries and, if they do go, they find them very foreign. Despite our incessant focus on the individual and what they do for a living being the definition of who they are, we do not exist in a vacuum and still need other people.

It is a very strange feeling seeking out someone else's family with them. For you it is just a puzzle, for them it is a really profound experience. I spent the first six years of my life with all four of my grandparents. I know how they died, I know where they lived and I know exactly where they all came from. I have never felt the need to visit Beckenham in Kent where my maternal grandmother was born and brought up, and I have never visited any of their graves since the funerals. My ancestors are not a mystery. It makes me very ill-equipped to know what someone else is going through in seeking to discover a family secret.

I know Sam as an incredibly competent, imposing woman capable of virtually anything. She wears wraparound dresses that even I know are Diane Von Furstenberg and she worked in film, getting them made, or selling them to distributors. Fed up with seeing scripts that she knew wouldn't sell, she then became a screenwriter. She has gone from flying round the world making deals with producers to sitting in rural Wales, in the area that her parents are from, to find out who she is, who her people are, and to become a better writer. She is seeking out this memorial stone in order to write.

We walked to the graveyard. It was the town's cemetery as well as one with Commonwealth graves and memorial stones. It was huge and had at least three different parts to it. We knew it was Division 4, Grave 612, but there were no signposts to mark any divisions or graves.

On the left-hand side, at the edge of the cemetery half-way up a hill, was a long row of white memorial stones. The rest of the cemetery was a muddle of graves of all different shapes and sizes facing different ways. These were all the same size and shape and in a perfect row – typical of Commonwealth War Graves Commission cemeteries across the globe. We made our way up. And there he was. Benjamin Jones was the first gravestone we came to, and then after that there were 12 more grouped together from the same plane. The youngest one was about 19 years old, the eldest in their mid-twenties. The names, ranks, dates of birth and dates of death were all there and nothing else. Someone must be charged with keeping them clean and tidy – the 13 of them, looking out onto the bay along with all the others, a memorial to dead young men that almost no one ever came to visit.

Afterwards we walked to the whisky shop in town. There are three distilleries in Campbeltown. Glen Scotia, which is owned by the Loch Lomond Group whose other distillery is up in Alexandria, and Springbank and Glengyle, which are owned by the Mitchell family, one of the old families of Campbeltown. They also own the shop and Cadenhead's bottlers, the oldest private bottler in Scotland. Mark Watt, who is the public face of Cadenhead's, was the man telling bad jokes at the Dramboree private bottlers tasting, so I asked at the shop if he was around so we could get a tour of the warehouse.

Mark is another example of the industry at its best. An unassuming man with a polo shirt, glasses and a walk like a swaying tree, he wears his considerable whisky knowledge very lightly. Mark says he does things for a laugh, says whisky is easy to understand and is far less complicated than wine and that a lot of things are guesswork.

Anyone who knows both Mark and whisky says his knowledge is phenomenal. Jason Standing, who organises Dramboree, speaks in awe of Mark and his ability to guess 80 per cent of the distilleries correctly in a blind tasting of malts. Although he pretends to be, Mark is anything but daft.

He arrives at the shop apologising for not being able to take us round the Cadenhead's warehouse properly because his mother has arrived for the weekend, but he says that he can show us round for about half an hour.

Sam looked slightly concerned at the idea of spending as much as half an hour trying whisky that she knows she doesn't like, but, bolstered by having found her grandfather's memorial stone, she remembers what we are here for and tells me that this part of the book, where she hates everything she tries, is going to be interesting for me to write. I smile at her. She has no idea that, as far as I am concerned, in making her first whisky experience a tour of Cadenhead's warehouse I have brought out the very big gun very quickly.

Although Campbeltown only has the three distilleries

left, you can easily see how integrated the whisky industry and the town were. Distilleries in other places in Scotland tend to be on the edges of towns and villages. The Black & White whisky bottling plant in Stepps that I grew up beside was beyond the places anyone in the village went, so far away it was beside the bus depot. Rural distilleries, like Glenkinchie in the middle of the Lothian countryside, have some houses alongside which were for the original distillery workers, but there is nothing else there. Even in Oban, a town that was built round the distillery, there is a definite demarcation between the beginning and end of the whisky production business and the rest of the town. Not so with Campbeltown. Cross a street and go from one pub to another and you walk past a warehouse. Along another road a Tesco and a retirement home now stand where distilleries once were. The nooks and crannies of Campbeltown, the dead ends and the cul-de-sacs all seem to be, or once have been, warehouses, malting rooms or distilleries. In the same way that the ghosts of medieval glory inhabit many a Majorcan village, reduced from hosting the Knights Templar to selling toys and trinkets to tourists, Campbeltown seems lost without its whisky.

The Mitchell family are the last knights standing in the former whisky metropolis, and they take their role as heirs to Campbeltown's legacy very seriously. That was one of the reasons they bought Cadenhead's bottlers in the 1970s.

Mark tells us about Cadenhead's. 'Although it was founded in 1842 in Aberdeen by George Duncan, the company was taken over and the name changed by William Cadenhead in

1858. It remained in the Cadenhead family until it was sold to the Mitchells [then Mitchell and Wright] in 1972.'

At the time, Cadenhead's was a very good customer of Springbank, as very few distilleries had their own brand of whisky. That they do today is a measure of how much the industry has changed.

'In the seventies distilleries generally didn't sell directly to the public, so buying Cadenhead's and moving the bottling site here helped create more employment as well as giving them the opportunity to sell more Springbank under the Cadenhead's label,' explained Mark.

Another reason the acquisition made sense was that, in the 1970s, there was an extreme shortage of glass and Cadenhead's had lots of glass bottles, Mark went on. 'It was almost worth buying the company for the glass alone.'

Seventy per cent of Cadenhead's stock is matured in Campbeltown, including all of the bottled Springbank. The rest is parked all over Scotland.

'There is a romantic image of us having Highland Park at Highland Park and Macallan at Macallan. That does happen, but I also know that we've got Glenrothes maturing at Glenfarclas distillery and we've got Glenfarclas at Glenrothes. It depends on where it is when we've bought it.

'Personally, I want to bring more casks into Campbeltown so that we can keep an eye on them properly. It costs a lot of money to get a sample of your own cask from a distillery, as much as £50 to get a 100ml sample of, say, Highland Park which becomes £50k a year if you are getting 1000 samples.

'We have whiskies from 108 distilleries all across Scotland.

We are in a lucky position, like MacPhail [Gordon & MacPhail, the private bottler based in Elgin], in that we've got time; we can buy a lot of young stuff and just lay it down in the warehouse, and we'll look at it in five, 10, 15 years' time.'

By this time we have wandered the five minutes from the shop to the warehouse, past some houses and shops in the middle of Campbeltown and into a long white building which is dark, damp and full of casks, most of them lying on the floor, some piled up in twos and threes.

Mark handed us a couple of glasses and Sam looked around at the casks in a slight panic. We needed our taste buds to 'warm up' before tasting from the cask, according to Mark.

'I don't believe in having a "fresh palate" and all that. This is 52 per cent alcohol. If you've not had any alcohol today your first sip just makes your tongue think, "What the hell is going on?" Your second sip is much nicer.

'You wouldn't go for a run without stretching; you need to warm up your palate.'

When he's trying 10 samples, Mark always goes back to the first later in the day, to make sure he has the 'full measure of its character'.

'Sam doesn't like whisky, Mark,' I said, throwing down the gauntlet.

I realise now his face went into the same mode that mine does when someone tells me they don't like whisky. It is a mixture of concern, pity and a girding of loins to rise to a challenge.

Drinking different whiskies is just such immense fun. It's like middle-age clubbing. You get that rush of joy from a beautiful whisky the way you used to from getting dressed up, going out and raving. Whisky is an adult's drink; teenagers drink vodka or gin. It's something to discover once the clubbing scene is full of people young enough to be your offspring and a babysitter is too expensive every Saturday night.

Whisky buffs feel genuine concern for people who drink spirits but say they don't like whisky. I now take great pride in finding a whisky for a non-whisky drinker. As you know, I fancy myself as a bit of a whisky whisperer. But more than proving to myself that everyone likes a whisky, I want to prove to the person in front of me there is a pleasure in life that they have been missing. That is what Mark's face said as soon as I told him about Sam.

'What is it you don't like about whisky?'

Sam got defensive. 'I don't mind rye whisky, it's just Scotch. Why would you want to drink anything that tastes of Toilet Duck and smoke?'

Mark put his head down and his thumb and forefinger on his chin. Then he lifted his head and strode purposefully towards a cask, removed the bung, took some whisky out of it using a valinch – the tube made specifically for the job – and put it in our glasses.

'Try that,' he said, looking intently at Sam.

If there is one thing I know about Samantha Horley it is that she is not a woman born to tell people what they want to hear. If she doesn't like something and you ask for her opinion, she will give it to you, no holds barred, honestly and concisely. If niceties and ego-soothing are what you are after, Sam is not your woman.

She didn't screw up her face in total disgust on smelling what was in her glass, so that was a good sign. Then she took a sip.

'That doesn't taste like Toilet Duck at all,' she said, with exactly the same expression as my friend Ramón 20 years previously, after his first taste of Macallan. 'That is delicious.'

Mark smiled the whisky buff smile that says, 'One more of us, one less of them.' His afternoon was made.

It was a Glentauchers 12-year-old in a sherry cask. It's a Speyside whisky owned by Pernod Ricard, with most of its produce going into blends. Mark described it as 'not a sexy distillery', mainly I think because it is very small and not a big brand. Being a private bottlers means you can get to taste distilleries that have either been closed or aren't generally commercialised.

But from a business perspective, surely it makes no sense for big companies like Pernod Ricard and Diageo to sell casks to private bottlers or individuals? Surely the thing is to take your own production to market and sell directly to the public?

'It's easy to knock "the dark side" [Diageo and Pernod Ricard] and I always say that there is a love-hate relationship between independent bottlers and distillers, in that we love them, they hate us. But if it wasn't for independent bottlers, no one would have heard of the rare whiskies that they know well now. They wouldn't be able to charge £7k a bottle for their Brora 40-year-old for example, so there is a need for it all.'

Another thing about inter-company selling is that big

companies also need to buy for their blends. Johnnie Walker is comprised of more than 33 malt whiskies, but Diageo only owns 28 malt distilleries. Despite being responsible for about a third of the whisky production in Scotland, even they need to buy casks from other companies to produce their biggest brands.

This long tradition of selling casks between companies seems, in part, to explain why the industry as a whole is so collegiate. The only person to actively encourage me to visit Campbeltown was a Diageo employee, who told me how tiny the Springbank bottling plant was compared to the Diageo one outside of Glasgow. In discussions with people in the industry, they all speak highly of other brands or new distilleries that are starting out. Owners of new distilleries have told me how people in other well-established distilleries have knocked on their doors offering help and advice on setting up and avoiding problems. There are rivalries, of course, but so much less than any other industry that I have seen. As a journalist friend up in Scotland to write a piece on whisky put it, 'Either this is the best industry in the world to work in, or it's a cult.'

Sam had finished her Glentauchers and was looking at her empty glass in wonder. Mark then poured us whiskies that sounded like a lightning trip round tiny villages on Speyside. Each one seems to Sam to be the one that would make the perfect Manhattan. She was very shocked that she liked so many; I knew what it was she wouldn't like.

We came to a cask filled with Springbank. Almost all Campbeltown whiskies are peated whiskies. They do not have the same level of peat in them as Islay whiskies, but they do have that distinctive peaty taste. Sam took a sip of it and spat it onto the floor then started coughing. 'See, that is just TCP and misery. Do people actually like that? Are there people who choose to drink that stuff of their own free will?'

Mark and I both nodded, both of us thoroughly enjoying the dram.

'The only thing you need to know about booze, Sam, is whether you like it or not. There is far too much rubbish spoken by, well, me – you should like this, you should get this. If you like it, that's all that matters,' said Mark.

'You obviously don't like anything with peat in it, so just avoid it; there's plenty of other stuff to try.'

He found a Château Lafite barrel that Cadenhead's had filled with Auchentoshan and gave her some of that to calm her down and get her back in a good mood.

'When we bottle this, it'll be for the German market, most definitely,' said Mark. 'They will love this. Everyone is going mental about markets in China at the moment and I sell a little bit in China, but it's only to four bars in Shanghai and it's pretty much what I can drink in a year. Our biggest market is Germany but that's because we have two shops in Germany. Our market is Germany, Japan, Taiwan and the USA. Andorra is my best market per head of population. Everybody in Andorra spends 37p a year on Cadenhead's whisky.'

After about eight whiskies Mark starts apologising that he can't spend any longer with us as he needs to get home to see his mum. He is particularly regretful that he can't show us his cocktail room. He and his wife, who used to work for Springbank herself, have dedicated an entire room in the downstairs of their house to cocktail making. We didn't get to see it that day and the promised photo of it never arrived, so it remains one of the mysteries of this book. He described it in ways that make me think it may be the nirvana of the home cocktail bar.

'It has a gin cupboard with 12 gins, a rum cupboard which is actually an old 78 record player and a ridiculous amount and variety of whisky.

'Then there are the vermouths, then all the bitters. I pick up different ones when I'm travelling. Then there is another cupboard for mixers, glasses and shakers. The chairs in the room are from the old cinema in the town, so are plush red velvet push-downs.

'We go there to have a drink once the kids are asleep.'

If you, dear reader, think that you could make, or already have, a better cocktail room than one full of booze with an old record player for a cupboard and cinema seats to sit on while you enjoy your drink, please let me know. Until then this is the one that I fantasise about whenever I make a cock-tail in my kitchen.

As Sam discovered she liked Scotch whisky after all, I thought it only fair that she give me a recipe for you. If you remember Wishaw with my father, the one I needed to phone and make up with, you will understand why I could never have written this. It's still a great recipe, though. Even if those things are not chips.

Sam's Steamed Mussels with 'Chips'

Serves 2

½ onion, very finely chopped
1 celery stick, very finely chopped
big knob of butter
200ml double cream
2 bay leaves
4 juniper berries, crushed
400g new potatoes, quartered lengthways
splash of olive oil
handful of fresh rosemary, roughly chopped
sea salt
60ml whisky
60ml water
1kg mussels, cleaned (discard any that are damaged or don't close when lightly tapped)

In a saucepan, sweat the onion and celery slowly in the butter until softened. Add the cream, bay leaves and juniper and heat carefully until just bubbling. Remove from the heat and put aside to infuse.

Preheat the oven to 200°C/fan 180°C/gas 6. Put the potatoes in a roasting tin and add the splash of olive oil and rosemary, coating thoroughly. Sprinkle with salt. Roast for about 40 minutes, turning every 10 minutes or so to avoid the potatoes sticking to the tin.

Just before the potatoes are ready, put the whisky and water in a wide lidded saucepan and bring to the boil. Add the mussels and cover with the lid. Cook for 4–5 minutes until the mussels have opened, shaking occasionally (discard any that stay shut). Drain the mussels, retaining the cooking liquor. Put the mussels back in the pan, with the lid on, to keep warm.

Pour the cooking liquor slowly through a fine-mesh sieve into the cream, making sure all sand and grit stays out. Warm through and pour over the mussels. Serve with a bowl of 'chips' on the side.

Friday night in Campbeltown was something of which I was slightly wary. *Whisky from Small Glasses* seemed like a warning about a place where everyone was crazy and full of drink. After a not very impressive dinner we wandered into the centre of town looking for a pub. Pubs in small towns are fiercely tribal. The village in which I spent my 18-month semi-rural fantasy had two – one you went to, and one you didn't.

Campbeltown has a lot more than two pubs, and like all towns they have their own language. When I was in primary school Susan Stirling and her family moved to Elie, a village on the east coast of Scotland. Her father got an opportunity to take over the chemist's there and, since it was a village they had all adored as a family, they jumped at the chance. When I visited, the first thing I learned was that everyone hated tourists, especially tourists from

Glasgow. The Edinburgh and Dundee ones were bad, but the Glasgow ones were beyond the pale. The worst atrocity, Susan's new school friend told me, was that a Glaswegian tourist had walked into one of the Elie pubs and spent the entire evening sitting on Dave the fisherman's bar stool. Every 12-year-old in Elie knew that stool was Dave's and they knew not to sit on it, or at least to stand up and move when Dave arrived.

Pubs in London where guys like Dave have their own stool are a dying breed, and the demographics of the city are changing due to gentrification so quickly that people there don't have locals so much anymore. The chances of an ever-changing bar staff knowing the name of any of the locals are remote, to say the least. In contrast, Campbeltown seemed like the town of a thousand Daves, all with their own place which we might steal.

We headed to a large hotel pub on the front hoping for some space. The tables were full of groups and the bar had a lone man at either side of it, drinking beer. We sat on two free stools near one of the men. He joined in our conversation on gin choices, pointing out the one that was made on Islay, and kept talking. He was a joiner who did most of his work in the Highlands. I asked him what people did for work in Campbeltown.

'The dole mostly,' he said, 'or work away and come back. There's no' a lot here ye can dae.'

He had worked at the Springbank distillery at least a decade previously and told us a trick to get whisky out of an empty barrel.

'It only works in summer mind, but you put the barrel in the sun wi' a clean paint tray underneath it and roll it around a wee bit and ye can get about a litre of whisky. That's what we used to do.'

He went on to tell us about having a heart attack and being saved by his 19-year-old son.

'He works as a lifeguard in the swimming pool over there,' he gestured with his glass behind our heads. 'I owe my life tae that boy, I wouldnae be here if it wasn't for him. He knew what was happening and saved me. I need to give him everything now, I mean, he's no' my son. I call him that but he's my wife's son. But I love him like he's mine.'

'Is your wife here?'

'Aye. She stays in the toon. We all dae, except me when I'm away working.'

Standing or sitting alone in a pub hoping that a stranger will come in and sit near enough to you to give you a chance to tell stories about yourself while your wife is at home has always seemed to me a strange pastime for a man, but Scotland is full of such men in pubs. It's a man's duty to prop up a bar by himself with no book to read, no phone to play with, and to drink while staring into space, kidding on that he's enjoying himself while he stares at his beer, stares at the bar and wonders how much life he's got left.

As a family company the Mitchells have done their level best to keep employment alive in the town.

I once met the salesman for the Springbank distillery in a pub in Glasgow. 'My job is to say no,' he told me.

'The Mitchells won't change the way they run the

distillery. Almost nothing is automated, everything is done on site. They employ 70 people to make less whisky than other distilleries, which employ no more than 20. They don't want to expand the production as they have lived through too many whisky booms and busts, so just keep it the way it is.

'When our customer in the US asks for more whisky than his designated amount I have to say no. Can you imagine having a sales job where most of the time you have to say, "No, I can't sell you that"?'

We went on a tour of the two whisky distilleries that the Mitchells own and discovered just how different things were compared to other distilleries. They malt their own barley on kiln floors the way Gordon on Islay had told me it was originally done. Their checks and measures are all done by hand; it was like looking at a distillery from the fifties. Not once was there even a hint that the company was interested in efficiency savings and improvements. The Mitchell family prioritised stability over all else.

When we arrived for the tour there was a group of four French people and 10 embarrassed-looking men joining us. The men all had blue polo shirts saying CampbellVegas on the front and their names on the back, except for one who was in pink, jeans cut to his knees, a rather flat tutu and had antlers on his head. They looked at Sam and me and the French four nervously; we looked at them nervously. Stag parties are not generally very quiet affairs, but they all shuffled slightly awkwardly round the distillery with their hands in their pockets, in almost complete silence.

After Springbank the French four left and there was just

the stag do, Sam and me. The men seemed to have lost their embarrassment and were talking about what they had seen and how they now understood why Springbank was so expensive. Most of them were from Campbeltown and they said that they had all thought local whisky was just too much money until today.

The Glengyle distillery is a massive 'up yours' on the part of one company to an industry body. As the whisky metropolis was reduced to just two distilleries, the Scotch Whisky Association intervened and decreed that, despite Springbank producing three brands of malt whisky – Springbank, the highly peated Longrow and the triple-distilled Hazelburn – two distilleries weren't enough for Campbeltown to keep its status as a distinct whisky region. The Mitchells were incensed but clearly something had to be done. At the time the Lowlands, another distinct whisky region, had only three malt distilleries, so the Mitchells saved the honour of Campbeltown and in 2000 built a third one.

Glengyle had been a distillery up until 1925 and the building was still intact so they bought it, got rid of the pigeons, cleaned it up and set about turning it back into a distillery. They got second-hand stills and distilling equipment from the Ben Wyvis distillery which, despite being closed in 1977, had kept the stills.

In 2004 the first whisky was made at Glengyle. Another company owns the Glengyle whisky brand and there is no tradition of Campbeltown whisky ever being called 'Glen', so the whisky produced is called Kilkerran after the Gaelic *Ceann Loch Cille Chiarain*, the name of the original settlement where

Saint Kieran had his religious cell and where Campbeltown now stands.

Now, imagine you have just saved the honour of your town and taken four years to build a distillery in the process. The logical thing to do would be to utilise it to its full capacity, making whisky round the clock. Everyone in the whisky world knows what you have done, so there is a lot of goodwill to trade on and your brand is sure to succeed. It's what any normal, sensible business would do.

Whisky at Glengyle is produced during six weeks of every year. Some of the distilling team at Springbank go over to Glengyle for six weeks and make whisky and then it stops until the next year. Six weeks. Just 35 days and then nothing.

You have to be pretty lucky to get hold of a bottle of Kilkerran. Springbank, Longrow and Hazelburn – all whiskies produced at Springbank – are more easily available and, when you drink one, remember the calibre of the people who make it.

We left the distillery, and the stag do went on to have a tasting of the full range of Springbank whiskies along with lunch before going off later for a barbecue on the beach. We had ended up the night before in various other town pubs and in one place in particular a group of middle-aged Campbeltonians had impressed on Sam the need to go back to her grandfather's grave and introduce herself. We had a 6.30 bus to catch to go to Arran the next morning, so whatever we were doing, we were doing it quietly.

We ended up on a bench looking out at the bay eating fish

and chips, and decided not to go to any of the pubs we had been to the night before in case we had another long session. There were only a couple of pubs we thought suitable to visit as we were either too old or not brave enough to go to the rest.

And it was while we were at the bar in a place about two streets away from the front, talking to yet another Campbeltown joiner who this time had an eight-year-old son who was biologically his, whose wife was at home with the child while he drank alone, when all of a sudden a male voice shouted out loud, 'Girls!'

We turned round and there were 10 men, nine of them in blue polo shirts and one in pink, still with the antlers on his head.

15

DREAMING OF DRAMS

'Happiness is having a rare steak, a bottle of whisky,
and a dog to eat the rare steak.'
JOHNNY CARSON

There are times in your life when you have to consider both
the choices you have made and the kind of person you are,
and lying on a bench in a covered-over bus shelter at a ferry
terminal with nothing but a bin, a Portaloo and very efficient
Wi-Fi was, for me, one of those moments.

I am very lucky to have such good friends. Wullie never
complained once when I dragged him round Kilmarnock
in the rain and never even started a fight. Sheri put up with
being chatted up by a man with his name tattooed on his
knuckles and a visit to a car park without a hint of protest.
And opposite me right at that moment was Sam, asleep on
a bench in a bus shelter, using her suitcase as a pillow as she

slept while waiting two hours for the first Sunday ferry from Claonaig to Lochranza.

The stag party, bored with one another, had commandeered us as fellow distillery travellers who therefore needed to spend the rest of the night with them. The groom, still in his pink polo shirt and antlers, wasn't getting married until September but that weekend was the only one they were all available, as all of his friends worked offshore in the merchant navy. They all worked in the North Sea, servicing the oil and gas industry and spending six weeks on a boat and six weeks onshore. They had come back from work the day before and most of them just wanted to be away from each other. Ian, the best man, had an 18-month-old baby and a wife who was six months pregnant, and he spent most of the time telling me that he just wanted to go home. He said organising stag parties in Amsterdam, Dublin and Barcelona had been easier than this one in their hometown. A few more minutes of conversation with Ian and it was very clear why he had organised so many. He was the type of kind, calm, organised person who is the reliable best man, great at crisis management and pouring oil on the troubled waters of even the most complicated wedding and stag do.

And this seemed as complicated a group as any. Apart from the friends, all of whom both lived in the area and worked offshore, the groom's father had the typical West of Scotland working-class male diseases of a heart condition, emphysema brought on by heavy smoking, and obesity. He had to sit down most of the time and needed to be taken the five-minute walk from Springbank to Glengyle in the car. The groom's two younger brothers were there, one of whom also worked on boats; the other was at university in Glasgow. The student obviously felt completely out of place at home. He had moved on, seen a bigger world where people could make money doing very different things. That he hadn't made any of that money yet, and was dependent on his elder brother financially, was evidently adding great tension to the dynamics of the day. The friends all felt the student was a waste of space; the father that his university-going child was the star of the three.

They all just looked like they wanted the day to end and so were very relieved to have two new faces to tell all their woes to. They promised they'd go to see Sam's grandfather's memorial once we had gone and made her get her photo out to see how much she looked like him.

When oil was discovered in the 1970s off the east coast of Scotland it was the saving of many a small community. Apart from the money for the Exchequer and the growth of Aberdeen, places like Campbeltown now had somewhere their men could work away but also stay at home. Before the oil boom, some 44,000 people a year were leaving Scotland to find work elsewhere in the UK or in the rest of the world. By the mid-1980s that number had halved, due exclusively to oil.

With communities like Campbeltown, where the only work is far away or in care homes and hotels, I sometimes think I am guilty of misplaced nostalgia. I have an idea of Spanish small towns where people live and work and hardly ever leave as my pattern of how things should be. But rural Spain is emptying. If you travel round villages in Castile, they are empty except during holidays when people who have moved to big cities come back for a visit. Norway, a place that has used all its oil money to build and maintain an infrastructure enabling people to stay in rural areas, now has an immigration campaign to get Dutch people to move to the 'good life' in rural Norway as its population is moving away from the countryside into cities.

The fact is that rural people have always moved, often to the city. They are not, however, always that keen on admitting it. As Derek Cooper said, 'Although the heart may be in the hills few expatriates in their right mind actually contemplated living there.'

''Tis my wish,' wrote Neil MacLeod, 'that Death should find me in my bonnie native glen.' But until that time he was happy enough in Edinburgh. And writing from the comparative comfort of Glasgow, Lauchlan MacLean Watt cried, 'O bury me in Dunvegan, in the country of MacLeod.' But he didn't mean he wanted to be buried there while he was still in the prime of life.

As Billy Connolly said in the seventies, 'Partick, that's my own wee place and I love it dearly. That's why I moved away. In fact, the further away I get from it, the more I love it.'

Traditional rural life has always involved temporary migration for work, be it the high seas, the coastal mainland or harvest picking. Scotland's fruit and cereal harvests needed seasonal migrant workers from other parts of Scotland well into the mid-19th century.

Orkney was almost totally dependent on the whaling industry, which meant men were away for long periods of time. The herring industry had young women from rural areas moving round from Ullapool in the West Highlands all the way down to Lowestoft, following the boats and the shoals of fish in order to salt and pack them into barrels. Many a Western Isles family was reliant on the money brought in by the herring girls for survival, so offshore working for Scotland's rural population is hardly something new.

If I was shocked at everyone in Campbeltown having to work away, I think it also betrayed my own assumptions that a fixed geographical life is the norm. Both my parents had respectable middle-class, public-sector jobs, which meant that my childhood was completely grounded geographically. Working-class jobs were, in my childhood, in mines or factories, so people were tied to these places for all of their working lives, often only leaving them for brief holidays either elsewhere in Scotland or somewhere sunny.

These young men working offshore in the oil and gas industry, the joiner at the pub having to travel up to the central Highlands for work, they are more in keeping with traditional Scottish life than my upbringing of two parents working in the same area and never having to leave.

After extricating ourselves from the party, soaked with gin and whisky, we still managed about two hours' sleep and to get on the only Sunday bus going anywhere near Claonaig. Sitting on the bus, clean but looking very much the worse for wear, we immediately cheered up when a young woman in her early twenties, with greying make-up and still pulling on her clothes, ran to get on the bus at the last minute. She looked at us and decided we were co-conspirators in the suffering of morning after the night before and declared: 'If I hadn't made this bus my mum would have killed me.'

'We're going to Arran,' I said, while offering her half of my sandwich purchased the day before. 'Somehow. We need to get the eight miles from Kennacraig to Claonaig, hitching once we get off the bus.'

She raised her eyebrows. 'At seven o'clock on a Sunday morning? That is a tiny wee single-track road. You'll be lucky.'

And we were. The bus driver dropped us off at the end of the road to Claonaig and, after five minutes, a big white van stopped and an engineer from Northern Ireland called Fintan, who was spending two weeks laying cable for a wind farm, took us to the ferry terminal, leaving us for two hours with nothing but wide benches, some shelter and an internet connection.

Sam is used to five-star hotels during the Cannes Film Festival, or luxury holidays in scuba-diving resorts, and there she was having a nap in a bus shelter in the middle of nowhere.

If you ever decide to go on any kind of road trip where you are dependent on public transport, take friends like Sam, Sheri or Wullie. Their patience and laughter at being cold, or being in a rubbish place, or sleeping on a bench; their ability to turn anything and everything into a joke left me marvelling at my good luck in knowing such people. Travel companions can be complicated, but the best ones are determined to enjoy themselves no matter what and aren't fazed by unexpected weather, travel arrangements or conversations with strangers.

After what seemed like an eternity, the tiny CalMac ferry arrived to take us the 15-minute trip from Claonaig to Lochranza on the isle of Arran, a place where I spent most of my childhood holidays. It's where I learned to ride a bike and where, a few years later, I raced a car down a hill on one and fell off and broke my wrist. It is where I learned I was hopeless at crazy golf and, most importantly, I learned that no sane person would ever go swimming in the sea off Scotland with only a swimsuit on.

We, like most families, always went to Arran on the other ferry from Ardrossan. It was a less than 50-mile drive from home in a car packed for a fortnight's holiday, which started off in a caravan in Whiting Bay and in later years graduated to a house in Brodick, before being abandoned altogether for holidays in Majorca. In common with a vast number of people from mainland Scotland and the North of England, for me a red and black Caledonian MacBrayne ferry means holidays the way for Proust a madeleine meant childhood.

When I first went back to Arran as an adult after an absence of over 20 years, I was rather shocked to see how fancy the Ardrossan to Arran ferry had become. Gone was the smoky, dusty cafe with its instant coffee in polystyrene cups and greasy bacon rolls fried in week-old lard that you ate with your eyes closed in the hope that you wouldn't see the end of cigarette ash the cook had accidentally dropped on your roll. In its place was a canteen selling a variety of dishes freshly made in clean kitchens using produce from around the West of Scotland. Menus on tables actively encouraged you to drink the freely available water instead of sugary fizzy drinks.

The TV screen no longer played a badly made film in which every inhabitant of Arran stopped whatever they were doing – be it catching lobsters, shearing sheep or mopping a floor – and turned to the camera, saying, 'Hello and welcome to Arran.' The lady at the tourist information office then said the same thing in three different languages in exactly the same West of Scotland accent. It had been replaced by BBC daytime telly with people flogging tat from their attic or looking for that elusive perfect house.

That first journey was a bit of a jolt. While the CalMac ferry from Ardrossan to Arran had joined the 21st century, a part of me longed for a smoky cafe and an ash-sprinkled bacon roll. But like most of these moments, my inner Presbyterian told me to get a grip; that progress, and a decent cup of coffee, is often a very good thing.

Arran is an island in the middle of the space between the Kintyre peninsula and the coast of Ayrshire. It has long been a holiday destination for Glaswegians, and many of the houses that were built in the late 19th century have a smaller one at the back or side that families moved to in order to rent their main houses out in the summer to visiting tourists. Having read thus far you'll not be surprised to know that most of the island's population are pensioners, retired from the central belt of Scotland or North of England, or slightly younger incomers running hotels, craft shops and cafes, chasing the dream of a Scottish island idyll.

Lochranza is at the northern end and looks like a dark village in the Highlands. When we got off the ferry and walked through the village we realised that it was in the middle of a rather heated flag war. Half of the houses had a flag at a window; a few had flagpoles of various sizes, either beside the gate or at the side of the house. The flags were mostly either Scottish saltires or British Union Jacks, but a few had the circle of yellow stars on a blue background of the EU. We walked past a low-built cottage with an old-fashioned slated roof that had a copper sign saying 'SNP' nailed to it.

A village of 200 people, most of whom are pensioners from other places, must have to learn to get along in the pub or the village hall coffee morning, since I imagine heated constitutional debates in either place would be frowned upon. While a villager may not wish to have an argument directly with their neighbour about the UK's place in Europe and Scotland's place in the Union, they still seemed very keen for everyone to know what side they were on.

Walking a mile up the road to the whisky distillery with our suitcases, our hangovers kicked in and counting the flags became an important distraction. We got to the distillery and ran upstairs to eat everything that was on the cafe menu.

Arran distillery was founded in 1994 by Harold Currie, a former director of Chivas, the last distillery on Arran having previously closed in the mid-19th century. Currie and his colleagues decided to open a distillery on Arran rather than Islay partly due to the competition of Islay distilleries, partly due to the quality of the water on the island and partly due to people like me. It's a popular tourist island. It sells itself as Scotland in miniature. Easier to get to than islands like Mull or South Uist, it is consequently also much busier. The marketing possibilities of being able to buy whisky from the

island of your childhood holidays was not lost on the owners.
In fact, Arran whisky could taste like sawdust and cigarette
butts and it would still have people like me queuing up to
buy it. We are fortunate that it tastes good.

One of the problems with opening a new whisky distillery
is that you cannot sell what you have produced for at least
three years and even then you will want to keep most of
your stock for longer. Some distilleries produce gin to have
an income while the whisky matures. Arran built a visitor
centre. We sat at the cafe and had sugary fizzy drinks, smoked
fish and bread, and a venison burger and chips, wondering
how the hell we were going to pull ourselves together enough
to be able to go on a distillery tour and tasting.

'We will rally,' Sam said. 'We can do this.'

If there is one thing that makes Arran my favourite distillery
to visit, it's the staff at the visitor centre. In most distilleries
they are either really young people starting off their careers in
whisky or students working the summer holidays. The staff at
Arran have an average age of around 73. Almost all of them
have retired to the island and after a few months realised that
they needed something to do that was both fun and part-time.
As a visitor you get a tour by a guide who is in a stress-free job,
clearly delighted to be there and to have you visit.

I had been to the distillery two years previously and met
a Yorkshireman called Dave. He had taken early retirement
from his job and moved to Arran as an experiment and an
adventure, getting a job in the distillery cafe. Two years later
he was running the reception desk and his wife was now
working in the shop. A group of them had gone on a boat trip

a few days before to Campbeltown, where they had visited the distillery, enjoyed lunch on the deck of the boat and sailed back to Lochranza.

Here was me, looking at towns and villages filled with pensioners in all areas of rural Scotland, thinking how sad it was that they were simply retirement homes and had no buzz to them. The pensioners themselves are having the time of their lives, with part-time jobs, afternoons out sailing across to the mainland and socialising all over the island.

'Every Tuesday morning there's a coffee morning in the village hall here in Lochranza,' one of the guides told me. 'There's about 32 people, and 28 of them are talking. The other four? Well, they're just catching their breath.'

Where I see lack of opportunity and hope, pensioners see a great social life. If whisky drinking is middle-aged clubbing, places like Lochranza are the bright lights and big city for pensioners. Dave's face when describing his life and the fun he and his wife were having was the face I see in people in their late twenties at the latest restaurant opening in Soho in London. They know that they are in the best place to be at exactly the right time. That Sam, at 46, had moved to rural Wales to write was a far more common trend for people our age than I realised. Her journey back to her roots followed a well-trodden path that could end up in a place like Lochranza, with a wee part-time job, an afternoon sail out on a friend's boat and a flag outside her house letting everyone know where she stood on constitutional matters.

Online technology has had a dramatic effect on a small whisky company's marketing strategy. Big malt brands like

Glenmorangie, Macallan or Glenfiddich can afford advertising, famous brand ambassadors and big PR campaigns. A small independent distillery like Arran needs to work out a strategy for sales and marketing with a far more limited budget and resources. One of the ways to do this is to have a large range of constantly changing limited editions, single-cask bottlings and different cask finishes. This keeps a brand's profile high in the online whisky world and whisky buffs will always know when you have something new to sell. Whisky fans are all familiar with sites like Whisky Fun, Whisky For Everyone and scotchwhisky.com, so when a new limited edition comes out they will often pounce. Arran's distillery also has great design and packaging, using the traditions of the island for their branding.

The previous distillery on Arran closed in 1837, when making money from a legal distillery was simply not possible. Arran was famous for having many tiny illegal stills making good-quality spirit that was then easily smuggled up the Clyde estuary and on to the ports of Greenock and Glasgow. In the last couple of years Arran has created some special Smugglers' Series bottlings to celebrate that heritage.

Like a lot of the modern whisky industry Arran does a range of second maturation, taking whisky from one cask and maturing it further in a different one. Private bottlers like Mark at Cadenhead's have done this for a long time, but it was a process started at Balvenie in Speyside in the early eighties. The result of that is the Balvenie DoubleWood range, which, as the name implies, is whisky stored in two different casks.

Putting a whisky into another wine or spirit cask is often

calculated guesswork and it's very difficult for a big distiller to maintain consistency when doing so. However, Glenfiddich is now producing a whisky finished in a cask previously filled with India pale ale, and Glenmorangie has a similar assortment. Smaller distilleries like Arran can create annual releases of cask finishes, as their customers know that each year the whisky will be slightly different and are perfectly happy with that.

The most common cask for a second maturation is port, but Arran also do Sauternes, Amarone and Madeira finishes. All of them taste slightly different, which means that one small distillery can produce a range of whiskies offering a variety of flavours that keeps them in the eye of the online whisky world.

If you are in a whisky bar with someone who doesn't like whisky because they think it is too fiery or too strong, then I would ask for a dram of a Sauternes cask finish. It is regularly my starting point when I am playing whisky whisperer and more often than not it works. Distilleries that produce quite a light whisky tend to mature casks in Sauternes, so it is a good place to begin.

The best way to find out which, if any, cask finishes you like is to ask at a bar which ones they have and work your way through them. Buying a round of Penderyn Madeira cask finish in a bar in Wales once earned me immeasurable kudos from both work colleagues and the hotel bar staff, so it is worth asking about them even if it's just to make friends.

After working our way through the ones on Arran, Sam surprised me by declaring her favourite to be the Amarone finish, so in tribute to the Italian origin, and specially for her, I made zabaglione with Amarone cask.

Zabaglione is normally made with Marsala, a fortified sweet wine, and in my opinion not often enough. For restaurants, the problem is that it cannot be made in advance and having a pastry chef make a dessert from scratch isn't something that most professional kitchens are set up for.

For chefs doing telly, whisking eggs and sugar with some kind of alcohol over a pan of simmering water doesn't look that exciting or innovative, so zabaglione has fallen out of favour.

It's a shame as it's a great dessert, easy to scale up or down. You can get everyone into the kitchen to take their turn at whisking the mix and once it's done you pour it into glasses and serve.

Zabaglione with Arran Amarone Cask

Per person
I egg yolk
I dessertspoon sugar
1 dessertspoon Arran Amarone Cask

Mix all the ingredients together in a saucepan that will fit over a second pan of simmering water without touching it and whisk continuously until the mixture is creamy and has increased by about four times in size.

Serve in individual dessert glasses.

Your friends and family will love you, I promise.

After the tasting we staggered onto the bus to take us round to the other side of the island and collapsed in a heap in the hotel. The next morning we went to Brodick and had an ice cream on a bench looking out towards the bay to make it a proper holiday and not just a research trip.

There is a sociological paper on whisky tourism written by Professor Karl Spracklen from Leeds Metropolitan University called 'Dreaming of Drams: Authenticity in Scottish whisky tourism as an expression of unresolved Habermasian rationalities'.

Now, if you are thinking, 'Hang on a minute, Rachel, I've read almost to the end and I can see you have taken your research very seriously, but isn't searching through academic papers taking things a wee bit too far?'

The truth is, the paper came to me. I was searching for whisky on the Radio 4 website and an episode of *Thinking Allowed*, the series on current sociological research, came up, with Professor Spracklen discussing it. Somehow I found it online, so obviously I read it.

The saddest thing about the paper is that 'Dreaming of Drams' is almost as good a book title as *Chasing the Dram* but now no one should really use it – just think of the kind of book you would read with a title like that. Then there is the problem of authenticity.

In the restaurant world, 'authentic' is given more abuse than the genitalia of a hormone-ravaged teenage boy. Almost every Spanish restaurant in almost every town in Britain says its food is authentic, but that may not mean it is any good. There are plenty of restaurants in Spain that serve badly made pre-prepared industrial food microwaved from frozen. And authenticity in Scotland is hard. The wilderness in Scotland, the kind you see on adverts for whisky, is often carefully managed shooting estates and as authentically wild as a prize-winning garden at the Chelsea Flower Show. As you know from the Keepers banquet, tartan and bagpipes are more Scott than Scotland, but we still have them everywhere all the time.

The paper suggests that middle-class Western tourists are in search of existentially authentic experiences – and here was me thinking I was just eating an ice cream looking over Brodick Bay.

Then I remembered all the conversations I have with people eager to find the 'authentic' Barcelona, when what they actually mean is that they want to be the only tourists in a place they visit. Food and travel journalists in London sometimes ask me for places in Scotland that are off the beaten track and I have to tell them that outside the central belt there is often only the one track to beat.

Once I had realised that I was never going to really get to grips with Habermasian rationality, so called after the German sociologist Jürgen Habermas, known for his theories on communicative reason and the public sphere, Spracklen's paper was remarkably like my own research, although what I called wandering round Scotland drinking whisky and talking to people he justified as fieldwork. He describes the Arran whisky brand as couching itself in the myths and legends of Scotland as part of its marketing plan, something you know the entire industry does to very great effect.

Whereas I went to Dramboree, his method involved studying the online whisky forums, and he says how they were 'keen to establish their Habermasian communicative freedom, which made their opinions more truly authentic than the instrumentalised consumption of the dupes taken in by marketing tricks' – a very fancy way of saying, 'These people think they know their stuff and sometimes think it makes them better than those who don't.'

One of his conclusions is that it is important for people to feel their experience as authentic to, in my words, truly feel the spirit of things.

Crossing back on the ferry to Ardrossan and the mainland, we sat on the deck in the sun drinking the bar's malt of the month, which was of course Arran 10-year-old, out of plastic cups, looking back at the island. It was the most existentially authentic experience that anyone could have wished for.

CONCLUSION

I made up with my father, although we are now banned from drinking whisky together. We tried going to the theatre, but we mistakenly went to a play set in an S&M dungeon and no one needs to watch a woman in tight black PVC trousers crack a whip astride a chair in front of their 70-year-old father, so it looks like we're going to have to bond over football. *Chasing the Ball: The Search for Sanity in Scottish Football* may be a book coming to a bookshop near you soon.

One of the people I met at Dramboree was a distiller called Lora. She is one of those friends that every whisky aficionado in training should have. Anyone who went to Dramboree was a suitable candidate, but a couple of months after whisky camp we were in Glasgow at the same time and met up at the Pot Still.

If you ask a proper whisky expert like Lora, someone who really knows their stuff, to choose you a whisky, they are not having a pissing contest. They are not trying to trick you, catch you out or make you feel stupid. They want you to drink something that you enjoy and they want you to start recognising flavours; they want you to realise that you know more about whisky than you thought and they want you to have a good time.

There are people who go to whisky events, and if it's a blind tasting the first thing they do is try to guess what whisky they are drinking, without paying attention to what flavours they are getting or whether they like the taste or not. They feel that if they don't guess correctly before anyone else they will lose some imagined, non-existent competition.

If you are in the presence of such people, remember that you, unlike them, are a decent enough human being to know that the correct place to piss is in the toilet and not at a table full of whisky glasses. Pay them no heed.

Likewise, if your whisky expert friend seems to want to catch you out rather than help you to educate yourself and have a better time drinking whisky, find another whisky friend. There are lots of them online, on social media and all kinds of virtual spaces. There will be one in your area; you just have to dig them out. Whisky people are like evangelical Christians – they love meeting new people who are either one of them or want to become one; they'll make you feel welcome and you can learn a lot from them.

Lora comes back with a pale-looking whisky that she won't tell me the name of and asks me what I can tell her about it.

Immediately I want to pee. I want to pee *high*. I want to piss out of the pub skylight and hit the moon.

I want to take a sniff and rattle off the name of a distillery, and maybe even the age of it or the fact it's the no-age-statement version, or just something that will make her see that I have learned, that I know, that I am so clever and so cool and so well versed in the ways of whisky that I will never, ever have to pee in public again.

The Pot Still has 700 whiskies. Even with all my research I have not tried all 700. Even if I had, there is no way I would remember the taste of 700 whiskies, especially given the state I would have been in while tasting some of them.

I am really nervous. I really, really, really want to be right.

It's a pale whisky; that means no added caramel and possibly reasonably young. I smell it. Slight turpentine, peat but not so much that it's the first thing you notice. It's definitely not a Laphroaig. It doesn't have the smoke of a Highland Park, though, and it's not a Lagavulin.

I give in, knowing that I'll never get it, and Lora tells me it's a Kilchoman, the distillery at the small farm on Islay.

Turned out I had learned two things researching this book. The first was a lot about whisky, almost all of which you have just read; the second was, present me with a mystery whisky to taste and I am as big a pain as the next person wanting to win the contest that doesn't exist.

If my geography of Scotland has become defined by distilleries, my friends have become defined by their whisky. Sheri is now intricately linked to Ben Nevis, Sam to Arran Amarone and Wullie to Johnnie Walker (I still need to get him a bottle).

People I have met up here include Kathleen, who drinks Ardbeg because it's where her father came from; Andrew, who drinks Lagavulin because he grew up in Argyll, across the water from the distillery; Kevin from Caithness, who drinks Old Pulteney or Highland Park; and every Aberdeenshire person I have met drinks Speyside. Despite whisky not having a terroir, Scots often gravitate to their origins when choosing a brand – that a doctor on North Uist receives only West Highland and Islay whiskies as presents from crofters is further evidence of this.

I started my research thinking I was going to splash some whisky in some food here and there and have ended up with a load of new friends and a new, unexpected passion.

And as for the food? The whisky in my cupboard is now an integral part of my cooking. I splash blends in onion and garlic bases, I cook mushrooms with all kinds of whisky and butter and nothing else. No one believes that three ingredients can taste that good. They insist that I must have used a different spice or herb, when all I have done is use a different whisky. It's become as normal for me as using wine is, my food is better for it and my friends are better friends.

Last week I went to Bristol to record a radio programme and stayed overnight at Jason from Dramboree's house. He had recently bought a special edition Glenfiddich and he opened the bottle for his wife, Liz, and me.

'The thing is, whisky is really about people,' he said. 'I mean, this is a great bottle. I bought it with some of my bonus from work but it's now the bottle we started when you were here. That'll now be what it means and when we drink it we'll think of you.'

Conclusion

I say my favourite whisky is Lagavulin, but do you know why? I went to the Islay festival on one of my first trips with Liz and we were outside the distillery, sitting on the pier in the sun drinking it, and I just thought, 'Yeah, this is the life I want.' And every time I drink Lagavulin I feel like I have a piece of it.

So please, close this book, go and enjoy a piece of the life you want with a whisky in your hand. It's what the spirit of it is.

Glossary of terms

ABV Alcohol by volume. Defined as the number of millilitres of pure ethanol present in 100 millilitres of solution at 20°C.

Age statement The age of the youngest whisky in a bottle. For example, Ben Nevis 10: it will have whiskies of many ages, but the youngest one in the bottle will be 10 years old.

Bitters Alcohol flavoured with bitter plant extracts, originally used as medicine, now mostly used in cocktails.

Blended malt A whisky made from malted barley from more than one distillery.

Bung hole The stopper on a cask.

Cask finish A whisky that has been put in a different cask for the last six months to two years before bottling. Examples: Arran Amarone finish and Glenfiddich IPA finish.

Cask strength Whisky bottled directly from the cask, generally with a higher ABV than other whiskies.

Chill filtration Cosmetic process to remove fatty acids that can make whisky cloudy when ice is added.

Chit Sprouted grain or tubercle, in whisky's case it is sprouted barley. Also called a culm.

Coffey still Patented still that distils alcohol by fractional distillation, used in the Scotch industry to make grain whisky.

Continuous still/column still Used to make grain whisky; the name given to a Coffey still (see above).

Cooper Professional cask/barrel maker.

Culm See **Chit**

Double distillation The process for almost all malt whisky production. Fermented wort is distilled then redistilled to make spirit.

Double wood Whisky that comes from two different casks. Example: Balvenie DoubleWood.

Feint The final spirit from the spirit still at the end of distillation, which is low in alcohol and redistilled.

Fèis Ìle The Islay music and whisky festival held every May. Be warned: spelled with an 'e' instead of an 'è' the word means shagging not festival. So, *'Deagh latha aig an fhèis'* – 'Have a good day at the festival' – has quite a different meaning without the accent.

Fermentation tank See **Washback**

Foreshot The first 5 per cent approx. of spirit to come off the spirit still is high in alcohol (75–80 per cent ABV), contains too many volatile compounds, and is redistilled.

Fractional distillation The method of distillation that most frequently takes place in a continuous/column still, the liquid is separated into fractions with differing boiling points.

Glossary of terms

Golden Promise barley Type of barley used by Glengoyne and Macallan distilleries and some of the Benromach bottling; known for its great taste but also its low yield and vulnerability to disease.

Grain still Continuous still used to make grain whisky.

Grain whisky Whisky made from a grain other than malted barley, normally wheat in present-day Scotland.

Japanese whisky Whisky that has been aged in Japan.

Keepers of the Quaich Invite-only organisation that recognises individuals who have done outstanding work for the Scotch whisky industry.

Malt whisky Whisky made from malted barley.

Maltsters Makers of malt barley.

New-make spirit Spirit from a still that is less than three years old. It can only be called whisky after it's been in a barrel for three years.

No age statement (NAS) Whisky from casks of unstated ages; the minimum will be three years as anything younger is not legally whisky.

Peat reek The name given to illegally distilled whisky in Scotland, something no one makes anymore and no one has ever tried.

Phylloxera A plant louse that feeds on vines. It destroyed many French vineyards in the 19th century.

Porteus mill A make of grain mill used by most older malt distilleries. It was so well made that almost no repairs or replacements were needed and the company went bankrupt.

Pot still Mostly used to make malt whisky, the distillation is done by batch method with heat being directly applied from beneath.

PPM Phenol parts per million. The higher the PPM, the peatier the whisky.

Quaich Shallow, two-handled drinking vessel sold in every tourist shop and distillery visitors' centre in Scotland.

Scotch Whisky that has been distilled and aged in oak barrels in Scotland for a minimum of three years.

Scotch Whisky Association Trade association body and lobbyist on behalf of the Scotch industry.

Silent distillery A distillery that has been closed, which the nostalgic refer to as 'fallen silent'.

Single cask Whisky bottled from one cask only.

Single-cask bottling A bottle of whisky that comes from only one cask.

Single malt Whisky made from malted barley from one single distillery.

Solera method Fractional blending in such a way that the finished product is a mixture of ages; most commonly used in the sherry industry, increasingly used in no-age-statement whisky. The method was pioneered by Glenfiddich, who use it for all their whiskies and age statements.

Special whisky bottlings Whisky brands now often blend casks to create limited edition special bottlings. Islay whiskies often do it for the whisky and jazz festivals.

Staves Thin, narrow piece of wood that forms part of a barrel or cask.

Triple distillation Technique whereby fermented wort is distilled then the resulting spirit is distilled and distilled a third time. Highly unusual in Scotch whisky; used by Auchentoshan.

Valinch A tube for drawing liquor from a cask via the bung hole.

Vatted malt More commonly called a blended malt nowadays, this is malt whisky produced from various distilleries.

Glossary of terms

Washback Container normally made of wood or steel in which yeast is added to wort and fermentation then takes place.

Whiskey Spelling generally used for Irish and American whisky.

Whisky Spelling generally used for Scotch, Canadian and Japanese whisky.

Whisky bar/pub After extensive research I have reached the conclusion that a whisky bar or pub is one with more whiskies than you want to drink or that you can comfortably drink in the one evening.

GLOSSARY OF WHISKY

Aberfeldy Built by the Dewar family and opened in 1898, this Highland malt was specifically created to be part of the Dewar's blend and once had a private railway line linking it with the firm's central operations in Perth. Now owned by Bacardi Martini, the malt has been recently repackaged and launched as a stand-alone malt.

Aberlour Speyside distillery built by farmer James Fleming in 1879, who had previously worked at Dailuaine distillery. It's currently owned by Pernod Ricard.

Aberlour A'bunadh Cask-strength no-age-statement special bottling from Aberlour which has been aged in oloroso sherry casks.

Abhainn Dearg Distillery on the Isle of Lewis first distilling in 2007; its name means Red River in Gaelic.

Allt-a-Bhainne Founded in 1975, this distillery was built to be run by one person. Owned by Pernod Ricard, most of the whisky goes into blends, although some bottlings are occasionally available.

anCnoc The brand produced by the Speyside Knockdhu distillery which was founded in 1894 in a place with easy access to barley and peat and right beside the newly built railway line. Current owners Inver House used the Gaelic for 'the hill' for the whisky to avoid confusion with Knockandhu.

Annandale Opened in the Lowlands in 1830 by George Donald, it was bought by Johnnie Walker in 1893 and was closed down in 1924. In 2007 Teresa Church and David Thomson purchased the site and, after extensive restoration, resumed whisky production in 2014.

Arbikie A family farm in Angus; after a night out in New York the three brothers decided to set up a distillery in 2015. Already selling gin and vodka, the whisky won't be released until it is at least 14 years old, in 2029.

Ardbeg An Islay whisky, the distillery was legally founded in 1815. Opened and closed several times, it was eventually bought by Glenmorangie (now in turn owned by LVMH – Moët Hennessy Louis Vuitton) in 1997, who invested heavily in upgrading the distillery. It is one of the peatiest and sweetest Islay whiskies on the market.

Ardmore Founded by Adam Teacher in 1898 for use in the Teacher's blend, the distillery, now owned by Beam Suntory, is still mostly used for the smoky notes in Teacher's, although there are some private bottlings.

Ardnamurchan The first legal distillery on the remote Ardnamurchan peninsula was opened in 2014 by Adelphi private bottlers; this distillery also aims to be the greenest and most efficient distillery in Scotland.

Arran whisky Isle of Arran is a privately owned distillery founded in 1994 in Lochranza. It has a range of bottlings, cask finishes and peated and unpeated whiskies. The company is building another distillery at the south end of the island near Lagg.

Glossary of whisky

Auchentoshan Lowland distillery on the outskirts of Glasgow. Legal distilling started here in 1817 but it wasn't until 1823 that the site got the name Auchentoshan. Unusually for a Scotch whisky, it is triple distilled, giving it a lighter flavour than even other Lowland malts. The distillery has passed through various hands at different times and is now owned by Beam Suntory.

Auchroisk Built in 1972 and now owned by Diageo, this whisky makes up an important part of the Singleton Malt range. Distillery bottlings are available, but mostly through private bottlers.

Aultmore Built in 1896, this Speyside malt forms a really important part of the Dewar's blend, although it is sometimes available as its own bottling. It is now owned by Bacardi Martini and is highly prized.

Balblair Founded in 1790, the Highland distillery was rebuilt in 1895 to be closer to the railway station. It fell silent from 1911 until after World War 2, when it was reopened to make whisky for the US market. Now owned by Inver House, bottlings have been sold since 2000. The distillery was also a location for the Ken Loach whisky film, *The Angels' Share*.

Ballantine's The second biggest-selling whisky in the world, Ballantine's is a blended whisky comprising 50 single malts and four single grains. It started life in 1827 when farmer's son George Ballantine opened a grocer's in Edinburgh and started blending and selling whiskies.

Ballindalloch Distillery built on the grounds of Speyside's Ballindalloch Castle in 2011 by the 23rd generation of the Macpherson–Grant family. The first whisky will be released in 2019.

Balmenach Founded in 1824 and now owned by Inver House, Balmenach's value for use in blends means that it has never been bottled as a single malt. Inver House also makes Caorunn gin there.

Balvenie Speyside distillery founded in 1893 by William Grant, who had previously worked at Mortlach. Still owned by the Grants, it is often seen as the little brother to Glenfiddich.

Ben Nevis Highland distillery based in Fort William founded in 1825 and now owned by Japanese company Nikka.

Ben Wyvis Highland distillery that functioned between 1965 and 1977 and then fell silent. The stills were eventually dismantled and sent to Glengyle in Campbeltown.

BenRiach Founded in 1897, the Speyside distillery was mothballed from 1899 to 1965 and eventually had its own bottling in 1994 but was closed again from 2001 to 2003 when it was sold to Inver House, who reopened it. Now owned by the same company that owns Jack Daniel's, BenRiach is in full production with its malting floor back in use from 2013.

Benrinnes Old-style Speyside distillery founded in 1835, now owned by Diageo; it is used in blends and is only available as a single bottling via private bottlers.

Benromach Speyside distillery near Forres originally built in 1898 and closed and reopened several times until it was closed in 1983. Taken over by Gordon & MacPhail in 1993, who started restoring the distillery in 1997 and began bottling whisky in 2008.

Berry Bros The oldest private bottlers in the UK, nowadays mostly wine merchants. Berry Bros created the Cutty Sark blend.

Black Bottle Whisky started in 1879 by Charles, David and Gordon Graham, members of a family of Aberdeen tea merchants who had branched out into whisky blending. The current Black Bottle style was produced from 2013 and is owned by the South African Distell Group.

Bladnoch Lowland distillery first built in 1817 that has been mothballed several times. In 2015 it was bought by Australian businessman David Prior, along with ex-Scotch Whisky

Association CEO Gavin Hewitt, who announced the purchase of Bladnoch and plans to restore the distillery.

Blair Athol Highland distillery built near the town of Pitlochry in 1798. Now owned by Diageo, it is one of the major components of the Bell's blend so single bottlings are relatively rare.

Bowmore Islay whisky with claims to have been founded in 1779 but which has had a distilling licence since 1816. A medium-peated whisky, it is one of the few distilleries with its own malting floor still in use. It has been owned by the Suntory Group (now Beam Suntory) since 1994.

Braeval Founded in 1973 by Chivas Bros and now owned by Pernod Ricard, it's a Speyside distillery that is used exclusively for brands so is very hard to find even with private bottlers. Braeval is, along with Dalwhinnie, the joint highest distillery in Scotland.

Brora Now-closed Highland distillery that was built in 1819 and known as Clynelish until the Clynelish distillery was opened in 1968. The distillery was closed in 1983 and in 2014 Diageo released a Brora 40-year-old with a retail price of £6,995.99.

Bruichladdich Islay whisky founded in 1881. It was mothballed three times before eventually closing in 1994 and then reopened in its present incarnation in 2000. It produces three brands: unpeated Bruichladdich, heavily peated Port Charlotte and the super-peated Octomore. The private owners sold the distillery to Rémy Cointreau in 2012.

Buchanan's Blend first developed by James Buchanan in 1884, now part of the Diageo group, it is hugely popular in Latin America.

Bunnahabhain Islay whisky founded in 1881. Historically it has been a major component of The Famous Grouse and Cutty Sark, and more recently a component of Black Bottle.

Cameronbridge Grain distillery in Fife, founded by John Haig in 1824 and where his cousin, Robert Stein, installed his continuous still a few years later. Mostly used in blends, the distillery also produces the Cameron Brig brand and the better-known Haig Club.

Caol Ila Islay whisky founded in 1846 and now owned by Diageo. So much of it was used in blends that until 2002 it was only available from private bottlers. It now has a range of aged malts, no-age-statements and special bottlings.

Cardhu Speyside whisky founded in 1824 by whisky smuggler John Cumming, it started as a farm distillery working on a seasonal basis after the harvest had been gathered. The distillery was run mainly by his wife Helen, who used to sell bottles of whisky to passers-by through the window of their farmhouse. It is now owned by Diageo and seen as the home of Johnnie Walker.

Chivas Started life in 1801 when John Forrest opened up a wine and grocery merchants in Aberdeen. In 1909 Chivas Regal 25-year-old, the world's first luxury blended whisky, was launched. In its first year, Chivas Regal became one of the most talked-about imported consumer goods among high society and, despite a few ups and downs, was later associated with Frank Sinatra and the Rat Pack.

Clynelish Clynelish was founded in 1819 as a money-making scheme by the Duke (although it was mostly the Duchess) of Sutherland at the height of the Clearances, and the original workers were evicted tenant farmers who were paid with the duke's coin which they could only use in the duke's shops. The distillery wasn't a success until the end of the 19th century when it became a highly prized malt. Now owned by Diageo, it is an important component of Johnnie Walker and is available in single bottlings as part of the Hidden Malts range.

Cragganmore A lightly peated Speyside malt founded in 1869 on a site that was near a good source of water and right beside the newly built Speyside railway. The founder, John Smith, had previously managed Glenlivet, Macallan, Glenfarclas and Wishaw distilleries. Now owned by Diageo, it's one of their Classic Malts but is also used extensively in blends.

Craigellachie Built in 1890 and part-owned by Peter Mackie of White Horse fame, it was used in White Horse and several other blends that were popular in Australia and South Africa. Now owned by Bacardi Martini, the Speyside malt has only really been marketed in single bottlings since 2014.

Cutty Sark Blended whisky first produced in 1923 by Berry Bros as a refined, softer alternative to the moonshine available in Prohibition-era USA. In 1961 it became the first Scotch to sell more than a million cases in America. Now owned by the Edrington Group, they have created various special releases, some based on its fame during Prohibition.

Daftmill Lowland farm distillery based in Fife and founded in 2005, the barley used in the whisky making is from the farm; the druff left over after fermenting the malt feeds their beef cattle and the water they use is from their own well. The distilling takes place on a part-time basis of two periods of three months a year.

Dailuaine Speyside distillery used mostly for blends, so generally only available from private bottlers. Has one spirit still bigger than the others and one wash still smaller than the others due to a mistake by coppersmiths 50 years ago.

Dallas Dhu Built in 1898, this Speyside distillery is now closed and has been a museum since 1986. There are still some stocks left which are hard to find and mostly owned by Diageo.

Dalmore Highland distillery founded in 1839 by Alexander Matheson, who had made his money in a firm that controlled the opium trade in China. An important part of Whyte &

Mackay blend, Dalmore is available in various expressions and is now part of the Whyte & Mackay Group who are owned by Emperador Inc. of the Philippines.

Dalwhinnie Speyside distillery founded in 1897 that in 1905, when it was bought by the American company Cook & Bernheimer, became the first Scotch distillery with non-British owners. Now owned by Diageo, it is part of the Classic Malts range.

Deanston Part of the Distell Group, the Highland malt was founded in 1965 in a converted mill. It uses organic barley in its mash and claims to be one of the greenest distilleries in Scotland. Its character is light and soft with a slight hint of caramel.

Diageo Largest drinks company in the world, formed in 1997 with the merger of Guinness and Grand Metropolitan; owner of the Johnnie Walker brand and over 20 distilleries.

Douglas Laing Glasgow-based private bottlers started in 1948; most recently produced a range of blended malts.

Dufftown Speyside distillery that was originally a mill, it was founded in 1896 and is now owned by Diageo, forming part of its Singleton range.

Eden Mill New Lowland distillery in Fife built on the site of an old grain distillery. Set up by businessman Paul Miller, who started the brewery in 2012 and started distilling malt whisky in 2014. It is the only combined brewery and distillery in Scotland at the moment.

Edradour One of Scotland's smallest distilleries, this Highland malt was founded in 1837 and still looks like a proper Victorian farm distillery. Now owned by the Signatory Vintage Scotch Whisky Company, it is one of the prettiest and most popular distilleries in Scotland.

Edrington Group International drinks company that acquired The Famous Grouse, The Macallan and Highland Park in 1999, and Cutty Sark from Berry Bros. & Rudd in April 2010.

Glossary of whisky

Famous Grouse The best-selling blend in Scotland, it started life in 1896, created by Perth wine and spirits merchant Matthew Gloag. Now owned by the Edrington Group, its home is Glenturret in Perthshire.

Fettercairn Founded in 1825 and bought in 1830 by former prime minister William Gladstone's father, this Highland distillery is now owned by Whyte & Mackay and Philippines-based Emperador Inc. and while it is used mostly in blends a limited range has been bottled.

Girvan Grain Single-grain whisky from the Grant's grain distillery at Girvan in Ayrshire in the Lowlands. Has only recently been bottled as a single-grain whisky and is gaining respect among whisky experts.

Glasgow Distillery Co. Small independent Lowland distillery located on an industrial estate on the Southside of Glasgow. It opened in 2012, and in 2015 started distilling malt whisky in Glasgow for the first time in over 100 years. Expected to produce a Speyside style, they are experimenting with full maturation in ex-port and ex-Sauternes casks.

Glen Elgin Founded in 1898, this Highland malt is now owned by Diageo and used exclusively in blends; although some was bottled at the beginning of the millennium they are a very rare find.

Glen Garioch A Highland whisky from the east of Aberdeenshire, it was officially founded in 1797 but was probably distilling long before that. After various owners and shutdowns, it is now owned by Beam Suntory and used only for single malt.

Glen Grant Founded in the 1840s in Speyside by the Grant brothers (not the same Grants as either the Glenfarclas or the Glenfiddich Grants – there were a lot of Grants starting distilleries in the Highlands of Scotland in the 19th century), it's now owned by the Gruppo Campari and is the biggest-selling malt whisky in Italy.

Glen Keith Speyside distillery built in 1957 to supply the brands Chivas, Passport and 100 Pipers, it was mothballed in 1999 and then reopened in 2013 after a refit by new owner Pernod Ricard. Still used almost exclusively in blends, there are a few bottles around from private bottlers.

Glen Moray Founded in 1897 on the outskirts of the Highland town of Elgin in a converted brewery, it was closed in 1910, reopened in 1923 and is now mostly used by French owner La Martiniquaise for its Label Five and Glen Turner blends.

Glen Ord Founded by the local laird, Thomas MacKenzie, in 1838, the Highland whisky has been used extensively in blends and had various brand names throughout the years, but it is now marketed as Singleton of Glen Ord by owner Diageo.

Glen Scotia Founded in 1832 in Campbeltown, Glen Scotia has had more than 10 owners in its history and is now part of the Loch Lomond Group, producing quite a soft Campbeltown style.

Glen Spey This Diageo-owned Speyside distillery was built in 1878 at the same time as its neighbour Glenrothes by James Stuart, who was also the licensee of Macallan at the time. Used mostly in blends, it has had some bottlings as part of Diageo's Flora and Fauna range, but bottlings can be hard to find.

Glenallachie Built in 1967 by a Scottish and Newcastle Brewers subsidiary, the Speyside distillery is now owned by Pernod Ricard and is mostly used in blends, although the Signatory Vintage Scotch Whisky Company does do some private bottlings.

Glenburgie One of the most important malts for the Ballantine's blend, the second biggest-selling Scotch whisky in the world, the Speyside distillery was originally built in 1829 but was rebuilt by Pernod Ricard in 2005. Due to its use in Ballantine's, as the scotchwhisky.com website says, you are more likely to see the Loch Ness monster than a single bottling of Glenburgie.

Glencadam Founded in the Highlands in 1825, the distillery was mothballed in 2000 then reopened in 2003. Now owned by Angus Dundee Distillers, it is beginning to emerge as a respected malt.

Glendronach A Highland distillery located just outside the Speyside border region, this distillery only stopped heating its stills by coal in 2005. Built by a consortium of local farmers in 1826, it is now owned by the Jack Daniel's producer Brown-Forman and is very popular in Taiwan.

Glendullan A distillery was first built on the site in 1897 but was closed in 1985 when the sister site built next door in 1972 took over all the production. Diageo-owned, it makes the US exclusive Singleton of Glendullan brand.

Glenfarclas Founded in 1836, this Speyside whisky is one of the few older whiskies to have remained in the hands of the same family since it was sold by Robert Hay's family to their neighbours, the Grants (not the ones who own Glenfiddich). The stills are still heated by gas burners and all the spirit is aged in oloroso sherry casks.

Glenfiddich The largest malt whisky distillery in the world, it was founded by W.S. Grant, former manager of Mortlach in Dufftown, in 1886 and now produces over 6.5 million litres of whisky a year. In 1963, after a dispute about grain supply, the Grants decided to start selling Glenfiddich under its own label and, in the late 1960s, it became one of the first malt whiskies available in the new duty-free outlets.

Glenglassaugh Now owned by Jack Daniel's producer Brown-Forman, the Highland distillery was built in 1874 by local businessman James Moir. It was closed from 1907 to 1960 and then again from 1986 to 2008. The post-2008 whisky is seen as very much a work in progress.

Glengoyne In continuous production since 1833, sold as single malt since the early 1990s and originally marketed as an unpeated

Highland malt. Owned by Ian Macleod since 2003, its distillery is a well-known tourist destination.

Glengyle The third distillery in Campbeltown founded by the Mitchell family in 2000 and opened in 2004. It produces the Kilkerran brand.

Glenkinchie A Lowland whisky, the distillery is about 15 miles from Edinburgh, founded in a glen of the Kinchie Burn in 1837. It started to be properly marketed as a stand-alone malt in 1989 and is part of the Diageo Classic Malts range.

Glenlivet Founded in 1824 by George Smith, The Glenlivet is the biggest-selling malt in the US and the second-biggest malt whisky in the world. Now owned by Pernod Ricard, the Speyside whisky is available in a wide range of age statements as well as no-age-statements and special bottlings.

Glenlossie Since its construction on Speyside in 1876, this whisky has been in great demand for use in blends so is rarely seen on the market, even via private bottlers, but owners Diageo do sell it as part of their Flora and Fauna range.

Glenmorangie Owned by Moët Hennessy Louis Vuitton, who also own Ardbeg, often marketed as having stills as tall as giraffes. Glenmorangie is one of the major pioneers of the cask finish and sells a wide range.

Glenturret As an illegal distillery was known to be here from 1775, it claims to be the oldest distillery in Scotland, but this small farm-style Highland distillery (with a very nice restaurant and cafe attached) has since 2002 been marketed as the home of The Famous Grouse blend, also owned by Edrington. Single malt bottlings are rarely available.

Glenrothes Founded in 1878, the distillery is owned by Edrington, and the single malt was recently acquired back from Berry Bros. It's an important component of Cutty Sark blend.

Glentauchers Built on Speyside by James Buchanan in 1897 to supply the Buchanan's and Black & White brands and now used mostly in Ballantine's. There are very few individual bottles sold and they are mostly through private bottlers.

Gordon & McPhail Private bottlers based in Elgin, thought of as the royalty of the whisky industry. Started in 1895, it is still owned by the Urquhart family. They also own the Benromach distillery.

Grant's The fourth best-selling Scotch blend in the world, it still belongs to the Grant family and is a well-known Speyside-style blend first sold in 1898.

Haig Club Launched in 2014, this grain whisky is made in the Lowlands at Cameronbridge distillery and is a partnership between Diageo, former footballer David Beckham and music mogul Simon Fuller.

Harris distillery A social distillery on the Isle of Harris in the Outer Hebrides which is community-owned; the whisky still first started working in January 2016.

Hazelburn Hazelburn was a distillery in Campbeltown between 1825 and 1925 and is now a triple-distilled unpeated whisky made at Springbank distillery.

Highland Park Orcadian whisky founded around 1798 which retains its malting floor and uses local peat to dry the malt. A highly regarded malt whisky owned by the Edrington Group, it is one of the ingredients of Famous Grouse; there are also many different Highland Park bottlings widely available.

Inchgower Built in 1871, this costal Speyside distillery was owned by the Buckie town council for a couple of years after the original owners, the Wilson family, went bankrupt in 1936. It was then bought by Arthur Bell and used in the Bell's blend as well as Johnnie Walker, and is now available as a single malt as part of owner Diageo's Flora and Fauna range.

Inver House Thai-owned whisky group, including malt distilleries Old Pulteney, anCnoc, Speyburn, Balblair and blended brands MacArthur's, Catto's and Hankey Bannister.

Invergordon Founded in 1959 in the Highland town of Invergordon in an attempt to create more industry in the Highlands, it is the only grain distillery in the region. Always used in the Whyte & Mackay blends as well as many other blended whiskies, it is now owned by the parent company of Whyte & Mackay, Emperador Inc. of the Philippines.

Johnnie Walker The best-selling Scotch in the world, it started life in a grocer's shop in Kilmarnock as Walker's Kilmarnock Whisky and now sells in excess of 20 million cases per year all over the world.

Jura Founded in 1963 by local landowners Robin Fletcher and Tony Riley-Smith to help stem the decrease in the island's population, now owned by Whyte & Mackay's parent company Emperador Inc. of the Philippines, it is a range of widely available bottlings.

Kilchoman Islay farm distillery founded in 2005, all of the malting, distilling, maturing and bottling is carried out on the island. Held in high regard by the whisky geeks.

Kilkerran Lightly peated Campbeltown malt made at the Glengyle distillery since 2004. The distillery is owned by the Mitchell family and only in use for six weeks of the year.

Kingsbarns Brainchild of former golf caddie Douglas Clement, who couldn't raise sufficient funds to build the distillery near St Andrews, the Wemyss family bought the company, made Clement a director and the Lowland distillery was built in 2013. It aims to produce the traditional light-tasting whisky of the Lowlands.

Kininvie Built on the same site as Balvenie in 1970 by the Grant family due to pressure on their malt stocks, this whisky is mostly used in blends although there have been some bottlings for Taiwan or for duty-free shops.

Knockando Founded in 1898, this distillery was built near the new railway for ease of access and designed to make the light Speyside style that was becoming very popular with blenders. Now owned by Diageo, it is one of the main malts in the J&B blend as well as being sold as a single bottling.

Lagavulin One of Diageo's Classic Malts range, the Islay whisky was founded in 1816 and is an important component of White Horse blend. A very popular malt, it has appeared in a range of Hollywood films and the American comedy series *Parks and Recreation* ended with character Ron Swanson buying 51 per cent of the distillery.

Laphroaig Founded in 1815, this Islay whisky is one of the strongest-tasting whiskies in Scotland. The distillery still has its own malting floor which malts about 20 per cent of its barley. Now owned by Beam Suntory, it has a royal warrant from Prince Charles.

Ledaig (Pronounced 'lay chick'.) The peated malt from the Tobermory distillery on the Isle of Mull, it was first released in 2007 using the original name of the distillery first built in 1798.

Linkwood A Speyside distillery built near the town of Elgin in 1821, it has been through various ownerships and openings, closings, refits and rebuilds throughout its history – including a new build and another distillery across the road in 1972. The latest rebuild took place in 2012 when the original building was knocked down. The whisky is part of owner Diageo's Flora and Fauna range and it's also found among a lot of private bottlers' collections, most notably Gordon & MacPhail.

Loch Lomond Distilleries Small whisky company that owns Loch Lomond and Glen Scotia distilleries.

Lochside Silent Highland distillery mothballed in 1992 and demolished in 2004–05, the occasional very expensive bottle can still be found of either the grain or the malt whisky.

Longmorn Speyside distillery founded in 1893 and one of the places where the father of Japanese whisky, Masataka Taketsuru, learned about making whisky. Most of the whisky is used in blending but there are some private bottlings available.

Longrow A heavily peated Campbeltown malt made at the Springbank distillery.

Macallan One of the first farm distilleries in Speyside, it went legal in 1824 and is now one of the biggest malt whisky producers in the world. Always important for blends, The Macallan was marketed as a stand-alone malt in the 1980s. Currently owned by the Edrington Group, it now has a range of bottlings and special releases.

Macduff Founded in 1960 in the Highlands by a group of Glasgow brokers, most of its whisky is used for the William Lawson blend, although some does get to private bottlers and it is now being sold directly under the brand Glen Deveron. It was bought by Martini & Rossi in 1972 and became part of the Dewar's range in 1993 when Barcardi and Martini merged.

Machrie Moor The peated whisky from the Isle of Arran distillery.

McDonald's A special edition whisky from Ben Nevis, created to celebrate their 185th year. It is an attempt at recreating the McDonald's Traditional Ben Nevis, which was a popular in the 1880s.

Mannochmore Built by a previous incarnation of owner Diageo, DCL, in 1971, it is used in the Dimple and Haig blends as well as the 12-year-old being sold as part of the Flora and Fauna range of single malts.

Miltonduff Speyside distillery which first went legal in 1824 and is now owned by Pernod Ricard and used mostly for the top notes of the Ballantine's blend. Private bottlings are available, mostly via Gordon & MacPhail.

Mortlach The first legal distillery in Dufftown founded in 1823 by farmer James Findlater, its complicated distilling method means that the whisky is distilled 2.81 times.

Nikka Japanese whisky company and owner of Ben Nevis distillery in Fort William.

North British Grain distillery in Edinburgh founded in 1885 to provide various different blenders with an alternative to DCL's grain distillery at Cameronbridge, it is now jointly owned by the Edrington Group and DCL's successor, Diageo. If anyone has a bottling of North British they aren't letting on as it all goes into blends.

Oban Single Malt First built in 1799 at the heart of the town plan of Oban, the small distillery was rebuilt in 1883. Now owned by Diageo, it forms part of their Classic Malts range.

Octomore The heavy-peated range from Islay distillery Bruichladdich.

Old Parr Blend created in 1909 by Greenlees Bros in London and now owned by Diageo; it's no longer available in the UK or Europe but is the most popular whisky in Colombia.

Old Pulteney Founded in 1826 in Wick, one of the most northerly towns on the Scottish mainland, the barley originally arrived by boat, the whisky left the same way and many of the distillery workers were also fishermen. Old Pulteney was first marketed as a stand-alone brand in the late 1990s by its owners, Inver House group, part of the International Beverage group.

Penderyn The only malt whisky made in Wales at the moment, it was founded in 2004 and now has various expressions including cask finishes.

Port Ellen Diageo-owned distillery which closed in 1983, its dwindling stocks of whisky command incredibly high prices.

R&B Distillers Small private whisky company set up in 2014 by Alisdair Day, selling the Tweeddale blend and building a distillery on the island of Raasay, with plans to build one on the Borders.

Roseisle A massive malt distillery on Speyside, it opened in 2013 and the harbingers of doom said that it was Diageo's attempt to create a super-distillery so they could close all their other ones. At the time of writing, all the others are still open and working to capacity. Like the much smaller Ardnamurchan, it has been built with a lot of environmental considerations: it has a biomass plant which means it generates a lot of its own energy, and a heat recovery system.

Royal Brackla Founded by Captain William Fraser in 1817, mostly to stop the locals from distilling illegally in the surrounding area, it was the first whisky to receive a royal warrant in 1835, earning the right to be called Royal Brackla. Closed between 1986 and 1991, it is now owned by Barcardi Martini as part of the Dewar's range and is available as various age statements.

Royal Lochnagar A small Highland distillery built in 1845, in 1848 it was granted a royal warrant after Queen Victoria and Prince Albert, who had recently bought Balmoral Castle and Estate nearby, had what must be the first recorded distillery tour. The queen sampled a dram which she declared she liked and went on to often have it mixed with claret. An important blend in Johnnie Walker Blue, it's also available as single bottlings and via private bottlers.

Scapa Built in 1885 on Orkney by blender John Townsend, it was closed from 1994 to 2004 when owners carried out extensive refurbishment and, after Pernod Ricard took over in 2005, it was released as a single malt.

Scotch Malt Whisky Society Edinburgh-based private bottlers and worldwide whisky club, started in 1983. Well known for their distinctive labelling with no mention of the distillery.

Speyburn Part of the Inver House group and ultimately owned by Thai Beverages, it's a Speyside malt that whisky buffs think is greatly underappreciated and very good value for money.

Springbank Campbeltown's biggest distillery which produces three whisky brands, Springbank, Longrow and Hazelburn. Family owned, it was founded in 1828 and is the only distillery to malt, distil, mature and bottle on site.

Starlaw Opened in 2010 by owners La Martiniquaise, this is the newest grain distillery in Scotland, although another one is planned in Girvan. Located in the Lowlands in the industrial town of Bathgate, it also has space for over 600,000 barrels.

Strathclyde A grain distillery on the Southside of Glasgow, it was originally built in 1927 to make gin, moving into whisky production in 1936. Now owned by Pernod Ricard, it makes grain spirit exclusively for whisky.

Strathearn Probably Scotland's smallest distillery (until someone builds an even smaller one), built in 2013 in disused farm buildings in the Highland village of Methven, owner Tony Reeman-Clark has promised that every batch of whisky made will be different due to the type of stills and the barrels used.

Strathisla The oldest licensed distillery in Scotland, it got its licence in 1786. A Speyside whisky, it is used mainly for the Chivas blends; although there are some single bottlings by owners Pernod Ricard, what little is available is mostly from private bottlers.

Strathmill A light Speyside malt founded in 1892, it is mostly used in the J&B blend but a small amount has been bottled directly by Diageo as part of its Flora and Fauna range. Most of the single bottlings are available from private bottlers.

Talisker Skye distillery founded in 1830 by the MacAskill brothers, who bought Talisker House and cleared the people off the land for more profitable sheep. They also decided to make money with a distillery. Now owned by Diageo and part of the Classic Malts series, it was Scottish writer Robert Louis Stevenson's favourite whisky.

Tamdhu A Speyside distillery built beside the new railway in 1897 by a consortium of blenders, it was closed for over two decades in the early 20th century and then open between 1948 and 2009 when it was mothballed until 2011, at which point it was bought by Ian Macleod Distillers who reopened it. A newly packaged and very popular Tamdhu 10 was launched at the Speyside Whisky Festival in 2013.

Tamnavulin Built in 1966 by a subsidiary of Invergordon distillery, it was closed between 1995 and 2007 and is now owned by Philippines-based Emperador Inc. There are a few bottlings from the 1970s and 80s around and some private bottlings, but the whisky is almost always used for blends.

Teaninich A North Highland distillery built in 1817 by famously benevolent landlords Captain Hugh and General John Munro, the original site was mothballed in 1984 with the second site, built in 1970, continuing to be expanded, and in 2000 it became the only distillery in Scotland to have a hammer mill and mash filter so has no mash tun to create the wort. In single bottlings, it is available as a 10-year-old in owner Diageo's Flora and Fauna blend and also through private bottlers.

Tobermory Founded in 1798, the distillery on the Isle of Mull has closed and reopened several times, finally reopening in 1991. It produces the unpeated Tobermory and peated Ledaig whiskies and is owned by the South African group, Distell.

Tomatin Founded in 1897 on a site that has probably distilled whisky since the 16th century, Tomatin has gone bankrupt, closed and reopened several times in its history, until it was finally rescued in 1986 by Takara Shuzo and Okura & Co and became the first

Japanese-owned Scotch distillery. Mostly used for the Antiquary blend, it is now sold as a Highland malt under its own name and has a peated range, Cù Bòcan.

Tomintoul Built in 1965 by a couple of whisky-broking firms beside the highest village in Scotland, the Speyside distillery is now owned by Angus Dundee. It has various age statements and bottlings as well as a peated range called Old Ballantruan.

Tormore Built on Speyside in 1959 to service the blending industry, current owners Pernod Ricard use it mostly in the Ballantine's blend, although a 12-year-old is now on the market and there are a few single-cask and private bottlings.

Tullibardine Built in 1949 in the Highlands on the site of the old Gleneagles brewery and mothballed from 1994 to 2003, it is now owned by the French group Picard Vins & Spiritueux and used in their blends. There have been a few single-bottling releases; currently the most popular is a no-age-statement malt that has been aged in bourbon casks.

Tweeddale A blended whisky made by Alasdair Day of R&B distillers in 2010 to an early 20th century recipe from his great-grandfather Richard Day's cellar (accounts) book for Coldstream grocer J&A Davidson.

VAT 69 Created by the Leith-born blender William Sanderson in 1882. The story is he vatted 100 casks and invited a panel of friends to taste them blind. The 69th cask was unanimously declared to be the best, and the name stuck. Now owned by Diageo, the blend is sold mostly in Spain, Australia and Venezuela.

Wemyss Malts Private bottlers based in Edinburgh set up by the well-known landed gentry Wemyss family in 2005. They also own the newly built Kingsbarns distillery in Fife.

White Horse First blended in 1861 by James Logan Mackie in

Edinburgh, the Diageo-owned blend now has its biggest market in Russia. The malt whisky Lagavulin is an important component of the blend.

Whyte & Mackay Charles Mackay and James Whyte founded a company as whisky merchants and bonded warehousemen in Glasgow in 1882, producing the W&M special blend. Now owned by Emperador Philippines, they produce the W&M range as well as Dalmore, Jura and Fettercairn single malts.

Wm Cadenhead Oldest private bottlers in Scotland, originally based in Aberdeenshire, now based in Campbeltown and owned by the Mitchell family.

Wolfburn Built in 2012 by Aurora Brewing on the site of the old Wolfburn distillery which had closed in the 1850s, Wolfburn is the most northerly distillery in mainland Scotland. The three-year-old releases have received a lot of plaudits and aficionados are eagerly awaiting the eight-year-old.

ACKNOWLEDGEMENTS

Firstly, thanks to my agent Nick Canham, who phoned me while I was heating pies in a pub oven for a friend's wedding to say, 'I think you have a strong idea here', and secondly my thanks to Iain MacGregor of Simon & Schuster for agreeing with Nick. Thanks also to Karen Farrington and Lorraine Jerram for editing, researching and structuring *Chasing the Dram* into a proper book.

That I owe a huge debt of gratitude to everyone mentioned in the book goes without saying but, within the whisky world, I would like to thank Dr Nick Morgan, Head of Whisky Outreach at Diageo – almost everything that is correct whisky knowledge in this book is because of him, the mistakes are my own. Ailana Kamelecher, Sarah Brown and Tarita Mullings of Story PR have also been invaluable with help, advice and logistics, Derek Sneddon with great advice, contacts and amazing food photos, and Annabel Miekle, Director of Keepers of the Quaich, has always bent over backwards to help.

Thanks to many of the people who feature in the book but aren't named, including Signe Johansen, Allan Jenkins, Anne Maxwell, Ronnie Swanson, Donald Colville, David Boyd, Professor Barry Smith, Lemn Sissay, Mr Jenny Landreth (aka Mark), Laura Goodman, Julie Hamilton and every distillery guide in every distillery that I have ever visited.

Lesley Johnstone Jones, Lucy Dichmont, Darby Dorras, Robert Abel, Jay Rayner, Annie Gray, Bea Vo, Deborah Robertson, Thane Prince, Diana Henry, Liz Vater, Victoria Shepherd and Victoria Stewart are all people who helped make this book possible in various different ways, often unbeknownst to them, but I owe them all a very big thanks.

Lastly thanks to Amro 'It's not Chekhov, is it' Gebreel for getting me through panic and procrastination, and above all to my mother, who stared at me warily and asked if she could talk to me now when I announced I had just sent off my first draft.